A HANDBOOK FOR
the Art and Science of Teaching

SUSTAINABLE
FORESTRY
INITIATIVE

Certified Fiber Sourcing

www.sfiprogram.org

A HANDBOOK FOR
the *Art* and Science of Teaching

Robert J. Marzano
John L. Brown

Alexandria, Virginia USA

1703 N. Beauregard St. • Alexandria, VA 22311-1714 USA
Phone: 800-933-2723 or 703-578-9600 • Fax: 703-575-5400
Web site: www.ascd.org • E-mail: member@ascd.org
Author guidelines: www.ascd.org/write

Gene R. Carter, *Executive Director*; Nancy Modrak, *Publisher*; Julie Houtz, *Director of Book Editing & Production*; Leah Lakins, *Project Manager*; Georgia Park, *Senior Graphic Designer*; Mike Kalyan, *Production Manager*; Keith Demmons, *Typesetter*; Carmen Yuhas, *Production Specialist*

PAPERBACK ISBN: 978-1-4166-0818-9   ASCD product #108049   n6/09
Also available as an e-book through ebrary, netLibrary, and many online booksellers (see Books in Print for the ISBNs).

Quantity discounts for the paperback edition only: 10–49 copies, 10%; 50+ copies, 15%; for 1,000 or more copies, call 800-933-2723, ext. 5634, or 703-575-5634. For desk copies: member@ascd.org.

Library of Congress Cataloging-in-Publication Data

Marzano, Robert J.
  A handbook for the art and science of teaching / Robert J. Marzano and John L. Brown.
      p. cm.
  Includes bibliographical references and index.
  ISBN 978-1-4166-0818-9 (pbk. : alk. paper) 1. Effective teaching—Handbooks, manuals, etc. I. Brown, John L., 1947- II. Association for Supervision and Curriculum Development. III. Title.

  LB1025.3.M342 2009
  371.102—dc22
                                      2009005307

20 19 18 17 16 15 14 13 12 11   5 6 7 8 9 10 11 12

To my lifelong friends and colleagues Debra Pickering and Diane Paynter, who have taught me a great deal about effective teaching.

Robert J. Marzano

To Rob A. Pennie, Marjorie Spirer, and Max C. West, for their support during the development of this handbook.

John L. Brown

A Handbook for the *Art* and Science of Teaching

Table of Contents

Module 1

Introduction

The Art and Science of Teaching (Marzano, 2007) was designed as a comprehensive framework for effective instruction to be used by teachers in every subject area at every grade level. As such, it is an update and amalgamation of previous works such as *Classroom Instruction That Works* (Marzano, Pickering, & Pollock, 2001), *Classroom Management That Works* (Marzano, Pickering, & Marzano, 2003), and *Classroom Assessment and Grading That Work* (Marzano, 2006). Given the complexity of teaching, it makes sense that a comprehensive framework would necessarily include and integrate other works that address specific aspects of teaching.

The title words *art* and *science* were carefully selected to convey a message—effective teaching is both art and science. It is art in the sense that it involves no specific script all effective teachers must follow. Indeed, effective teachers are as varied in their characteristics and behaviors as are effective students. It is science in the sense that there are strategies that research over time has shown to have a high probability of enhancing student achievement. These "high probability" strategies are the tools in an effective teacher's tool box. Not every teacher uses these tools in the same way and with the same frequency. However, most effective teachers probably have developed a facility with them.

In keeping with the variety and flexibility that characterize the domain of effective teaching, *The Art and Science of Teaching* is presented as a series of design questions (see Figure 1.1). These questions are used by teachers as reminders of what should be addressed during a unit of instruction and the lessons within those units. Again, different teachers will answer these questions in different ways with comparable results.

FIGURE 1.1

Design Questions for *The Art and Science of Teaching*

1. What will I do to establish and communicate learning goals, track student progress, and celebrate success?
2. What will I do to help students effectively interact with new knowledge?
3. What will I do to help students practice and deepen their understanding of new knowledge?
4. What will I do to help students generate and test hypotheses about new knowledge?
5. What will I do to engage students?
6. What will I do to establish or maintain classroom rules and procedures?
7. What will I do to recognize and acknowledge adherence and lack of adherence to classroom rules and procedures?
8. What will I do to establish and maintain effective relationships with students?
9. What will I do to communicate high expectations for all students?
10. What will I do to develop effective lessons organized into a cohesive unit?

The Structure of the Handbook

This handbook is organized into modules. There are two or more modules for each of the 10 design questions. Figure 1.2 lists the modules that relate to each design question. Each module begins with a section titled Reflecting on Your Current Beliefs and Practices. This section is intended as a set of preview questions that not only stimulate your background knowledge regarding the content in the module but also provide a framework for digesting the information in the module. Each module ends with a section titled Checking for Understanding. This section provides a brief summary of the module content in the context of self-assessment questions that ask you to consider what you understood well and what might require some reexamination on your part.

FIGURE 1.2

Design Questions and Modules

Design Question 1: What Will I Do to Establish and Communicate Learning Goals, Track Student Progress, and Celebrate Success?

- Module 2: Establishing and Communicating Learning Goals
- Module 3: Designing and Using Formative Assessments

Design Question 2: What Will I Do to Help Students Effectively Interact with New Knowledge?

- Module 4: Identifying Critical-Input Experiences and Using Previewing Strategies

- Module 5: Using Cooperative Learning, Curriculum Chunking, and Descriptions, Discussions, and Predictions
- Module 6: Helping Students Elaborate on New Content, Summarize and Represent Their Learning, and Reflect on Their Learning

Design Question 3: What Will I Do to Help Students Practice and Deepen Their Understanding of New Knowledge?

- Module 7: Examining Similarities and Differences and Identifying Errors in Thinking
- Module 8: Helping Students Practice Skills, Strategies, and Processes
- Module 9: Using Homework and Academic Notebooks to Deepen Student Understanding

Design Question 4: What Will I Do to Help Students Generate and Test Hypotheses About New Knowledge?

- Module 10: Teaching Students to Support Claims and Assertions with Evidence
- Module 11: Hypothesis Testing and Higher-Order Thinking
- Module 12: Engaging Students in Task Design, Cooperative Learning, and Self-Evaluation

Design Question 5: What Will I Do to Engage Students?

- Module 13: Using Games and Inconsequential Competition to Promote Student Engagement
- Module 14: Rules of Engagement: Questioning, Physical Movement, and Pacing
- Module 15: Additional Cognitive, Affective, and Social Interaction Strategies for Promoting Student Engagement

Design Question 6: What Will I Do to Establish or Maintain Classroom Rules and Procedures?

- Module 16: Effective Classroom Organization
- Module 17: Establishing and Maintaining Classroom Rules and Procedures

Design Question 7: What Will I Do to Recognize and Acknowledge Adherence and Lack of Adherence to Classroom Rules and Procedures?

- Module 18: Acknowledging Students' Adherence to Classroom Rules and Procedures
- Module 19: Acknowledging Students' Lack of Adherence to Classroom Rules and Procedures

Design Question 8: What Will I Do to Establish and Maintain Effective Relationships with Students?

- Module 20: Communicating Appropriate Levels of Concern and Cooperation
- Module 21: Communicating Appropriate Levels of Guidance and Control

Design Question 9: What Will I Do to Communicate High Expectations for All Students?

- Module 22: Identifying High-Expectancy and Low-Expectancy Students
- Module 23: Changing Behavior Toward Low-Expectancy Students

Design Question 10: What Will I Do to Develop Effective Lessons Organized into a Cohesive Unit?

- Module 24: Identifying the Focus of a Unit
- Module 25: Developing Effective Lessons

Each module presents information in small, digestible bites or "chunks." This is in keeping with a basic principle of effective teaching discussed in Design Question 2: *What will I do to help students effectively interact with new knowledge?* After each chunk of information, you will find an activity box that asks you to react to the information that has been presented or to describe how you might use that information. To illustrate, consider Figure 1.3, which is one of the activity boxes from Module 5: Using Cooperative Learning, Curriculum Chunking, and Descriptions, Discussions, and Predictions. This module is one of three within Design Question 2.

FIGURE 1.3

Sample Activity Box from Module 5

Activity Box

The examples in this section demonstrate two different types of "chunking." The first example demonstrates how a teacher might chunk the content during a single lesson—a small piece (i.e., a chunk) of information is presented to students, which they then process in small groups. The next two examples illustrate a second approach to chunking. Here new information is organized into chunks across different lessons during a unit. It is important to note that during these lessons information would also be chunked into small digestible bites. Describe how you have used or could use each of these two approaches to chunking.

How to Use the Handbook

This handbook is intended as a self-study guide for the 10 design questions underlying *The Art and Science of Teaching*. Although it is possible to use this handbook without having first read the book, we strongly recommend that you do so, particularly if you are interested in the research and theory that form the foundation for the recommendations in this handbook.

One way to use the handbook is to read it independently. In doing so, the design questions can be addressed out of order but will be more fluid if read in order. Another useful approach is to form study teams. We believe this is the most effective way to study the specifics of the design questions in *The Art and Science of Teaching* because it allows colleagues to compare perspectives. These study teams might be impromptu groups, grade-level groups, departmental groups, or an entire faculty. To stimulate dialogue we recommend that each participating member of a study team independently complete the activity boxes within a module. The team can then compare answers to these queries. In short, the activity boxes within each module can serve as the basis for an analytic discussion by colleagues of each module's content.

Regardless of how the handbook is used, a careful reading of it along with a reading of *The Art and Science of Teaching* should provide you with a thorough grounding in the strategies identified by the science of teaching as highly likely to enhance student achievement. Using these strategies in a way that enhances the achievement of your particular students is the domain of the art of teaching that must be thought of as a personal journey of reflective practice over a number of years. We hope this handbook will serve as a road map on that journey.

Design Question 1

What Will I Do to Establish and Communicate Learning Goals, Track Student Progress, and Celebrate Success?

Module 2

Establishing and Communicating Learning Goals

Module 3

Designing and Using Formative Assessments

Design Question 1

What Will I Do to Establish and Communicate Learning Goals, Track
Student Progress, and Celebrate Success?

Module 2

Establishing and Communicating Learning Goals

This module and the next deal with establishing and communicating learning goals, tracking student progress, and celebrating success. Arguably the starting place for all effective instruction is designing and communicating clear learning goals. Although this might seem self-evident, actually executing this behavior is anything but routine for a number of reasons. First, there is a good deal of confusion about the difference between learning goals and instructional activities or assignments. All are important, but all have distinguishing characteristics. Once learning goals are clearly identified, they should be stated in a form that provides clear direction for students. Here we present a scale or rubric format. Well-written rubrics set the stage for assessments (addressed in Module 3) and can be used to provide students with effective feedback (also addressed in Module 3). Finally, the teacher should not be the only one setting learning goals during a unit of instruction. Students should be asked and invited to establish their own learning goals that complement those established by the teacher.

Reflecting on Your Current Beliefs and Practices

Before examining the strategies in this module, take some time to examine your current beliefs and practices by answering the following questions:

1. How clear are you about the distinction between a learning goal and a learning activity or an assignment? How do you communicate the difference to students?

_____

_____

_____

_____

2. To what extent do you communicate learning goals in a way that makes explicit to students how they can improve?

_____

_____

_____

_____

3. To what extent do you have students restate rubrics in their own words?

_____

_____

_____

_____

4. To what extent do you have students design their own learning goals for units of instruction? If you do not, how might you do so?

_____

_____

_____

_____

Recommendations for Classroom Practice

This module addresses the following instructional strategies for Design Question 1:

- Clearly articulating learning goals as opposed to activities and assignments
- Creating scales or rubrics for learning goals
- Rewriting scales in student-friendly language
- Having students identify individual learning goals

Clearly Articulating Learning Goals as Opposed to Activities and Assignments

There is a great deal of confusion regarding the differences between learning goals and activities and assignments. There is also confusion regarding how they interact. Essentially, activities and assignments are used to help students achieve learning goals. Consider the following list of elements, all of which are activities or assignments:

- Students preview the chapter on the adverse effects of smoking before reading it.
- Students compare and contrast the use of technology in World War I and World War II.
- Students complete the word problems at the back of Chapter 4.
- Students read a chapter of a novel and write a brief summary.
- Students read about the experiment for tomorrow's class and create a hypothesis as to its outcome.

Everything in the list represents something students will do to help them learn new information or new skills. We call these activities or assignments. Activities are typically things that are completed during a single lesson. For example, the first element, previewing the chapter on the adverse effects of smoking, would most likely be an activity. It would be done in class in preparation for reading a chapter in the textbook. The last element, about the experiment for tomorrow's class, might also be an activity done in class; however, it could also be an assignment. Typically, assignments are done outside of regular class time, although students may begin assignments during class time. The second element, involving comparing and contrasting the use of technology in World War I and World War II, would most likely be an assignment because it would probably take more than one class period. Frequently, assignments turn into homework. (We address the issue of homework in a subsequent module.)

We have worded the activities and assignments in the list somewhat formally. However, teachers usually record activities and assignments in a shorthand fashion in their planning books. For example, a teacher might simply write "preview chapter" to remind herself that she will have students preview the chapter on the harmful effects of smoking before reading it.

Activity Box

Identify one activity and one assignment you have used with students. Remember that activities are completed in a single class, whereas assignments are not.

Learning goals or objectives state what students should learn over the course of a unit (or a lesson or an entire semester). Consider the following list:

- Students will understand key aspects contributing to the outcomes of World War I and World War II.
- Students will be able to factor and simplify quadratic equations.
- Students will understand plot, theme, conflict, and resolution of the novel.
- Students will be able to create a reasonable hypothesis for a simple experiment and compare their hypothesis to the experiment's outcome.

As the list illustrates, learning goals have a very specific format:

Students will understand _____.
or
Students will be able to _____.

The format "students will understand . . ." is used when information is the target of a learning goal. Technically, information is referred to as *declarative knowledge*. Declarative knowledge includes information such as vocabulary terms, facts, generalizations, and principles. The following are examples of declarative knowledge:

- Incidents leading to the U.S. involvement in World War II
- The concept of plot
- A specific plot in a specific story

The format "students will be able to . . . " is used when a process is the target of a learning goal. Technically, processes are referred to as *procedural knowledge*. Procedural knowledge includes processes such as skills, heuristics, and strategies, as well as complex processes such as writing. The following are examples of procedural knowledge:

- Factoring and simplifying quadratic equations
- Creating reasonable hypotheses for simple experiments
- Using specific word processing software

For a more detailed discussion of learning goals for declarative and procedural knowledge, see *Designing and Assessing Educational Objectives* (Marzano & Kendall, 2008).

Occasionally a learning goal will include both declarative and procedural knowledge. In these cases the following format can be used:

Students will understand _____ and be able to _____.

To illustrate, a physical education teacher might design the following learning goal, which includes both declarative and procedural knowledge:

Students will understand the dynamics involved in stretching the hamstring muscle and be able to demonstrate the proper form.

It is important to note that the rules we are presenting regarding how to write objectives can be relaxed after a teacher understands the difference between declarative and procedural knowledge. This is illustrated in the next section of this module and in the next module for Design Question 1.

Distinguishing between learning goals versus activities and assignments as well as writing effective goals are important aspects of effective teaching. Figure 2.1 provides more examples. In the figure, the language arts and the science examples involve learning goals that incorporate both declarative and procedural knowledge. Note that each learning goal is associated with a specific activity or assignment or both. Making sure that learning goals are linked to specific activities and assignments is a critical aspect of the art and science of teaching.

FIGURE 2.1

Learning Goals and Activities/Assignments

Subject	Learning Goals	Activities and Assignments
Social Studies	Students will understand . . . • How the antebellum period affected the Civil War. • The crucial events of the Civil War. • The immediate and lasting effects of the Civil War on the United States.	Students read Chapter 10 of the biography of Mary Todd Lincoln.
Math	Students will be able to . . . • Use an ordered pair to plot a point on a graph and vice versa. • Identify and solve linear equations from looking at a graph.	Students time each other in groups to see who can plot the most points on a graph.
Language Arts	Students will understand the rules of capitalization and will be able to correct capitalization mistakes in their own writing.	Students identify capitalization mistakes on a teacher handout.
Science	Students will understand how weather patterns change locally and be able to measure those changes using basic tools.	Students write the weather forecast information, the high and low temperatures, and the precipitation in a daily journal.

Examples

Elementary Art. This elementary art teacher is working on the concept of perspective with her art students. She wants them to understand two different ways perspective can be established in paintings or photographs. She states her learning goal as follows: *Students will understand two approaches to establishing perspective.* To help students accomplish this goal, she plans an activity in which students will be shown paintings exemplifying the two types of perspectives that are the focus of the learning goal.

High School Technology. This technology teacher designs a unit devoted to helping students understand the characteristics of Web sites that demonstrate academic rigor. He establishes two learning goals: (1) *Students will understand the characteristics of academically rigorous Web sites,* and (2) *Students will be able to screen Web sites for their academic rigor.* He plans a series of initial activities that will exemplify characteristics of academically rigorous Web sites. He also identifies assignments that teach students how to analyze specific Web sites.

Activity Box

Identify a learning goal you have addressed recently. Describe one assignment and one activity that might accompany that goal.

Creating Scales or Rubrics for Learning Goals

While activities and assignments are being deployed in class, students should have opportunities to see their progress through formative assessments. We address how to design formative assessments and track students' progress in Module 3. In this section we consider how to translate learning goals into a scale that can be used to design and score formative classroom assessments. We should note that in the remainder of this handbook we will typically use the term *scale* as opposed to *rubric*. For a detailed discussion of why the term *scale* is preferred, see *Classroom Assessment and Grading That Work* (Marzano, 2006).

The first step in creating a scale for a learning goal is to identify knowledge that is easier than the learning goal and knowledge that is more complex than the learning goal. To illustrate, consider the following learning goal for reading at the middle school level:

Students will describe complex causal relationships in grade-appropriate passages.

Notice that the format for this learning goal is different from those used previously. Recall that we said that once teachers have become familiar with the distinctions between declarative and procedural knowledge, the rules we've established regarding writing goals can be relaxed. This is particularly true for declarative knowledge, which is the subject of the learning goal above regarding causal relationships in grade appropriate passages. In fact, this goal could have been written in the following way: *Students will understand complex causal relationships in grade appropriate passages.* However, when writing goals for declarative knowledge it is very helpful to use verbs that specify how students will demonstrate understanding. In this case that verb is *describe*. Other verbs commonly used when designing goals for declarative knowledge include *recognize, select, identify, exemplify, name, list, label,* and *state*. For a comprehensive list of such verbs, see *Designing and Assessing Educational Objectives* (Marzano & Kendall, 2008) and *Designing and Teaching Learning Goals and Objectives* (Marzano, 2009). For a thorough discussion of the ways in which learning goals can be written once an understanding of declarative and procedural knowledge has been acquired, see *The New Taxonomy of Educational Objectives* (Marzano & Kendall, 2007).

After designing the learning goal, the teacher would identify content that is an aspect of the learning goal but a simpler version of it or a prerequisite for it. In this case the teacher might identify the following content:

Students will identify literary clues that signal a cause-effect relationship.

At this level students can't explain complex cause-effect relationships but can identify terms and phrases within a passage that indicate a cause-effect relationship is present.

Next the teacher would identify content that is a little more complex than the learning goal, such as the following:

Students will explain the relationship between complex causal relationships in one story and those in other stories.

At this level students not only can describe explicit cause-effect relationships in a particular story (i.e., can demonstrate competence in the learning goal), but also can explain how the identified relationship is similar to those in other stories.

Activity Box

Select a learning goal you have used in class. Next, identify easier content that is an aspect of that learning goal or a prerequisite for that learning goal. Finally, identify related content that is more complex than the learning goal.

Learning goal:

Easier or prerequisite content:

More complex content:

With a clear learning goal identified along with content that is more complex and more simple, a scale can be readily designed. To illustrate, consider Figure 2.2. To understand the scale in the figure, let's start with the whole-point scores.

- The 0.0 score value is the lowest on the scale; it is assigned to a student who shows no understanding of the content whatsoever, even with help.
- The next whole-point step up is a score value of 1.0; it is assigned to a student who shows some knowledge of the simpler and more complex content when given help.
- To receive a score of 2.0, a student shows understanding and skills regarding the simpler content but makes major errors or omissions when it comes to the more complex content.
- A score of 3.0 is the next step up. It means that a student demonstrates knowledge of all the content (simple and complex) that was explicitly taught.
- Finally, a score of 4.0 applies to a student who is able to demonstrate knowledge that goes above and beyond what was explicitly taught in class.

FIGURE 2.2

Scale for Learning Goals

Score 4.0		In addition to Score 3.0 performance, in-depth inferences and applications that go beyond what was taught.
	Score 3.5	In addition to Score 3.0 performance, in-depth inferences and applications with partial success.
Score 3.0		No major errors or omissions regarding any of the information and processes (simple or complex) that were explicitly taught.
	Score 2.5	No major errors or omissions regarding the simpler details and processes (Score 2.0 content) and partial knowledge of the more complex ideas and processes (Score 3.0 content).
Score 2.0		No major errors or omissions regarding the simpler details and processes but major errors or omissions regarding the more complex ideas and processes (Score 3.0 content).
	Score 1.5	Partial knowledge of the simpler details and processes (Score 2.0 content) but major errors or omissions regarding the more complex ideas and processes (Score 3.0 content).
Score 1.0		With help, a partial understanding of some of the simpler details and processes (Score 2.0 content) and some of the more complex ideas and processes (Score 3.0 content).
	Score 0.5	With help, a partial understanding of some of the simpler details and processes (Score 2.0 content) but not the more complex ideas and processes (Score 3.0 content).
Score 0.0		Even with help, no understanding or skill demonstrated.

This generic scale can be used to translate any learning goal for which simpler and more complex content has been identified and placed into a scale. To illustrate, consider Figure 2.3, which translates the learning goal for identifying complex causal relationships and its simpler and more complex content into a scale. In Figure 2.3 the content for the learning goal regarding comprehension of complex causal relationships has been placed in the Score 3.0 position. The simpler content has been placed in the Score 2.0 position, and the content that is more complex than the learning goal has been placed in the Score 4.0 position. This simple protocol can be used to design a scale for any learning goal in any subject area.

FIGURE 2.3

Scale for the Learning Goal of Understanding Causal Relationships

Grade 8		
Score 4.0	**In addition to Score 3.0 performance, in-depth inferences and applications that go beyond what was taught, such as** • Explaining how a complex causal relationship in one story is similar to that in another story.	
	Score 3.5	In addition to Score 3.0 performance, in-depth inferences and applications with partial success.
Score 3.0	**While engaged in grade-appropriate reading tasks, the student demonstrates an ability to** • Describe complex causal relationships (*e.g., observing that the plight of Anne Frank in* The Diary of Anne Frank *is the result of causes ranging from the policies of the Nazis in Amsterdam to the childhood of Adolph Hitler*). **The student exhibits no major errors or omissions.**	
	Score 2.5	No major errors or omissions regarding the Score 2.0 elements and partial knowledge of the Score 3.0 elements.
Score 2.0	**No major errors or omissions regarding the simpler details and processes, such as** • Identifying literary clues that indicate complex causal relationships (*e.g., recognizing specific words and phrases that signal complex causal relationships*). **However, the student exhibits major errors or omissions with Score 3.0 elements.**	
	Score 1.5	Partial knowledge of the Score 2.0 elements but major errors or omissions regarding the Score 3.0 elements.
Score 1.0	**With help, a partial understanding of some of the Score 2.0 elements and some of the Score 3.0 elements.**	
	Score 0.5	With help, a partial understanding of some of the Score 2.0 elements but not the Score 3.0 elements.
Score 0.0	**Even with help, no understanding or skill demonstrated.**	

Examples

Eighth Grade Science. This 8th grade science teacher is planning a unit on the structure and properties of matter. Her learning goal is for students to understand the characteristics of various elements. She identifies some content that is easier and more difficult than this target information and writes the following scale, which she will present to students.

Score 4.0	In addition to Score 3.0 performance, in-depth inferences and applications that go beyond what was taught, such as	
	• Describing patterns in the composition, atomic number, melting point, and boiling point of a set of elements.	
	Score 3.5	In addition to Score 3.0 performance, in-depth inferences and applications with partial success.
Score 3.0	While engaged in tasks that address the structure and properties of matter, the student demonstrates an understanding of important information, such as	
	• General characteristics (composition, atomic number, melting point, boiling point) of various elements (*e.g., explaining general information known about a specific element, such as explaining that the boiling point of nitrogen is 77.36 K [-195.79° C, -320.42° F]*).	
	The student makes no major errors or omissions.	
	Score 2.5	No major errors or omissions regarding the Score 2.0 elements and partial knowledge of the Score 3.0 elements.
Score 2.0	No major errors or omissions regarding the simpler details and processes, such as	
	• Recognizing and recalling specific terminology, such as – conservation of mass, – atomic arrangement, and – thermodynamic system.	
	• Recognizing and recalling isolated details, such as – the atomic number of an element is equal to the number of protons, which defines the element.	
	However, the student exhibits major errors or omissions with Score 3.0 elements.	
	Score 1.5	Partial knowledge of the Score 2.0 elements but major errors or omissions regarding the Score 3.0 elements.
Score 1.0	With help, a partial understanding of some of the Score 2.0 elements and some of the Score 3.0 elements.	
	Score 0.5	With help, a partial understanding of some of the Score 2.0 elements but not the Score 3.0 elements.
Score 0.0	Even with help, no understanding or skill demonstrated.	

Activity Box

Using the form below, design a rubric for a recent goal you have addressed in class by filling in the content for Scores 4.0, 3.0, and 2.0.

Score 4.0		
	Score 3.5	In addition to Score 3.0 performance, in-depth inferences and applications with partial success.
Score 3.0		
	Score 2.5	No major errors or omissions regarding the simpler details and processes (Score 2.0 content) and partial knowledge of the more complex ideas and processes (Score 3.0 content).
Score 2.0		
	Score 1.5	Partial knowledge of the simpler details and processes (Score 2.0 content) but major errors or omissions regarding the more complex ideas and procedures (Score 3.0 content).
Score 1.0	**With help, a partial understanding of some of the simpler details and processes (Score 2.0 content) and some of the more complex ideas and processes (Score 3.0 content).**	
	Score 0.5	With help, a partial understanding of some of the simpler details and processes (Score 2.0 content) but not the more complex ideas and processes (Score 3.0 content).
Score 0.0	**Even with help, no understanding or skill demonstrated.**	

Rewriting Scales in Student-Friendly Language

Learning goals and the scales that go with them are typically written for teachers. Another way of saying this is that they are written in "teacher language." It is highly useful to translate them to "student language." To illustrate, consider Figure 2.4. It contains the scale shown in Figure 2.3, but this time the content for Scores 4.0, 3.0, and 2.0 has been stated in student language. This revision was done via a class discussion in which students and teacher jointly decided how best to rewrite the content for Scores 4.0, 3.0, and 2.0. Also note that specific examples are provided. These examples give students clear illustrations of what is expected of them.

FIGURE 2.4

Student-Friendly Scale for the Learning Goal of Understanding Causal Relationships

Score 4.0	In addition to Score 3.0 performance, in-depth inferences and applications that go beyond what was taught, such as	
	• Being able to describe what caused what in one story and explain how it is the same in another story. For the story we read about the landslide that wiped out the town because the people didn't take care of the vegetation on the hills, we would have to show how this is the same as the story about the baseball player who didn't take care of his health and lost his position on the team.	
	Score 3.5	In addition to Score 3.0 performance, in-depth inferences and applications with partial success.
Score 3.0	While engaged in grade-appropriate reading tasks, the student demonstrates an ability to	
	• Describe exactly what led to something happening. For example, in the story about the landslide that wiped out the town, we have to start right from the beginning when the townspeople didn't plant any new plants on the hills after the fire, and then explain how the rainy season was much worse than they thought, and keep showing how one thing led to another right up until the disaster.	
	The student exhibits no major errors or omissions.	
	Score 2.5	No major errors or omissions regarding the Score 2.0 elements and partial knowledge of the Score 3.0 elements.
Score 2.0	No major errors or omissions regarding the simpler details and processes, such as	
	• Being able to describe the parts of a story or the language in a story that lets us know the story is now talking about something making something else happen.	
	However, the student exhibits major errors or omissions with Score 3.0 elements.	
	Score 1.5	Partial knowledge of the Score 2.0 elements but major errors or omissions regarding the Score 3.0 elements.
Score 1.0	With help, a partial understanding of some of the Score 2.0 elements and some of the Score 3.0 elements.	
	Score 0.5	With help, a partial understanding of some of the Score 2.0 elements but not the Score 3.0 elements.
Score 0.0	Even with help, no understanding or skill demonstrated.	

Examples

Middle School Geography. This 7th grade social studies teacher has designed a scale for a learning goal regarding the difference in human and animal migration. She has students break into small groups and rewrite the Score 4.0, 3.0, and 2.0 elements from the scale. Groups share their responses, and the class as a whole comes up with a student-friendly version of the scale created by the teacher.

Primary Reading. This teacher has presented students with a scale for a learning goal regarding writing a composition with a clear beginning, middle, and end. Using previous compositions students have written, the teacher provides examples of compositions, or "anchor papers," for Scores 4.0, 3.0, and 2.0. These are posted on the board right next to the scale. Students can clearly see what Score 4.0, 3.0, and 2.0 papers look like.

Activity Box

Using the Score 4.0, 3.0, and 2.0 values from the activity box containing the rubric you designed, rewrite the content in a way that would be more student friendly. Remember to provide an example of a response for each Score 4.0, 3.0, and 2.0 value.

Rewritten Score 4.0 content:

Rewritten Score 3.0 content:

Rewritten Score 2.0 content:

Having Students Identify Individual Learning Goals

It's probably safe to assume that students are more engaged in a unit of instruction when they have personal goals regarding the content that is addressed. Consequently, it is beneficial to ask students to articulate personal learning goals. To illustrate, suppose a social studies teacher has set as a goal for a unit of instruction that students will understand the implications of major compromises considered by the delegates during the Constitutional Convention. After presenting this learning goal, the teacher would ask students to identify related goals of their own. One student might set a goal to learn more about specific people who attended the Constitutional Convention. Another student might set a goal to learn more about the place where the Constitutional Convention was held.

Whereas some students might quickly and easily generate personal goals related to the Constitutional Convention, it is probably true that many students would not. In this case a teacher must be willing to provide some concrete guidance. For example, the teacher might explain that the general theme they will be studying is that when something new is being developed, the rules and regulations that are established commonly have a profound effect on what happens in the future. The teacher would then encourage students to identify a personal goal regarding anything that is related to this general theme: *What are some things you are interested in right now that have rules and regulations? Who created those rules and regulations?*

One student who is interested in figure skating might decide that her personal goal is to learn more about the rules established for competitive figure skating to determine why they were established and how these initial rules have affected the sport over the years. Another student who likes basketball might do the same—learn about why specific rules were first established for basketball and how those rules have affected the sport throughout the decades. A student who is interested in computers might wish to determine how the early thinking about computing machines shaped the development of computers.

While students were learning about the Constitutional Convention, the teacher would continually help them make linkages between their personal learning goals and the overall class goal. To help students state their own learning goals in a precise manner, the following format can be used:

When this unit is completed I will better understand _____.
or
When this unit is completed I will be able to _____.

As is the case with teacher goals, student learning goals should be accompanied by a scale that can be used to track progress. We have found it useful to provide students with a generic scale like that in Figure 2.5.

FIGURE 2.5

Generic Scale for Student Goals

4 = I did even better than the goal I set.

3 = I accomplished my goal.

2 = I didn't accomplish everything I wanted to, but I learned quite a bit.

1 = I tried, but I didn't really learn much.

0 = I didn't really try to accomplish my goal.

Examples

Secondary Physical Education. A high school physical education teacher is addressing personal fitness. After she presents the learning goals for the unit and passes out the scales associated with those goals, she has each student identify a personal learning goal regarding physical fitness.

Elementary Social Studies. An elementary teacher has presented students with a scale for his learning goal regarding understanding the importance and history of the U.S. Constitution. He explains that the general theme they will be studying is how the U.S. Constitution was a document that changed the course of world history. For their personal learning goal, he invites students to learn about other documents or other events that changed the course of history.

Activity Box

Identify a learning goal you have used in a unit of instruction. Describe the directions you might have given students to help them identify personal learning goals that are related to the overall classroom goal.

Checking for Understanding

Use the following rating scale to assess your current understanding and comfort level regarding key strategies and processes presented in this module:

4 = I understand and already fully implement this strategy in my classroom.

3 = I understand this strategy, but I need to practice using it in my classroom.

2 = I can explain this strategy, but I am not fully confident that I can use it.

1 = I do not understand this strategy, and I do not currently use it in my classroom.

____1. Clearly articulating learning goals as opposed to activities and assignments
Based on my rating, I may need to revisit the following:

___ 2. Creating scales or rubrics for learning goals
   Based on my rating, I may need to revisit the following:

___ 3. Rewriting scales in student-friendly language
   Based on my rating, I may need to revisit the following:

___ 4. Having students identify individual learning goals
   Based on my rating, I may need to revisit the following:

Design Question 1

What Will I Do to Establish and Communicate Learning Goals, Track Student Progress, and Celebrate Success?

Module 3

Designing and Using Formative Assessments

The Scale for Learning Goals introduced in Module 2 (see Figure 2.2) was designed with formative assessment in mind. In this module we address how this scale can be used to design and score formative assessments and how those assessments can be used to provide students with feedback that can dramatically enhance their learning.

Typically a teacher will progress through a unit of instruction and give an assessment at the end to summarize the learning of students. Although the teacher might give some shorter quizzes along the way, the clear emphasis is on the assessment at the end of the unit. End-of-unit assessments typically are referred to as "summative assessments." The problem with relying on summative assessments only is that they don't provide students with feedback while they are learning new content. If teachers knew exactly how each student was progressing through a unit, they might be able to provide additional assistance. Likewise, if students knew how they were progressing, they would have the opportunity to work harder or to ask for assistance. An approach that provides student with feedback right from the beginning is referred to as "formative." Formative assessments are both powerful measurement tools and powerful instructional tools.

Reflecting on Your Current Beliefs and Practices

Before examining the strategies in this module, take some time to examine your current beliefs and practices by answering the following questions:

1. How well do you understand the defining characteristics of formative assessments? What are those characteristics?

_____

_____

_____

_____

2. How do you use formative assessments in your classroom?

_____

_____

_____

_____

3. What do you do to provide feedback to students consistently throughout a unit of instruction?

_____

_____

_____

_____

4. What do you do to show students that they have gained in knowledge throughout your units of instruction?

_____

_____

_____

_____

5. How do your grading policies support formative assessment?

_____

_____

_____

_____

Recommendations for Classroom Practice

This module addresses the following strategies for Design Question 1:

- Designing and scoring formative assessments
- Using a variety of types of assessments
- Keeping track of student progress over time

- Celebrating final status and knowledge gain
- Grading in a formative system

Designing and Scoring Formative Assessments

In Module 2 we introduced the scale depicted in Figure 3.1. In Module 2 we also explained that this generic scale should be translated into a specific scale for each learning goal in the unit. If a unit has two learning goals, two scales should be constructed. This is much easier than it might seem because a teacher need only identify content for Scores 2.0, 3.0, and 4.0.

FIGURE 3.1

Scale for Learning Goals and Formative Assessments

Score 4.0	In addition to Score 3.0 performance, in-depth inferences and applications that go beyond what was taught.	
	Score 3.5	In addition to Score 3.0 performance, in-depth inferences and applications with partial success.
Score 3.0	No major errors or omissions regarding any of the information and processes (simple or complex) that were explicitly taught.	
	Score 2.5	No major errors or omissions regarding the simpler details and processes (Score 2.0 content) and partial knowledge of the more complex ideas and processes (Score 3.0 content).
Score 2.0	No major errors or omissions regarding the simpler details and processes but major errors or omissions regarding the more complex ideas and processes (Score 3.0 content).	
	Score 1.5	Partial knowledge of the simpler details and processes (Score 2.0 content) but major errors or omissions regarding the more complex ideas and procedures (Score 3.0 content).
Score 1.0	With help, a partial understanding of some of the simpler details and pro-cesses (Score 2.0 content) and some of the more complex ideas and pro-cesses (Score 3.0 content).	
	Score 0.5	With help, a partial understanding of some of the simpler details and processes (Score 2.0 content) but not the more complex ideas and processes (Score 3.0 content).
Score 0.0	Even with help, no understanding or skill demonstrated.	

To illustrate, assume that an elementary social studies teacher is teaching a unit on local economics. One of the learning goals she identifies is that students will understand how local economics contributes to the community. The specific scale the teacher might design for this learning goal is shown in Figure 3.2. As described in Module 2, this scale would be translated, with teacher guidance, into student-friendly language. For Score 4.0, 3.0, and 2.0 content, the class as a whole would generate specific examples so that students have clear guidance as to expected outcomes.

The next task for the teacher is to design assessments that address the content in the scale. If a scale is well written, this is a fairly straightforward process, requiring only that

FIGURE 3.2
Scale for Local Economics

Score 4.0	In addition to Score 3.0 performance, in-depth inferences and applications that go beyond what was taught, such as • Explaining how local economics has helped or hindered a specific business.	
	Score 3.5	In addition to Score 3.0 performance, in-depth inferences and applications with partial success.
Score 3.0	While engaged in tasks that address economics throughout the world, the student demonstrates an understanding of important information, such as • Examples of uses of revenue in the local community (*e.g., explaining and exemplifying how revenue in the community can be used for a specific purpose like staffing and maintenance of a community recreation center*). The student makes no major errors or omissions.	
	Score 2.5	No major errors or omissions regarding the Score 2.0 elements and partial knowledge of the Score 3.0 elements.

Score 2.0	No major errors or omissions regarding the simpler details and processes, such as
	
	• Recognizing and recalling isolated details, such as
	  – permit fees help provide revenue to many local communities,
	  – some industries decline over time, and
	  – some types of work are available in each community throughout a state.
	
	However, the student exhibits major errors or omissions with Score 3.0 elements.	

	Score 1.5	Partial knowledge of the Score 2.0 elements but major errors or omissions regarding the Score 3.0 elements.
Score 1.0	With help, a partial understanding of some of the Score 2.0 elements and some of the Score 3.0 elements.	
	Score 0.5	With help, a partial understanding of some of the Score 2.0 elements but not the Score 3.0 elements.
Score 0.0	Even with help, no understanding or skill demonstrated.	

the teacher follow the content described in Scores 2.0, 3.0, and 4.0. To illustrate, the teacher who designed the scale in Figure 3.2 might write the following item for Score 2.0:

> Provide an example or illustration for each of the following statements:
> - Permit fees help provide revenue to many local communities.
> - Some industries decline over time.
> - Some types of work are available in each community throughout a state.

For Score 3.0, the teacher might construct the following item:

> Write a short paragraph explaining how revenue in the local community can be used for a specific purpose. Provide examples of the type of revenue that would most likely be used for that purpose.

Finally, for Score 4.0, the teacher might construct the following item:

> Select a specific business in the local community and analyze how the local economy has helped or hindered that business. Justify your reasons for making that determination.

These items would be combined in a single assessment like that in Figure 3.3.

Questions for Score 2.0 content typically employ the following formats: true-false items, multiple-choice items, fill-in-the-blank items, and short-answer items. Questions for Score 3.0 and Score 4.0 content typically employ constructed-response formats.

FIGURE 3.3

Three-Part Assessment

Part 1. Provide an example or illustration for each of the following statements:

    a. Permit fees help provide revenue to local communities.

    b. Some industries decline over time.

    c. Some types of work are available in each community throughout a state.

Part 2. Write a short paragraph explaining how revenue in the local community can be used for a specific purpose. Provide examples of the type of revenue that would most likely be used for that purpose.

Part 3. Select a specific business in the local community and analyze how the local economy has helped or hindered that business. Justify your reasons for making that determination.

Examples

Secondary Civics. This high school civics teacher has created a scale for the topic of personal responsibility in a democratic society. Using her scale, she creates items for the Score 2.0 content, the Score 3.0 content, and the Score 4.0 content. She has 10 multiple-choice questions for Score 2.0 content, three questions for Score 3.0 content that ask students to explain and exemplify some generalizations addressed in class, and one item for Score 4.0 content that asks students to make and defend a prediction based on what they have learned. She organizes these items into a single assessment with sections of the assessment designated for each level.

Elementary Mathematics. This 3rd grade mathematics teacher has developed a scale for data organization and interpretation. Given her specificity in describing the Score 4.0, 3.0, and 2.0 content regarding this topic, she finds it easy to develop an assessment that includes items for all components of the scale. She organizes the assessment into three sections—one each for Score 2.0 items, Score 3.0 items, and Score 4.0 items.

Activity Box

For a specific learning goal you have used or will use, identify Score 2.0 content, Score 3.0 content, and Score 4.0 content, and then write a sample assessment item for each.

Score 2.0 item:

Score 3.0 item:

Score 4.0 item:

Looking at Response Patterns

To score the assessment in Figure 3.3, the teacher would examine the pattern of responses across the three types of items—Score 2.0 items, Score 3.0 items, and Score 4.0 items. To illustrate, we'll consider the score values of 2.0, 3.0, and 4.0 and their related half-point scores.

Suppose a particular student answered items in Part 1 correctly but did not answer correctly the items in Part 2 or Part 3. The student would receive a score of 2.0 on the assessment. If the student answered items in Part 1 and Part 2 correctly but not Part 3, he would receive a score of 3.0. If the student answered all items in all three parts correctly, he would receive a score of 4.0.

Now let's consider some other patterns. Suppose a student answered some of the items in Part 1 correctly but no others. The student would receive a score of 1.5, indicating partial credit on the simpler details and processes (i.e., the Score 2.0 elements). Now assume the student answered all items in Part 1 correctly and received partial credit on the items in Part 2. The student would receive a score of 2.5. Finally, assume the student answered the items correctly in Part 1 and Part 2 and received partial credit on the items in Part 3. The student would receive a score of 3.5. In summary, by analyzing the pattern of responses across the three different types of items (Score 2.0 items, Score 3.0 items, and Score 4.0 items), scores of 1.5 to 4.0 can be assigned. However, scores of 0, 0.5 and 1.0 require teacher-student interaction.

One thing common to the score values of 0, 0.5, and 1.0 is that they all include the phrase *with help,* meaning that the teacher must interact with students to determine these score values. We should make one caveat here. The implication is *not* that a teacher must meet with every student after every assessment. Rather, a teacher would meet only with those students whose responses on the assessment indicated no knowledge of the content. There will probably be very few such students for any given assessment. With these students, the teacher might go over specific assessment items, giving guidance and hints. For example, consider again the assessment in Figure 3.3. With a particular student the teacher might say, "Maria, let's go over a few of these items. I know you understand a great deal of this because I've heard you answer some of these same questions in class. Let's take the first question. Tell me what you remember about the permit fees. Let me give you some clues . . . ."

Based on the interaction with the student, the teacher could assign a score of 1.0, 0.5, or 0. If the student was able to answer some Score 2.0 items and some Score 3.0 items with help, she would receive a 1.0. If the student was able to answer, with help, Score 2.0 items correctly but not Score 3.0 items, she would receive a score of 0.5. If the student could not answer any of the items correctly even with help, she would receive a score of 0.

Examples

Elementary Geography. This elementary teacher is scoring a test she designed on the characteristics of political regions versus economic regions. She notices that a majority of her students have missed items that were supposed to be easy—Score 2.0 content. She realizes that this situation means she either didn't do a very good job teaching that content or it was much harder than she thought. For this particular test, she recalibrates the item, now counting it as Score 3.0 content. She will discuss the item and review that content with students when she returns their papers tomorrow.

Middle School Science. This middle school science teacher has given a test on the topic of mutualism. One of her students has done quite poorly on the test, attempting to answer only a few questions. During a conference with the student, she goes over some of the items, reminding the student of discussions in class. With the teacher's guidance and help, the student is able to answer some of the Score 2.0 items and Score 3.0 items. The student is assigned a score of 1.0 on the assessment.

Activity Box

Contrast the method of designing and scoring formative assessments described in this section with the method you use.

Designing Individual Score-Level Assessments

The scale in Figure 3.2 regarding local economics deals with content that is based on information. It is declarative knowledge. Let's consider content that is more process or skill oriented (content that is procedural knowledge)—and, at the same time, consider designing individual score-level assessments. To illustrate, recall the scale for causal relationships presented in Module 2. It is reproduced in Figure 3.4.

To assess the content in Figure 3.4, the teacher might have students read a particular story such as *The Outsiders*, which depicts the struggles between two classes of students in an urban high school in the 1960s. The teacher might give students two weeks to read the book. Instead of developing one assessment for this learning goal, she would design an assessment at the beginning of the unit to determine students' knowledge of the Score 2.0 content—in this case, students' ability to recognize parts of the text that provide information about important causal relationships. This might be done by providing students with questions like the following:

> In the first chapter of the book, the author provides us with some specific clues that something will happen later on. What are some of those clues? What specific events look like they will cause other things to occur later on? What are some words or phrases that tell you something might cause something else to happen?

All students would answer this question, and the teacher would score their responses. For this assessment, the highest score students could receive would be a 2.0 because the assessment addresses only this level of the scale.

FIGURE 3.4

Scale for the Learning Goal of Understanding Causal Relationships

Grade 8		
Score 4.0	**In addition to Score 3.0 performance, in-depth inferences and applications that go beyond what was taught, such as** • Explaining how a complex causal relationship in one story is similar to that in another story.	
	Score 3.5	In addition to Score 3.0 performance, in-depth inferences and applications with partial success.
Score 3.0	**While engaged in grade-appropriate reading tasks, the student demonstrates an ability to** • Describe complex causal relationships (*e.g., observing that the plight of* Anne Frank in The Diary of Anne Frank *is the result of causes ranging from the policies of the Nazis in Amsterdam to the childhood of Adolph Hitler*). **The student exhibits no major errors or omissions.**	
	Score 2.5	No major errors or omissions regarding the Score 2.0 elements and partial knowledge of the Score 3.0 elements.
Score 2.0	**No major errors or omissions regarding the simpler details and processes, such as** • Identifying literary clues that indicate complex causal relationships (*e.g., recognizing specific words and phrases that signal complex causal relationships*). **However, the student exhibits major errors or omissions with Score 3.0 elements.**	
	Score 1.5	Partial knowledge of the Score 2.0 elements but major errors or omissions regarding the Score 3.0 elements.
Score 1.0	**With help, a partial understanding of some of the Score 2.0 elements and some of the Score 3.0 elements.**	
	Score 0.5	With help, a partial understanding of some of the Score 2.0 elements but not the Score 3.0 elements.
Score 0.0	**Even with help, no understanding or skill demonstrated.**	

After students had read the entire book, the teacher would design a second assessment, this time focused on Score 3.0 content. The question posed to students might be this:

> In the end, the "rich kids" and the kids from the "other side of the tracks" saw that they were more alike than different. Describe the specific events that led to this awareness on both sides.

Again the students' responses would be scored, but this time the highest score a student could receive would be a 3.0 because the assessment was designed for the 3.0 level of the scale.

Finally, at the end of the unit, the teacher would provide an assessment that addressed Score 4.0 content. It might be something like this:

> We have studied other books that involved complex causes. Select something we have read in class or something you have read on your own and explain how the events in that work are similar to and different from the events in *The Outsiders*.

This method of designing and scoring formative assessments is different from the method described earlier. In the example involving local economics, the teacher designed one assessment that included Score 2.0 items, Score 3.0 items, and Score 4.0 items. To score the assessment, students' patterns of response were examined. On that one assessment, then, students could receive scores ranging from 0.0 to 4.0.

The second example involving *The Outsiders* is quite different. In this case, the first assessment contained Score 2.0 content only. Thus, the highest score a student could receive is 2.0. The next assessment involved Score 3.0 content. This would be administered only after students had demonstrated their competence at Score 2.0 content. Finally, the third assessment dealt with Score 4.0 content. This would be administered after students had demonstrated competence with Score 3.0 content.

Examples

Elementary Writing. This language arts teacher has designed a scale for writing compositions with paragraphs that are logically related and have good transition sentences. Score 2.0 on the scale requires students to provide transition sentences for related paragraphs that are provided for them. The teacher's first assessment deals with this level only; she gives students paragraphs and they provide the transitions. Once students seem comfortable with this content, she moves up to Score 3.0 content, which requires them to write a five-paragraph essay in which they must write the paragraphs and the transitions. After that she designs assessments that address the Score 4.0 content.

High School Mathematics. This high school mathematics teacher has designed a scale for polynomials. Her first assessment is for the Score 2.0 content—simple polynomials with one variable. After that she moves to Score 3.0 content, which addresses polynomials with two variables. The final part of her unit will address Score 4.0 content, which requires students to model real-life situations using complex polynomials.

Activity Box

Which of the two methods of designing and scoring formative assessments do you like better—the one in which assessments include Score 2.0, 3.0, and 4.0 content or the one in which Score 2.0 content is assessed separately from Score 3.0 content, and Score 3.0 content is assessed separately from Score 4.0 content? Explain your reasoning.

Using a Variety of Types of Assessments

Formative assessments as described in this module will use a variety of types of items and tasks. Certainly many formative assessments will use traditional types of paper-pencil formats that involve true-false items, multiple-choice items, fill-in-the-blank items, and short constructed-response items. In addition to these traditional approaches to assessment, a teacher should include some nontraditional techniques. Here we consider three: (1) the probing discussion, (2) unobtrusive observation, and (3) student-generated tasks.

The Probing Discussion

As its name indicates, the probing discussion involves the teacher talking with a student one-on-one and asking the student to explain something or demonstrate something. The advantage to this approach is that the teacher can obtain very specific information about a particular student's knowledge. For example, a social studies teacher working on a learning goal involving local economics would simply sit down with a student and ask her how the money made in the community might be used by the community for specific projects. While doing so, the teacher could probe more deeply and determine the depth of the student's knowledge by asking clarification questions. The teacher could also guide the inquiry to cover all aspects of the topic. If the Score 2.0 components on the scale addressed information about permit fees, the decline of certain industries, and specific types of work available in the community, the teacher could make sure these elements were addressed by the questions she asked. The student's response to the probing discussion would be scored using the scale and entered into the teacher's grade book. In short, a probing discussion can provide a comprehensive picture of a student's knowledge because of the flexibility it provides the teacher in terms of addressing all the content in a particular scale.

Unobtrusive Observation

Unobtrusive observation means that the teacher observes a student demonstrating a particular type of knowledge without necessarily interacting with the student. For example, assume that a teacher has a learning goal that deals with solving a particular type of mathematics problem, such as computing the area of irregular shapes. The teacher might observe a student working on a problem of this type and notice that his methodology and answer are both correct. The teacher would score the student using the scale designed for this objective and enter the score into the grade book.

Student-Generated Tasks

A powerful assessment alternative is to have students generate their own tasks to demonstrate competence for specific values of the scale. To use this approach, a teacher would typically begin by designing and administering an assessment on a specific learning goal. Each student would have a score on this initial assessment. For example, one student might have a score of 2.0, indicating knowledge of the basic content, and another student might have a score of 3.0, indicating knowledge of the basic content and the more complex content that is explicitly taught. Next, the teacher would ask students to identify or design tasks that would warrant their moving up to the next score value. The student with a score of 2.0 might propose that she will write a brief explanation of the Score 3.0 content to move to that level. The student with a score of 3.0 might propose that he give a brief oral presentation involving the Score 4.0 content to justify moving to that level. The point here is that students take the responsibility for providing evidence that they should move to the next level of the scale.

Examples

Middle School Art. This teacher has designed a scale for a specific brushstroke technique. She notices that Andre is using the technique precisely while working on a specific painting and is even making adaptations beyond what was taught. In her grade book she records a score of 4.0 for this unobtrusive observation.

Elementary Science. As a form of formative assessment, this science teacher periodically asks individual students to come up to her desk and has a discussion with them about a specific learning goal. She does not provide hints or clues to the student. Rather, she asks the student to go into more depth regarding specific topics and to clarify specific answers. This type of interaction allows her to address the full range of content in a scale during one discussion with a student. She uses these discussions as a valuable form of formative assessment.

Activity Box

Describe ways you might use probing discussions, unobtrusive observations, or student-generated tasks to assess students.

Keeping Track of Student Progress over Time

Throughout a unit, students should graph their progress on specific learning goals. A graph of this sort is depicted in Figure 3.5. In this example, six scores have been recorded. The first assessment was on February 5; the next assessment was on February 12, and so on. The student's first score was 1.5, then 2.0, and so on. The student's final score in the set was 3.0. Graphically displaying student progress like this can be a powerful motivational tool because students can see their progress over time.

FIGURE 3.5

Tracking Student Progress

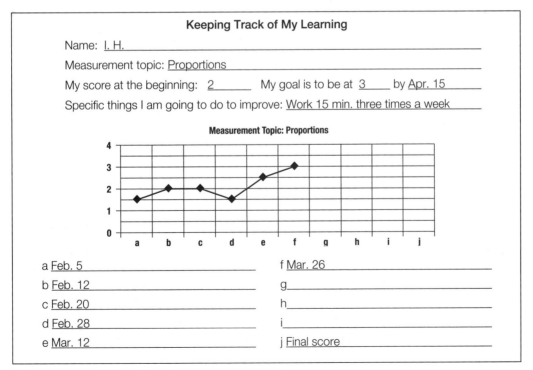

Keeping Track of My Learning

Name: I. H.

Measurement topic: Proportions

My score at the beginning: 2   My goal is to be at 3   by Apr. 15

Specific things I am going to do to improve: Work 15 min. three times a week

Measurement Topic: Proportions

a Feb. 5   f Mar. 26
b Feb. 12   g
c Feb. 20   h
d Feb. 28   i
e Mar. 12   j Final score

It is important to note that the teacher must assign a final score (the last column in Figure 3.5) for a learning goal based on her best judgment of the student's final status. Certainly the student's final score in the set (see Column f) is a good candidate for the final score. In this case that final score is a 3.0. If the teacher believes this is an accurate representation of the student's true level of understanding or skill relative to the topic, then, indeed, 3.0 should be the final score. However, assume for a moment that the sample student depicted in Figure 3.5 received a final score on March 26 of 2.0. Would it be fair to assign this as the final score when the previous score is a 2.5? Students will vary in the scores they exhibit across a given topic for many reasons other than their knowledge. Sometimes they have good days; sometimes they have bad days. This is why teachers must use judgment when assigning a final score. If a student has a final score that is lower than previous scores or markedly higher than previous scores, the teacher should seek further information from the student so as to make an informed judgment about the student's final status.

Examples

Secondary Social Studies. This social studies teacher is having students track their progress on their ability to analyze an opinion paper for bias. Students track their scores on the assessments on their individual progress charts. Periodically, students meet with the teacher to discuss how they might demonstrate competence at the next level of the scale.

Elementary Reading. This reading teacher has designed a scale to track students' fluency while reading aloud. Periodically throughout the grading period, students read aloud in class and the teacher scores the students using the scale. Additionally, the students score themselves. Comparing and discussing these scores, the teacher and student come up with a score that reflects the student's true status at that point in time.

Activity Box

Describe how you might use or adapt the graphing approach to tracking student progress.

Celebrating Final Status and Knowledge Gain

A unit of instruction should not end without celebrating student success. There are two approaches to doing so. The first and most common is to recognize final status—simply recognizing and celebrating each student's final score on a scale for each learning goal.

In this scenario all students who received final scores of 4.0 for a given learning goal would be recognized, then all students who received a final score of 3.5, and so on.

A very different approach is to recognize knowledge gain for each student. Knowledge gain is the difference between where a student began the unit and where the student ended up. For example, consider the student in Figure 3.5. She started with a score of 1.5 and ended up with a score of 3.0. This represents a gain of 1.5 points on the scale. Over a unit or a quarter, the learning gain for each student on each learning goal can be represented on a bar graph.

One of the most powerful aspects of recognizing and celebrating knowledge gain is that virtually every student will have something to celebrate. One student might have started at a score of 2.0 for a given learning goal and ended up with a score of 3.5. Another student might have started with a score of 1.0 and ended up with a score of 2.5. Even though the final status for these two students is quite different (3.5 versus 2.5) their knowledge gain is the same—1.5 scale points.

Examples

Elementary School Science. This elementary science teacher has kept track of two learning goals over a three-week unit. At the end of the unit he has a celebration recognizing all students who attained final scores of 4.0 and 3.0 on the two objectives. He also acknowledges knowledge gain. He hands out certificates for gains of 0.5 points, 1.0 points, and so on. He finds that virtually every student has something to be proud of.

Middle School. All the teachers at Jefferson Middle School keep track of student progress on specific learning goals. At the end of each grading period, the school has two honor rolls. The first is traditional, celebrating final status on learning goals. The second is called the "on-a-roll." It acknowledges and celebrates those students who have exhibited exceptional knowledge gain over the quarter.

Activity Box

Describe what you consider to be the relative merits of celebrating knowledge status and knowledge gain.

Grading in a Formative System

The final topic we address in this module is grading. Specifically, we address the following question: How does one grade when using rubrics or scales to track progress on learning goals? The most straightforward approach would be to numerically summarize student status across various learning goals. For example, assume that for a given grading period a teacher addressed six learning goals. Two were addressed during the first three-week unit, two during the next three-week unit, and two during the last three-week unit. Also assume that a particular student received the following final scores for those six goals: 2.5, 3.0, 2.0, 4.0, 3.0, and 3.5. The numeric average of 3.0 would be a viable summary score representing typical final status for the student across the six learning goals.

In some schools teachers are required to use a scoring system like this:

Advanced
Proficient
Basic
Below Basic

To report student status using a system like this, a translation is required. Figure 3.6 shows one possible translation. To use this translation, the teacher would compute an average score for a student across the six learning goals as before, but she would then translate that average using the conversion shown for the four status categories. In this case, the student's average score of 3.0 across all six learning goals translates to the status of Proficient.

Many districts and schools use traditional *A*, *B*, *C*, *D*, and *F* letter grades. Again, a simple translation allows for this:

A = 3.00 to 4.00
B = 2.50 to 2.99
C = 2.00 to 2.49
D = 1.00 to 1.99
F = Below 1.00

Finally, some districts and schools require an overall percentage score. To do this, the conversion scale in Figure 3.7 (or an adaptation of it) might be used. When translating to percentage scores, we recommend that teachers first translate scores for individual learning goals to a percentage score and then average those percentages. To illustrate, reconsider the following six rubric scores on six learning goals:

Learning Goal 1 = 2.5 = 80 percent

Learning Goal 2 = 3.0 = 90 percent

Learning Goal 3 = 2.0 = 70 percent

Learning Goal 4 = 4.0 = 100 percent

Learning Goal 5 = 3.0 = 90 percent

Learning Goal 6 = 3.5 = 95 percent

Average percent = 87.5 percent

Here the score of 2.5 on Learning Goal 1 translates to 80 percent, the score of 3.0 on Learning Goal 2 translates to 90 percent, and so on. The average of these percentage scores is 87.5 percent.

FIGURE 3.6

Conversion to Advanced, Proficient, Basic, and Below Basic

Advanced	**Score 4.0: In addition to Score 3.0 performance, in-depth inferences and applications that go beyond what was taught.**
	Score 3.5: In addition to Score 3.0 performance, in-depth inferences and applications with partial success.
Proficient	**Score 3.0: No major errors or omissions regarding any of the information and processes (simple or complex) that were explicitly taught.**
	Score 2.5: No major errors or omissions regarding the simpler details and processes (Score 2.0 content) and partial knowledge of the more complex ideas and processes (Score 3.0 content).
Basic	**Score 2.0: No major errors or omissions regarding the simpler details and processes but major errors or omissions regarding the more complex ideas and processes (Score 3.0 content).**
	Score 1.5: Partial knowledge of the simpler details and processes (Score 2.0 content) but major errors or omissions regarding the more complex ideas and processes (Score 3.0 content).
Below Basic	**Score 1.0: With help, a partial understanding of some of the simpler details and processes (Score 2.0 content) and some of the more complex ideas and processes (Score 3.0 content).**
	Score 0.5: With help, a partial understanding of some of the simpler details and processes (Score 2.0 content) but not the more complex ideas and processes (Score 3.0 content).
	Score 0.0: Even with help, no understanding or skill demonstrated.

FIGURE 3.7

Conversion Scale to Percentages

Scale (Rubric) Score	Percentage Score
4.0	100
3.5	95
3.0	90
2.5	80
2.0	70
1.5	65
1.0	60
Below 1.0	50

Examples

Elementary Language Arts. Over a nine-week period, this elementary language arts teacher has obtained final status scores for her students on five learning goals. Her school requires that she assign one of the following categories to each student: Advanced, Proficient, Basic, or Below Basic. These categories must be assigned as an overall language arts score. The teacher averages the five final status scores for each student and then translates the average score to the categories required by the district.

High School Biology. This biology teacher has tracked students' progress on seven goals over the nine-week quarter. He has to use percentage scores on the report cards, so he converts the final scores on learning goals into percentages. Even though the report card in his school is very traditional, he believes he has a powerful system that allows students to see not only their final status on specific learning goals but also their knowledge gain.

Activity Box

Which of the grading techniques presented in this section do you prefer? Explain your answer.

Checking for Understanding

Use the following rating scale to assess your current level of understanding and your comfort level regarding the key strategies and processes presented in this module:

4 = I understand and already fully implement this strategy in my classroom.
3 = I understand this strategy, but I need to practice using it in my classroom.
2 = I can explain this strategy, but I am not fully confident that I can use it.
1 = I do not understand this strategy, and I do not currently use it in my classroom.

___ 1.   Designing and scoring formative assessments
Based on my rating, I may need to revisit the following:

___ 2.   Using a variety of types of assessments
Based on my rating, I may need to revisit the following:

___ 3.   Keeping track of student progress over time
Based on my rating, I may need to revisit the following:

___ 4.   Celebrating final status and knowledge gain
Based on my rating, I may need to revisit the following:

___ 5.   Grading in a formative system
Based on my rating, I may need to revisit the following:

Design Question 2

What Will I Do to Help Students Effectively
Interact with New Knowledge?

Module 4

Identifying Critical-Input Experiences
and Using Previewing Strategies

Module 5

Using Cooperative Learning,
Curriculum Chunking, and
Descriptions, Discussions,
and Predictions

Module 6

Helping Students Elaborate on
New Content, Summarize and
Represent Their Learning, and
Reflect on Their Learning

Design Question 2

What Will I Do to Help Students Effectively Interact with New Knowledge?

Module 4

Identifying Critical-Input Experiences and Using Previewing Strategies

This module and the next two (Modules 5 and 6) address helping students effectively interact with new knowledge. To fully address this design question, a teacher must keep a number of things in mind, including the following:

- Identifying critical-input experiences that involve a variety of mediums
- Previewing content before a critical-input experience
- Using grouping to enhance students' active processing of information
- Presenting new information in small chunks
- Using descriptions, discussions, and predictions to enhance student understanding of new information
- Asking questions that require students to elaborate on information
- Having students write out their conclusions
- Having students represent their learning nonlinguistically
- Asking students to reflect on their learning

All of these activities will take place in a single lesson. For ease of discussion, we've organized these activities into three modules:

- Module 4 (this module) addresses identifying critical-input experiences and previewing new content.
- Module 5 addresses breaking content into small chunks of new information and organizing students into small groups to facilitate the processing of information.

47

- Module 6 deals with ways students can elaborate on what they have learned, summarize and represent their learning, and reflect on their learning.

Reflecting on Your Current Beliefs and Practices

Before examining the strategies in this module, take some time to examine your current beliefs and practices by answering the following questions:

1. How do you typically introduce students to new content?

_____

_____

_____

_____

2. To what extent do you emphasize a variety of learning modalities to introduce students to new content?

_____

_____

_____

_____

3. How do you preview new content with your students?

_____

_____

_____

_____

Recommendations for Classroom Practice

This module addresses the following strategies for Design Question 2:

- Identifying critical-input experiences that involve a variety of mediums
- Previewing content before a critical-input experience

Identifying Critical-Input Experiences That Involve a Variety of Mediums

Teachers provide input to students on a daily basis. However, that input is much more important to student learning at some times than at others. For example, when a teacher is introducing a new type of problem in a mathematics class, it is critical that students begin with a strong foundation on the basics of solving that type of problem. Consequently, the first few lessons on the new problem-solving strategy are critical experiences for them. Similarly, when a teacher is introducing new information about the Bill of Rights, it is important that students have a good grounding in the essential elements of this information. We call these experiences "critical-input" experiences because of their importance in the process of teaching and learning new content.

Using a variety of learning modalities and focusing on experiential learning are important considerations when designing critical-input experiences. In particular, involving students in visual, dramatic, and narrative activities can greatly enhance their learning. Visual activities require students to create mental pictures of significant information they are encountering for the first time. Similarly, dramatic tasks involve students in dramatizing content, storing that content in the highly effective episodic memory system. Stories are another powerful way of introducing new content. In general, any new content that has a story attached to it will most probably be remembered by students for quite a while.

In general, critical-input experiences should be fast moving and engaging. To illustrate, a high school history teacher might want her students to understand the enduring impact of the 1929 stock market crash and the effects of the Great Depression on life in the United States following it. She is especially interested in helping students make connections between these earlier historical events and contemporary economic, social, political, and cultural issues. Her introduction to this unit includes a series of reflective and dramatic activities that frame key concepts and issues. First, she asks students to watch a series of short excerpts from silent and talking movies depicting the Roaring Twenties. She asks, "What impression of this era do these movies convey? To what extent do you find them realistic? How do they relate to circumstances today?" Next, students view a series of Work Progress Administration (WPA) photographs depicting life in the rural South and Midwest, including shots of Dust Bowl farmers leaving their homes for California. The teacher asks, "How do these photographs compare to the movie excerpts we just saw?" Finally, students participate in a series of brief dramatizations involving scenarios depicting life during the 1930s in the United States. Through these three interrelated critical-input experiences, students frame their understanding of key issues and the contrasting perspectives they will investigate during this unit on one of the worst economic disasters the United States has experienced.

As this example illustrates, sometimes a number of critical-input experiences are strung together serially to provide a rich and varied introduction to new content. As the following additional examples illustrate, critical-input experiences come in many forms.

Examples

Elementary School Unit on Rain Forests. A 3rd grade teacher wants her students to understand the significance of the rain forest as an environmental habitat as well as a source of survival for our planet. As she prepares to teach this unit, she decides to engage her students in a series of visual, dramatic, and verbal input tasks. In combination, these critical-input experiences will frame students' conceptual grasp of key unit concepts (e.g., ecological interdependency, rain forests as the "lungs of our planet," deforestation) as well as activate a variety of memory systems, including their episodic memory (the memory that retains personal narratives and emotional connections) and procedural memory (the memory that retains physical skills and procedures). Students will begin by imagining they are explorers in the Amazon rain forest. They will view an excerpt from a National Geographic video highlighting the living organisms—including animals and plants—that can be found there. They then will break into teams to classify what they have observed and report back to the class on their classification system.

Middle School Mathematics Unit on the Pythagorean Theorem. Rather than mechanically presenting the Pythagorean theorem—or lecturing on its applications at the beginning of the unit—a mathematics instructor chooses to engage students in a right-triangle treasure hunt. They are asked to observe their classrooms, school, home, and other areas they encounter, identifying places where right triangles are clearly evident in architectural or related structures. This assignment begins in class but ends at home. The next day, students discuss the universal presence of right triangles in visual displays in their world, including buildings, visual arts, advertisements, clothing, and other areas. This initial critical-input experience reinforces the significance of this geometric shape—and prepares students for understanding the significance of the Pythagorean theorem as part of measuring everyday objects and spaces.

Activity Box

Which of the three examples presented in this section is most similar to what you have done or would like to do? Explain why.

Previewing Content Before a Critical-Input Experience

Before the presentation of new content via a critical-input experience, students benefit from previewing it so that they can activate prior learnings associated with the new content. We have identified a variety of previewing strategies and experiences that can be used with virtually all learners.

What Do You Think You Know?

This strategy activates students' prior knowledge and experiences in relationship to new content. It is especially useful in helping the teacher observe the level of familiarity students have with new content as well as diagnose significant gaps in their knowledge and skills. For example, during an English/language arts lesson, an elementary school teacher working with her students on varying sentence structure previews key content. She asks students to think about what they already know about types of sentence structure. Then, students pair up and share their ideas. Each pair, in turn, is asked to create an example of the types of sentence structure the pair has identified. The previewing experience concludes with students sharing their writing as a whole group, with the teacher then presenting examples and explanations of simple, compound, and complex sentences. At the end of the session, students reexamine their initial ideas about what they thought they knew.

Overt Linkages

In this previewing strategy, the teacher helps students identify connections between content they have previously studied and content they will learn about in an upcoming critical-input experience. A high school civics teacher, for example, might preview for students the distinctions between criminal and civil law by asking them to think about events and incidents they have observed in recent news stories as well as first-hand events involving legal issues. As students brainstorm and list these events, they speculate on which category—criminal law or civil law—might be appropriate for each event. The teacher can ask them to revisit prior lessons and units dealing with legal concepts to help them finesse and fine-tune the distinctions emphasized during the unit.

Preview Questions

Engaging students in discussions of preview questions before a critical-input experience can greatly increase their understanding and activation of prior knowledge related to it. As middle school students prepare to read the first chapter of George Orwell's allegory *Animal Farm*, for example, students are asked to keep the following questions in mind and be prepared to answer them later: (1) *What works of literature have you read in which central characters represent human virtues and vices?* (2) *What popular films have characters that represent the forces of good and evil?* (3) *Which animals in* Animal Farm *seem to be the main characters?*

Brief Teacher Summary

Teachers can use oral and written summaries before a critical-input experience to help students anticipate key ideas and patterns. At the beginning of an algebra unit on polynomials, for example, a mathematics teacher might have students preview the chapter, summarizing key concepts for students. As he moves through this summary, he helps students understand the importance of the content and its connections to their prior learning in the course. Similarly, an elementary science teacher might introduce a unit on cloud formations by showing students photographs of the major categories they will study, highlighting simple ways for them to distinguish among these categories.

Skimming

This process is closely aligned with surveying text in the SQ3R (survey-question-read-recite-review) method. Teachers in all content areas can use guiding questions such as the following: (1) *As you skim this chapter (or passage), what are its major section headings?* (2) *What do these headings tell you about the main ideas and important concepts you will learn about?* (3) *Does the chapter (or passage) contain subheadings? If so, what does the text for each subheading tell you?* (4) *As you finish previewing this chapter (or passage), how would you summarize what you think it is about?* (5) *How familiar are you with its content? What do you expect to learn, based upon your initial preview of this material?*

Teacher-Prepared Notes

This strategy requires the teacher to provide students with an outline of important content associated with an upcoming critical-input experience. Students work with the teacher to review the notes and to identify initial questions or areas of confusion. The notes can function as a kind of advance organizer for students as well as serve as a road map throughout the critical-input experience. A middle school language arts instructor, for example, might preview a unit on figurative language in poetry by providing students with an outline of key concepts and examples for key terms they will investigate, such as *metaphor, simile, oxymoron,* and *hyperbole*. Students can refer to this outline as they read and discuss various forms of poetry. They can also enhance their understanding by revisiting the outline during various critical-input experiences the teacher uses throughout the unit and adding further examples from the poems they read and analyze.

Examples

Secondary Science Lesson on Fossil Evidence. Before watching a film on how the age, history, and changing life forms of the earth can be determined by fossils and the area around them, a secondary science teacher provides students with a brief summary of what they will see.

Elementary Mathematics Lesson. Before modeling a strategy for front-end rounding, an elementary mathematics teacher asks students what they think they already know about rounding. As students call out their thoughts, the teacher records them on the whiteboard. At the end of the lesson, the teacher reviews the comments on the whiteboard to determine which ones proved to be accurate and which ones did not prove to be accurate.

> ### Activity Box
>
> Describe how you have used at least two of the previewing strategies listed in this section.

Checking for Understanding

Use the following rating scale to assess your current understanding and comfort level regarding key strategies and processes presented in this module:

4 = I understand and already fully implement this strategy in my classroom.
3 = I understand this strategy, but I need to practice using it in my classroom.
2 = I can explain this strategy, but I am not fully confident that I can use it.
1 = I do not understand this strategy, and I do not currently use it in my classroom.

___1.   Making a distinction between critical-input experiences and other types of activities
Based on my rating, I may need to revisit the following:

___2.   Using a variety of mediums to present new content
Based on my rating, I may need to revisit the following:

___3.   Previewing content using the "What do you think you know" strategy
Based on my rating, I may need to revisit the following:

___ 4.   Previewing content using overt linkages
Based on my rating, I may need to revisit the following:

___ 5.   Previewing content using preview questions
Based on my rating, I may need to revisit the following:

___ 6.   Previewing content using brief teacher summaries
Based on my rating, I may need to revisit the following:

___ 7.   Previewing content using skimming
Based on my rating, I may need to revisit the following:

___ 8.   Previewing content using teacher-prepared notes
Based on my rating, I may need to revisit the following:

Design Question 2

What Will I Do to Help Students Effectively Interact with New Knowledge?

Module 5

Using Cooperative Learning, Curriculum Chunking, and Descriptions, Discussions, and Predictions

In this module we continue to explore techniques for helping students interact with new knowledge. All three of the modules in this section address Design Question 2: *What will I do to help students effectively interact with new knowledge?* As we saw, this design question involves a number of components. In this module we address the need to present new information and skills in small chunks so that students have time to process it and explore with other students their evolving reactions and perspectives. We also consider the need to engage students in a variety of small-group tasks to help them interact during critical-input experiences.

Reflecting on Your Current Beliefs and Practices

Before examining the strategies in this module, take some time to examine your current beliefs and practices by answering the following questions:

1. To what extent do you use cooperative learning and related small-group activities to help students process new information, skills, and procedures?

_____

_____

_____

---

2. To what extent do you chunk new knowledge in small increments?

---

3. How do you use students' descriptions, discussions, and predictions to reinforce their processing of new information, skills, and procedures?

Recommendations for Classroom Practice

This module addresses the following strategies for Design Question 2:

- Using grouping to enhance students' active processing of information
- Presenting new information in small chunks
- Using descriptions, discussions, and predictions to enhance students' understanding of new information
- Using formal techniques for critical-input experiences

Using Grouping to Enhance Students' Active Processing of Information

Cooperative learning and other small-group processes allow students to experience content from multiple perspectives. Group interaction not only facilitates knowledge development but also creates awareness that is difficult if not impossible to achieve without interaction. We believe pairs and triads are the most effective grouping configurations as students process new information and skills. However, larger groups may also be used effectively. These intimate settings provide students with multiple reference points, including opportunities to see how others view new content. Students can also benefit from seeing how others react to their own processing of new information.

Small-group activities can be used before a critical-input experience. They can also be used throughout a critical-input experience. In either case it is important to help students apply operating rules such as the following, which are essential to group success:

1. Be willing to add your perspective to any discussion.
2. Respect the opinions of other people.
3. Make sure you understand what others have added to the conversation.
4. Be willing to ask questions if you don't understand something.
5. Be willing to answer questions other group members ask you about your ideas.

The following examples illustrate how cooperative grouping might be used in conjunction with critical-input experiences.

Examples

World History Unit on Ancient World Civilizations. At the beginning of the academic year, this high school history class is preparing to investigate a variety of early world civilizations, including Mesopotamia, Egypt, the Indus River Valley, Mali, Songhai, and Ghana. The teacher breaks students into small groups of four to five. They are asked to brainstorm the characteristics they associate with the term *civilization*. Next, they are responsible for developing a consensus-driven definition of *civilization*, which they will then present to the whole class. Their teacher then leads the class in creating an operational definition they will apply to each of the world civilizations they will explore in this unit. The next day the teacher has students read about a specific civilization. Each group discusses how their definition of a civilization matches what they have read. The class revisits their definition, refining and modifying it as they examine each civilization, its unique and universal characteristics, and its enduring legacy.

World Language Unit on Teenage Customs. This Level 1 Spanish class is beginning a unit on what it means to be an adolescent in Spanish-speaking countries throughout the world. The teacher knows that the unit will emphasize both this cultural dimension and some difficult verb conjugations as part of its content. To pique their curiosity, she asks students to form "travel teams" that will work together throughout the unit, including participating in an initial WebQuest investigation of adolescent customs in a country they are assigned. As a prelude to this critical-input experience, each travel group is asked to generate a "top 10 list" of the traits, behaviors, and attitudes they associate with being a teenager in the United States today. After sharing their initial list with the whole group, each travel team will compare their initial list with characteristics of adolescence in their assigned country. Throughout the unit, travel teams will meet to explore how the language elements—including verb conjugations—they are learning in the unit might contribute to their ability to communicate with Spanish-speaking adolescents in other countries.

Elementary School Unit on the Parts of Speech. A majority of students in this 3rd grade class continue to have difficulty understanding the distinctions among the eight parts of speech. Observing this, their teacher decides that students will benefit from processing key concepts and skills in cooperative-learning groups. She has students break into triads and assigns them two interactive tasks: (1) *Use your grammar books and group knowledge to find a way to teach younger students the key elements of each of the parts of speech. For example, how can you help a 1st grader tell if something is a noun, a verb, an adjective, or an adverb? How would you teach the 1st grader the difference between a preposition and a conjunction? (2) As you conclude your first activity, we will draw out of a hat the particular part of speech your group will be responsible for presenting. In your two- to three-minute presentation, model for the class how you would teach a 1st grader your assigned part of speech.* The day after students make their presentations, the teacher illustrates each part of speech. Each triad examines its presentation for accuracy in light of the teacher's presentation.

Middle School Physical Science Unit on Newton's Laws. Students in this class are about to investigate Newton's laws, a unit their teacher knows from experience to be challenging for early adolescents. This year he decides to use a series of small-group experiential-learning activities before presenting the abstractions of Newton's principles. He first breaks students into pairs, with each team responsible for observing a series of demonstrations he conducts with simple machines, toy cars, and balloons. Each pair records its observations and is given time to reflect on what those observations reveal about motion, energy transfer, and how objects affect and are affected by them. At the conclusion of this observation cycle, pairs are asked to share their observations with another pair near them. During a final whole-class debriefing session, the entire group determines what they agree about concerning motion, energy transfer, and objects. As students read about the laws of motion in the textbook, each pair of students continually refines its initial understanding of these laws.

Activity Box

Which of the examples of the use of cooperative grouping presented in this section is most similar to the ways you have used grouping? Explain how. What are some ideas you have for ways you might use cooperative groups?

Presenting New Information in Small Chunks

Our working memory—where we process new information—is small and can handle only a few bits of information at one time. Too much information swamps our working memory. Therefore, students need to actively process new content in small chunks or increments based upon their readiness levels and background knowledge. In effect, the more students know about the new content they are to study, the larger the chunks can be. This is why effective teachers plan for how they will "chunk" new information for students.

Using curriculum chunking effectively requires teachers to distinguish between the declarative and procedural knowledge that may be new to students. It also requires informal but careful pre-assessment of what students know about the content. In general, the more students know, the larger the chunks can be; the less students know, the smaller the chunks should be.

Examples

Demonstration of Ecological Interdependence (Declarative Knowledge Focus). In this biology class, students are studying the concept of symbiosis and interdependence within ecosystems. The teacher begins his presentation by showing them a series of photographs and short DVD clips of a specific type of ecosystem found throughout the planet. He then stops his presentation and asks students to form groups of three to discuss the information presented. The focus of their discussion becomes identifying key concepts and structural components of each of the systems presented. As the teacher presents additional system descriptions, students in each triad select a letter: *A*, *B*, or *C*. Member A summarizes the information presented in that segment. Then students B and C add to or modify what student A has said. At the conclusion of this activity, groups share their conclusions and questions they would like answered for clarification. The entire class then brainstorms predictions about what they may encounter as they learn about the next ecosystem. They continue this process as they explore each of the major ecosystems they will investigate in the course.

Introduction to Designing a PowerPoint Presentation (Procedural Knowledge Focus). Students in this computer applications class are learning to create a basic PowerPoint presentation on a subject of their choice. The teacher carefully chunks her introduction of key skills and strategies students might use. The first chunk involves a demonstration with follow-up small-group debriefing and application of the range of slide formats that can be chosen and the purpose for each. The second chunk involves the creation of a slide involving a title and illustrative bulleted items. The final chunk models and allows students to practice their use of various visual techniques, such as the fade and fly-in strategy. Between each segment of teacher demonstration and modeling, students debrief on what they have learned, collaborate on trying out specific strategies, and discuss clarifying questions (e.g., *What are the key skills and procedures you learned in this segment? How would you teach someone else to use these skills and procedures? Are there areas you would like revisited or modeled? How can you apply what you learned in this segment to the PowerPoint presentation you will be designing?*). Students also make predictions about what they will learn in the next segment.

Lesson on Editing for Subject-Verb Agreement (Declarative and Procedural Knowledge Focus). This English teacher is committed to helping students apply what they learn in lessons on grammar and usage to their own writing and editing process. Therefore, she chunks the curriculum content so that students move incrementally from the least complex to the most complex concepts, skills, and procedures in this mini-unit on subject-verb agreement. As students progress through the unit, she uses diagnostic and formative assessment data to differentiate instruction using flexible grouping. For students who quickly demonstrate proficiency in the declarative and procedural content of each segment, she creates independent activities, learning centers, and opportunities for students' direct application to their own compositions. For other students who require extra coaching or tutorials, she creates opportunities for them to receive the direct support. As students progress through the course, she uses peer-response group activities to help them revisit key ideas related to subject-verb agreement.

Activity Box

The examples in this section demonstrate two different types of chunking. The first example demonstrates how a teacher might chunk the content during a single lesson—a small piece (i.e., a chunk) of information is presented to students, which they then process in small groups. The next two examples illustrate a second approach to chunking. Here new information is organized into chunks across different lessons during a unit. It is important to note that during these lessons information would also be chunked into small digestible bites. Describe how you have used or could use each of these two approaches to chunking.

Using Descriptions, Discussions, and Predictions to Enhance Students' Understanding of New Information

After each small chunk of information is provided, students should work in their small groups to describe, discuss, and make predictions regarding new information. For example, assume that a physical education teacher has provided a small chunk of information regarding the proper technique for warming up before strenuous exercise. This is an example of procedural knowledge—something students will be expected to actually do. After presenting the first few steps of the technique (i.e., a small chunk), the teacher would stop and ask students to try those steps and discuss with their partners what they are clear about and what they are not clear about. After a short while the teacher would ask students to interact as an entire class. At that point the teacher would take questions from the groups to clear up confusion. The teacher would also ask students to speculate about the upcoming parts of the technique that have not yet been demonstrated or about how the technique as understood thus far might affect performance. When students appear to have a good grasp of the content in a particular chunk, the teacher would move on to the next chunk.

An elementary language arts teacher might present students with new information about the genre of tall tales by having students watch a short videotape illustrating a few of the genre's basic characteristics. This content is more declarative in nature. The teacher would organize students into pairs or triads. In their groups, students would be asked to review the information they had observed and identify key points. Groups would be invited to pose questions to the teacher. They would also be asked to make some predictions about other characteristics of tall tales that might be presented in upcoming chunks.

These illustrations for declarative and procedural knowledge have some common elements. One common element is that students must briefly summarize what they have heard, read, or observed. In their small groups, students simply restate the new information, making distinctions between more important versus less important information. Next, students identify and address confusing issues. They might work through these confusing elements in their groups, or they might ask the teacher questions. Finally, during this small-group discussion, the teacher might ask students to make predictions about what will be presented next. These three components—(1) summarizing, (2) clearing up confusion, and (3) predicting—are the elements that guide interactions among small groups.

Examples

High School Swimming Lesson. During this lesson on how to execute the butterfly stroke, the teacher first demonstrates the kicking motion that goes along with the stroke. Using float-boards for their upper body, students try the motion themselves and then meet with their pre-assigned swim partners to discuss what they understand and don't understand. While standing in the water, pairs ask questions of the teacher. Additionally, the teacher asks questions of the students regarding the kicking technique. Next the teacher demonstrates the arm movements of the butterfly stroke. Students try the arm motion in conjunction with the kicking motion. Again they meet with their partners to discuss the stroke and then ask questions of and answer questions from the teacher. Interacting about each chunk provides students with a firm foundational understanding of the stroke.

Elementary Social Studies. While presenting information about families, the teacher periodically stops and asks the triads of students she has formed to interact. One student summarizes what was presented. Then each triad identifies what they are confused about and tries to clear up their confusions. Many of the triads ask the teacher questions directly. Finally, the groups speculate as to what will come next in the presentation.

> **Activity Box**
>
> Describe how you have engaged or might engage students in activities that help them summarize, clear up confusions, and make predictions after they have heard, read, or observed new information.

Using Formal Techniques for Critical-Input Experiences

The previous illustrations depicted how summarizing, clearing up confusion, and predicting within small groups can help students process information. These three techniques can be applied in a variety of ways by teachers. Additionally, there are three formal techniques teachers might use that employ these same basic elements. The techniques are (1) reciprocal teaching, (2) jigsaw cooperative learning tasks, and (3) concept attainment.

Reciprocal Teaching

Reciprocal teaching involves having small groups of students be responsible for discussing and analyzing key sections of a text. They take turns serving as the discussion leader who raises and facilitates responses to questions such as these: *What are the main ideas here? What questions do we have? Are there areas we need to clarify? What predictions can we make?* Someone from the group summarizes content read during each segment of the reciprocal teaching process before transitioning to a new leader. In addition to helping students deepen their understanding of key unit knowledge, this process is an ideal strategy for enhancing students' reading comprehension and analytical reasoning skills.

Jigsaw Cooperative Learning Tasks

In this cooperative learning structure, students are assigned (or self-assigned) to a four-person group responsible for becoming experts on significant curriculum content. To achieve this goal, each person becomes an expert on a particular aspect of the assigned topic or topics. Students investigating the same aspect meet in groups to discuss their findings, conclusions, and questions. When they have finished, they return to their base groups and teach key content to their group members. We recommend that jigsaw activities include opportunities for groups to ask the teacher clarifying questions. They can also make predictions about what they will discover or learn when information from expert groups is shared with the base group.

Concept Attainment

This strategy asks students to induce an awareness and understanding of a new concept by responding to examples and nonexamples of that concept. All examples should clearly reflect the essential characteristics or attributes associated with the concept. The nonexamples should clearly demonstrate the absence of those attributes. Students should be reminded to look for patterns and connections common to all of the examples but missing in the nonexamples. When students think they have discovered the concept and its attributes, they should then provide an additional example and nonexample to confirm their understanding.

Examples

Reciprocal Teaching in an Elementary Language Arts Class. In this 4th grade classroom, the teacher is exploring ways to engage student interest in folk literature, particularly the African tradition of Anansi tales depicting a trickster spider. She begins the unit by reading students a sample Anansi tale, modeling the kinds of questions students will use when they break into reciprocal teaching teams. Her questions include these: *Who is the main character? How would you describe him? What does he appear to stand for or symbolize in human nature? What do you predict will happen next? What moral or lesson does this tale seem to be teaching us?* After modeling the use of this process with another Anansi tale, the teacher prepares students to replicate this questioning process in small groups. She asks them to take turns serving as group leader and facilitator as well as official summarizer. At the conclusion of the lesson, students have read and analyzed at least three new Anansi tales. The lesson concludes with students being asked to summarize what the class learned about trickster tales in the Anansi tradition.

Cooperative Learning Jigsaw in a Middle School Consumer Science Class. Students in this middle school class are learning about the quilting process, including its history, its cultural roots, and techniques for sewing and stitching a quilt. Their teacher uses cooperative learning groups and jigsaw structures to enhance student engagement and understanding. Students form groups of four by drawing numbers from a bag. Their initial configuration is their base group. Throughout the unit, students leave their base group and move toward expert groups responsible for learning about and then teaching base group members key content. During one segment, expert groups become knowledgeable about a particular quilting tradition and its historical origins. Another expert group segment allows different groups to develop expertise in a particular sewing technique. At the conclusion of every expert group investigation, members return to their base groups and teach the other members what they have learned.

Concept Attainment in a High School World Geography Class. As students in this classroom explore different world regions, their teacher makes a concerted effort to help them understand cultural traditions and nuances. When introducing students to a major world religion, for example, she uses concept attainment strategies, asking students to discover patterns in examples reflecting the specific religion (e.g., icons, spiritual concepts, architecture, and statements of belief) and contrasting nonexamples. When a particular unit requires students to understand and apply a key concept or idea from physical geography, the teacher uses visual examples and nonexamples related to the concept (e.g., isthmus, biome, and peninsula). Through this process, students reinforce their understanding and insight into the main ideas of the course. At key juncture points, the students are encouraged to create concept attainment activities to share with the rest of the class. This strategy proves especially useful when students are reviewing material and preparing for summative assessments such as end-of-unit tests.

Activity Box

Which of the three formal strategies described in this section—reciprocal teaching, jigsaw, and concept attainment—have you used in the past? Describe how you have used it. Also, describe how you might employ one or more of the strategies you haven't used before.

Checking for Understanding

Use the following rating scale to assess your current understanding and comfort level regarding key strategies and processes presented in this module:

> 4 = I understand and already fully implement this strategy in my classroom.
> 3 = I understand this strategy, but I need to practice using it in my classroom.
> 2 = I can explain this strategy, but I am not fully confident that I can use it.
> 1 = I do not understand this strategy, and I do not currently use it in my classroom.

___ 1.   Using grouping to enhance students' active processing of information
Based on my rating, I may need to revisit the following:

___ 2. Presenting new information in small chunks
Based on my rating, I may need to revisit the following:

___ 3. Using descriptions, discussions, and predictions to enhance students' understanding of new information
Based on my rating, I may need to revisit the following:

___ 4. Using the formal techniques of reciprocal teaching, jigsaw, and concept attainment
Based on my rating, I may need to revisit the following:

Design Question 2

What Will I Do to Help Students Effectively Interact with New Knowledge?

Module 6

Helping Students Elaborate on New Content, Summarize and Represent Their Learning, and Reflect on Their Learning

This module continues our exploration of strategies for helping students interact with new knowledge. In the previous two modules we addressed strategies for identifying critical-input experiences, previewing new content, presenting new content in small chunks, organizing students into small groups, and facilitating interaction about new content. In this module we address asking questions that require students to elaborate on new knowledge, having students write out their conclusions and represent their learning nonlinguistically, and having students reflect on their learning.

Reflecting on Your Current Beliefs and Practices

Before examining the strategies in this module, take some time to examine your current beliefs and practices by answering the following questions:

1. How do you use questions to help your students process new information, skills, and procedures?

_____

_____

67

_____

_____

2. How do you use questions and follow-up probes to encourage students to elaborate on insights and inferences they have drawn in response to new knowledge, particularly new content they have learned in critical-input experiences?

_____

_____

_____

3. To what extent do you have students write out their conclusions about their experiences?

_____

_____

_____

4. How do you use nonlinguistic representations such as graphic organizers as tools for students' elaboration on new knowledge?

_____

_____

_____

5. To what extent are students in your classroom actively engaged in self-reflection and self-monitoring about their acquisition and application of new knowledge?

_____

_____

_____

Recommendations for Classroom Practice

This module addresses the following strategies for Design Question 2:

- Asking questions that require students to elaborate on information
- Having students write out their conclusions
- Having students represent their learning nonlinguistically
- Having students reflect on their learning

Asking Questions That Require Students to Elaborate on Information

Questioning techniques have always been considered one of the most robust tools in a teacher's arsenal. Here we address two general categories of questions: (1) general inferential questions and (2) elaborative interrogations.

General Inferential Questions

General inferential questions come in two types: default questions and reasoned inference questions. Default questions ask students to fall back on (i.e., default to) their own background knowledge. At the conclusion of a videotaped introduction to deserts, for example, students might be asked to draw on their knowledge of deserts as living systems: *What kinds of organisms do you think we will find there? How do these plants and animals survive in this harsh environment? What are some things you know about deserts?* Questions involving reasoned inferences require students to use information from critical-input experiences to speculate on what is likely to be true about something they have studied. For example, students who have listened to a brief introduction to romanticism in English poetry might be asked questions such as this: *Based on what you heard in this introduction, what do the terms "romanticism" and "romantic" mean?* When answering this question, students would be expected to explain which parts of the introduction led them to their answer. With these types of questions, students are describing the inferences behind their answer—hence the name "reasoned inference." The answer to a question is not something they already know. Rather, it is constructed from information provided in the critical-input experience. To answer a reasoned inference question, students must point out the information that led them to the conclusion.

Elaborative Interrogations

Elaborative interrogations extend reasoned inference questions to a level that requires students to provide logical support for their conclusions. With the reasoned inference questions described earlier, students simply point out the information they used to construct their answers. However, when answering elaborative interrogations, students must explain and defend their logic. Elaborative interrogation questions have the following forms:

- Why do you believe this to be true?
- Why do you think that is so?
- What are some typical characteristics or behaviors you would expect of _____?
- What would you expect to happen if _____?

To illustrate, as students provide answers to questions about a historical figure they have been studying, a social studies teacher might ask questions such as these: *Why do you believe this to be true about the historical figure? What is the evidence supporting your conclusions?* As part of this process, the teacher attempts to clarify and articulate the thinking process he has heard the student use to arrive at the inference. Similarly, during a chemistry lab, the teacher might ask students to respond to the following question: *Based on what you have observed in previous labs, what would you expect to happen if we combine the following chemicals?* When students provide their answers, the teacher would ask them to justify the supporting logic.

Examples

High School Composition. After having students study the writing process and use it to compose well-written essays, the teacher asks students the following question: *What generalizations about effective writing can you make? Explain the facts that support your generalizations.* Because the teacher does not ask students to justify the reasoning behind their answers, this is not an elaborative interrogation. However, it is a reasoned inference question because students must state the information that led to their conclusions.

Elementary Mathematics. After studying the concepts of area and perimeter, the teacher poses the following question: *If you change the dimensions of a square but keep it as a rectangle with the same unit area, how will its perimeter change? Explain why your answer has to be true based on what we know about the relationship between area and perimeter.* This elaborative interrogation question requires students to show their logic and defend why it is accurate.

Activity Box

Construct one general inferential question and one elaborative interrogation question you might use in class.

Having Students Write Out Their Conclusions

As students extend and refine their knowledge of new content, they can more deeply process the new information by participating in a variety of writing tasks. Here we emphasize note-taking strategies and student notebooks.

Note-Taking Strategies

Students benefit enormously by using a combination of note-taking strategies, including taking purposeful running notes combined with summaries and nonlinguistic representations of key ideas, concepts, and processes. We emphasize the interactive nature of effective note taking, allowing students to process what they are hearing or observing. During a series of critical-input experiences, for example, when the instructor deliberately chunks key information, students can be encouraged to write down key ideas, terms, and generalizations.

One important recommendation we support is that students not try to take notes while new information is being presented in small chunks (see Module 5). When information is new to students, they should be allowed to concentrate on understanding it. Trying to take notes will distract them and decrease their comprehension. After students have had a chance to process the small chunks of content, they can turn their attention to taking notes.

When students start taking notes, we recommend that they be afforded a great deal of flexibility and variety in the way they take notes. The following are some options for note taking.

Informal Outline. When using the informal outline, students use indentation to indicate big ideas and the ideas that support them. This approach is depicted in Figure 6.1.

FIGURE 6.1

Example of an Informal Outline

Periodic Table of Elements
A group is a vertical column in the periodic table
    18 groups
    Some groups contain elements with very similar properties
    Number of valence shell electrons determines group
A period is a horizontal row in the periodic table
    7 periods
    Some periods also show similar properties
    Total number of electron shells determines period
Elements are listed in order of increasing atomic number
    Number of protons in atomic nucleus

Free-Flowing Web. When using the free-flowing web, students use a web of connected circles with radiating spikes to represent information. This approach is depicted in Figure 6.2.

FIGURE 6.2

Example of a Free-Flowing Web

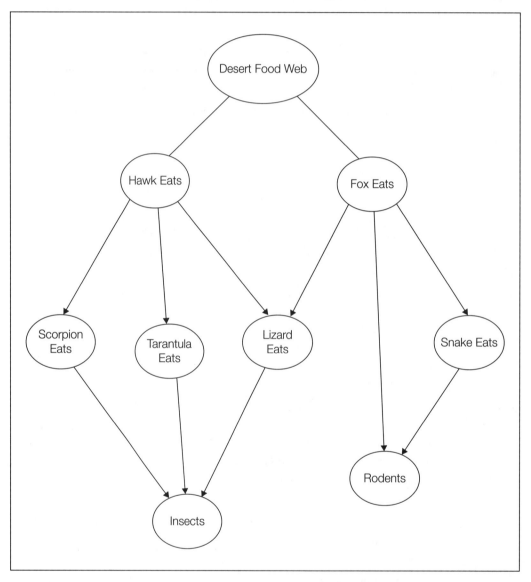

Combination Notes, Pictures, and Summary. In this approach, students record their written notes in the left-hand panel; they draw pictures or pictographic representations of the content in the right-hand panel; and they write a summary in the panel at the bottom. This technique is depicted in Figure 6.3.

FIGURE 6.3

Example of Combination Notes, Pictures, and Summaries

Human Reproduction	
Humans have a life cycle—birth, growth, reproduction, and death.	
Human babies are born to a male and female.	Birth
All humans grow at individual rates.	
Reproduction happens when a male and female engage in sexual intercourse and the male sperm fertilizes the female egg. Some humans do not reproduce, either by choice or circumstance.	Death Growth
A boy or girl is born within about 9 months of conception.	Reproduction **Circle of Life**
The human life span varies greatly, some living past 100 years old.	
Human beings are unique. They share a common life cycle, though the specific duration and details of the life cycle vary.	

Academic Notebooks

Academic notebooks can function as a compilation of entries that provide partial records of instructional experiences students have had. These notebooks can help students reflect on and assess their evolving thinking as they progress through a grading period or an academic year. By providing a sequential record of students' understanding of content, academic notebooks allow students to make corrections in their own thinking.

Students in all content areas can use academic notebooks to record their growing knowledge related to the course or grade-level content they are studying. In a middle school mathematics class, for example, students can divide their notebook into sections that parallel specific classroom tasks and activities. They may have a section devoted to introductory learning tasks (i.e., critical-input experiences) in which they date entries that summarize their reactions, questions, and growing understanding of key unit content. Another section may be devoted to two-column notes in reaction to class lectures and presentations. As part of this section, they may include periodic review and reflection activities in which they assess what they have learned, how they have progressed, and emerging questions they need answered. Their teacher may also require them to keep a reflective journal as part of their academic notebook. In this section, students would enter end-of-class, lesson, and segment reflections on their conclusions, reactions, and insights related to key content they study. Overall, their work with their notebooks becomes an organic and living interaction with the knowledge they are acquiring.

Examples

High School History. In a unit on the American Revolution, students are encouraged to devote a section of their academic notebook to a running record of their evolving knowledge, skills, and understanding. At key juncture points in the unit, their teacher has them pair with another student to compare their growing insights, conclusions, and questions based upon their shared notes. Periodically, students are asked to synthesize what they conclude about changes in their thinking related to the revolution, using their notes as a kind of archival record of their growth and progress.

Elementary School. As an activity in most of her critical-input lessons, this elementary school teacher has students work in pairs or triads to develop notes with pictures and summaries on sheets of chart paper. Each pair or triad then explains its notes to the whole class.

Activity Box

Which of the strategies for note taking described in this section most closely matches how you have used note taking in the classroom? What are some new ideas you might try?

Having Students Represent Their Learning Nonlinguistically

As educators we might have a tendency to underemphasize students' ability to use signs and symbols to process their experiences and visualize how they are internalizing new knowledge. Graphic organizers and other visual representations greatly enhance students' processing of information, skills, and procedures. They are also highly effective ways to assess students' accuracy and depth of understanding about key concepts. Students should use a range of graphic organizers (e.g., characteristic patterns, sequence patterns, process-cause patterns, problem-solution patterns, and generalization–supporting detail patterns) to help them deepen their insight and understanding. The use of a wide range of graphic representations also enhances students' reading comprehension and critical reasoning skills. Figure 6.4 shows common types of graphic organizers.

FIGURE 6.4

Common Graphic Organizers

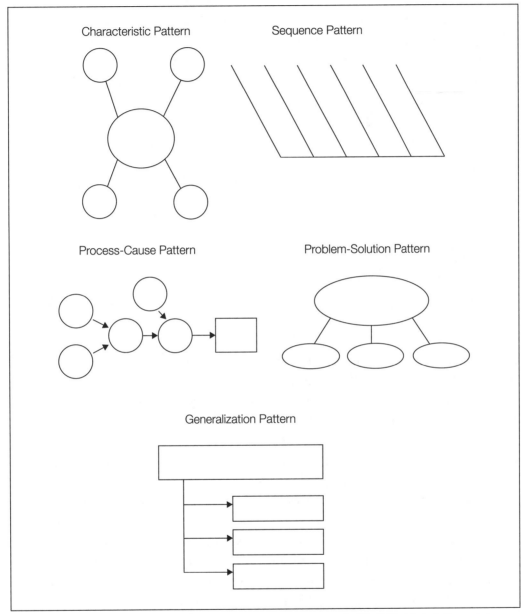

Source: From *The Art and Science of Teaching* (p. 53), by R. Marzano, 2007, Alexandria, VA: ASCD. Adapted with permission.

Similarly, students' participation in dramatic enactments can contribute significantly to their retention of knowledge and their cognitive processing of it. In effect, students can become human representations of key concepts they are studying. This process is both engaging to learners and highly memorable.

Finally, students' retention of key information can be enhanced through their use of a variety of mnemonic devices using imagery. We recommend two especially effective strategies: (1) rhyming pegwords—associating items in a list with imagery assigned to numbers (e.g., 1 = bun, 2 = shoe, and so on); and (2) link strategies—linking symbols and substitutes together in a chain of events or a narrative.

The *rhyming pegword method* is a simple system that can be used to remember information organized in a list. The method uses a set of words easily remembered because they rhyme with the numbers 1 through 10:

1 is a bun
2 is a shoe
3 is a tree
4 is a door
5 is a hive
6 is a stack of sticks
7 is heaven
8 is a gate
9 is a line
10 is a hen

The pegwords *bun, shoe, tree,* and so on are easy to remember and are also concrete and easy to picture. If a student wanted to connect information to pegword 1 (*bun*), she would form a mental image of the bun interacting with that information. For example, if a student wanted to remember the steps involved in a specific mathematical proof, she would visualize the first step occurring in a large hot dog bun; she would visualize the second step occurring in a shoe, and so on. (For a more detailed discussion, see *The Art and Science of Teaching*, Marzano, 2007, p. 55.)

The *link strategy* is a mnemonic device that involves linking symbols and substitutes together in a chain of events or a narrative story. To illustrate, assume that a unit of instruction focuses on the 13 original American colonies: Connecticut, Delaware, Georgia, Maryland, Massachusetts, New Hampshire, New Jersey, New York, North Carolina, Pennsylvania, Rhode Island, South Carolina, and Virginia. A football jersey represents New Jersey, and the Empire State Building is used as a symbol for New York. The name *George Washington* sounds like *Georgia*, and the words *Christmas carols* provide good reminders for the two Carolinas; dinnerware is used as a symbol for Delaware, and so on. Students link the mental images for each of the 13 original colonies into one story. For example, students picture George Washington (Georgia) wearing a football jersey (New Jersey). Next, students imagine George holding dinnerware (sounds like Delaware) as he stands on top of the Empire State Building (New York) and sings two Christmas carols (North and South Carolina). With his left hand, George is using the dinnerware to cut into a Virginia ham (Virginia and New Hampshire). In his right hand, George is holding a pen

(Pennsylvania) and connecting dots (Connecticut) on a puzzle. These dots join to form a picture of a road (Rhode Island), and Marilyn Monroe (Maryland) is riding on this road on her way to Mass (Massachusetts).

Examples

Graphic Organizers. Students engaged in a unit on John Steinbeck's novel *Of Mice and Men* use a variety of graphic organizers (as shown in Figure 6.4) to track and monitor their reactions to the novel and their changing conclusions about its structure and meaning. They include these graphic organizers in a section of their academic notebooks and modify the representations as they read Steinbeck's work. They use descriptive pattern organizers (a variation of Characteristic Pattern) to record key aspects of characterization. The large circle contains the name of a specific character, and the spoke-and-ball extensions represent character attributes (e.g., motivation, physical appearance, relationships). They identify key components of plot structure using the Sequence Pattern organizer, and they analyze cause-effect patterns in the novel using the Process-Cause Pattern graphic. Finally, as they prepare for an assessment in which they will create an analytical essay, they use the Generalization Pattern graphic to establish their thesis statement and supporting claims and assertions.

Dramatic Enactments. In this 5th grade history unit on the Industrial Revolution, the teacher periodically engages students in dramatic enactments. She assigns each of them a poster with the name of an individual or an event associated with the era. Larger posters are placed throughout the room, identifying significant historical trends and outcomes. Students are asked to form cause-and-effect lines, visually and physically depicting their perceptions about how the individual or event they represent is aligned with or contributed to the larger trends and outcomes. Students are asked to give a "headline" explanation of what their individual poster represents and why they placed themselves in the particular location in the room that they did. Their teacher has them revisit this process multiple times throughout the unit, culminating in a final composition and short presentation synthesizing what they perceive to be the most significant cause-effect patterns associated with this important historical era.

Mnemonic Devices Using Imagery. Elementary science students are asked to memorize a list of significant scientific concepts associated with important processes in the human body. For each process, their teacher asks them to create a mnemonic device to store and access key information. To remember systems in the human body, they are asked to create symbols that will substitute for each system and help them to make each system's formal name memorable to them. As students learn about important structural features within each system, their teacher has them use a link system to memorize the features in the cause-effect order in which they are found within each system. As students progress through the unit, they are periodically asked to share mnemonic devices they have created to memorize significant content knowledge in the unit. At the conclusion of the unit, their teacher asks them to reflect in their academic notebooks on which mnemonic devices and related imagery were the most effective in helping them store key information—and why.

Activity Box

Describe how you have used or might use graphic organizers, dramatic enactments, and mnemonic devices.

Having Students Reflect on Their Learning

The final step in a comprehensive approach to actively processing information is student self-reflection, which is particularly useful at the end of critical-input experiences. Once again, we stress the importance of questioning as a catalyst for success in this process. Questions that might be asked include these: *What were you right and wrong about? How confident are you about what you have learned? What did you do well during your learning experience and what could you have done better?*

In a broader sense, using reflective questions and other strategies can enhance students' capacity for metacognitive introspection. Specifically, all learners benefit from being asked to self-monitor and self-regulate, including continually examining how well they comprehend what they are learning and why they are learning it. Students should also play a central role in assessing their own progress toward proficiency relative to identified learning goals, asking questions such as these: *How am I doing? What do I understand better now? What am I still confused about? How could I have completed this task differently?* Here we consider three ways to stimulate student reflection.

Reflective Questions and Journals

At the end of a lesson or key unit segments, students can be asked to return to the section of their academic notebooks that functions as their reflective journal. As a closure activity, the teacher would ask them to respond in a four- to five-minute free write to a reflective question she poses. Here are some examples: *What were you right about in today's lesson? Which aspects did you get wrong or have trouble with? How well do you understand the major ideas we are studying in this unit? What did you do well today? What could you have done better?*

Think Logs

A variation of reflective questions and reflective journal entries is a more special-ized form of student self-reflection. A think log can be a part of a reflective journal or a separate section of students' academic notebooks. Each entry in a think log asks students to reflect on their understanding and use of a key cognitive skill. The teacher selects the focus of a particular think log entry based on what she emphasized with students during a particular lesson or unit segment. Here are some examples: *How would you explain classi-fication to a friend? How comfortable are you with drawing inferences? What aspects of the decision-making process we used in class did you feel most—and least—comfortable with? How well did you use your creativity and self-regulation habits of mind today?* Periodically, students can also be asked to share think log entries and compare their responses with those of their classmates.

Exit Slips

A simple but effective self-reflection strategy is the closure activity called an "exit slip." At the conclusion of a lesson or a class period, students are asked to respond to a specific reflective question that the teacher feels is particularly relevant to that lesson. As their title implies, exit slips are required for students to leave the class. Typically, students respond on a half-sheet of paper or a note card, reacting to a variety of questions such as these: *What do you consider the main ideas of today's lesson? Why? As we are moving through this unit, what do you feel most and least sure about? What suggestions could you make for helping us get the most out of this unit? Do you have specific questions about this content that you would like answered? Which aspects of your class work today do you consider most successful? Are there things you might do differently in the future to improve your performance?*

Examples

Primary Language Arts. In this 1st grade class the teacher frequently ends a critical-input lesson by asking the students to stand up one at a time and tell the class something new they have learned during the class. She also asks them to state a question they have about what they learned.

Secondary Science. This science teacher has students create a reflection section in their academic notebooks. Systematically, she gives students time to record their thoughts in this section. She invites them to share their thoughts with the rest of the class or to give her their notebooks to take home and read if students have a private communication they want to express.

> ## Activity Box
>
> Describe how you have used or might use reflective questions and journals, think logs, and exit slips.

Checking for Understanding

Use the following rating scale to assess your current understanding and comfort level regarding key strategies and processes presented in this module:

4 = I understand and already fully implement this strategy in my classroom.

3 = I understand this strategy, but I need to practice using it in my classroom.

2 = I can explain this strategy, but I am not fully confident that I can use it.

1 = I do not understand this strategy, and I do not currently use it in my classroom.

_____ 1.   Using general inferential questions
Based on my rating, I may need to revisit the following:

_____ 2.   Using elaborative interrogation questions
Based on my rating, I may need to revisit the following:

_____ 3.   Using a variety of ways for students to write out their conclusions
Based on my rating, I may need to revisit the following:

___4. Having students represent their learning nonlinguistically

Based on my rating, I may need to revisit the following:

___5. Having students reflect on their learning

Based on my rating, I may need to revisit the following:

Design Question 3

What Will I Do to Help Students Practice and
Deepen Their Understanding of New Knowledge?

Module 7

Examining Similarities and
Differences and Identifying
Errors in Thinking

Module 8

Helping Students Practice Skills,
Strategies, and Processes

Module 9

Using Homework and Academic
Notebooks to Deepen Student
Understanding

Module 7

Examining Similarities and Differences and Identifying Errors in Thinking

Design Question 2 deals with the initial presentation of information. Design Question 3, addressed in this module and the next two (Modules 8 and 9), deals with activities that help students practice and deepen their knowledge. Once again, it is important to keep in mind the distinctions and connections between declarative and procedural knowledge. Procedural knowledge (i.e., skills, strategies, and processes) is developed through a process of initial modeling followed by shaping (guided practice involving rehearsal and correction of missteps and misunderstandings) and eventual internalization of the procedure. Internalization is equivalent to *automaticity*, the capacity to independently apply a new procedure. In contrast to procedural knowledge, declarative knowledge (i.e., key information such as facts, generalizations, and principles) is developed through activities that require students to systematically review their initial understanding of information.

This module explores strategies for helping students develop their knowledge through a variety of comparison, contrast, and classification activities. This module also addresses a critically important but frequently overlooked aspect of teaching for understanding: direct instruction of rules of logic and logical fallacies.

Reflecting on Your Current Beliefs and Practices

Before examining the strategies in this module, take some time to examine your current beliefs and practices by answering the following questions:

85

1. How do you ensure that students deepen their understanding of new knowledge?

_____

_____

_____

_____

2. How do you help students reorganize knowledge so that they produce new insights?

_____

_____

_____

_____

3. How do you use comparison, contrast, and classification activities to support students' understanding of new knowledge?

_____

_____

_____

_____

4. How do you help students identify and correct errors in reasoning in their own thinking and that of others?

_____

_____

_____

_____

Recommendations for Classroom Practice

This module addresses the following strategies for Design Question 3:

- Comparing
- Classifying
- Creating similes and metaphors
- Creating analogies
- Identifying errors in thinking

Comparing

Comparing involves actively identifying and analyzing the significance of similarities and differences among or between things and ideas. A variety of strategies can be used for designing comparison tasks, including sentence stems, Venn diagrams, double-bubble diagrams, and comparison matrices.

Comparison Sentence Stems

Teachers can encourage students to find and defend similarities and differences by giving them sentence-completion tasks involving comparison. At the conclusion of a unit on fairy tales, for example, elementary students might be asked to complete the following sentence stems:

_____ and _____ are alike as fairy tale characters because they both _____. They are different as fairy tale characters because they _____.

Figure 7.1 provides an example from physical education.

FIGURE 7.1
Example of Completed Sentence Stems

Baseball and *fastpitch softball* are *similar* because they both . . .

- Have 4 bases in a diamond shape.
- Have 9 defensive players.
- Have the same ball/strike counts: 4 balls = walk; 3 strikes = out.

Baseball and *fastpitch softball* are *different* because . . .

- In *baseball*, the baselines are 90 feet, but in *fastpitch softball*, the baselines are 60 feet.
- In *baseball*, the pitching distance is 60 feet, 6 inches; but in *fastpitch softball*, the pitching distance varies between 40 and 46 feet depending on the level of play.
- In *baseball*, the pitcher throws overhand, but in *fastpitch softball*, the pitcher throws underhand.

Venn Diagrams

Often used in a variety of classroom situations, a Venn diagram requires students to identify parallel but different characteristics of two items in opposing sections of two circles, and to identify areas of similarity in the section of the diagram where the circles intersect. Students in a science classroom, for example, might identify differing aspects of two ecosystems they have studied and place those aspects in the outer sections of the two circles (e.g., differences among mammals, plants, physical terrains found in the two systems); they then might identify similarities and place those in the intersecting part of the two circles (e.g., commonalities among biological needs, physiological systems, chemical reactions). Figure 7.2 depicts a Venn diagram using the physical education example.

FIGURE 7.2

Example of a Venn Diagram

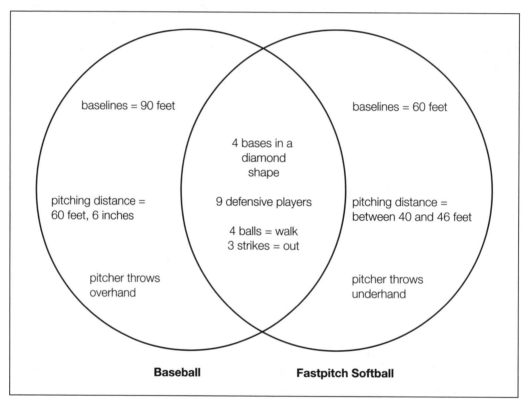

baselines = 90 feet

baselines = 60 feet

4 bases in a diamond shape

pitching distance = 60 feet, 6 inches

9 defensive players

pitching distance = between 40 and 46 feet

4 balls = walk
3 strikes = out

pitcher throws overhand

pitcher throws underhand

Baseball

Fastpitch Softball

Double-Bubble Diagrams

David Hyerle's (1996) variation on the Venn diagram involves students placing the names of the two items they are comparing in two parallel bubbles and areas of similarity in bubbles placed between them. Students identify areas of difference in bubbles to the left and right of the items that are being compared. Students in a foreign language class, for example, might compare teenage customs and practices in their own country and a country that uses the language they are studying as a primary language. Parallels or similarities in customs and practices are placed in bubbles going down the center of the page. Areas of difference are placed to the right and left of the two country bubbles. Figure 7.3 illustrates the double-bubble diagram using the physical education example.

FIGURE 7.3

Example of a Double-Bubble Diagram

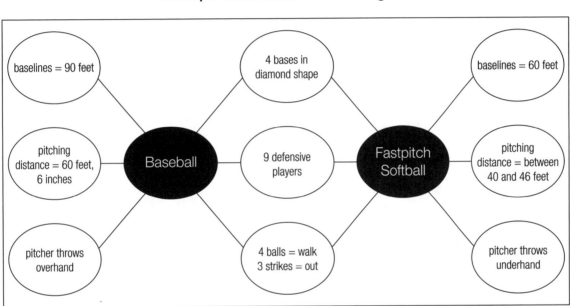

Comparison Matrix

A more formalized way to reinforce students' work with comparison involves the use of a matrix in which items being compared are listed at the top of the matrix and questions about areas of similarity and difference are listed vertically on the left side of the page. Students in a history class, for example, might collaborate with their teacher to create a bulletin board featuring a comparison matrix that visually synthesizes similarities and differences among eras they are studying. Across the top, they might list such eras as the Middle Ages, the European Renaissance, and the Age of Enlightenment. Vertically placed questions might include these: *What are the major forms of government in each era? What is the enduring legacy of each era? How did class structures change during each era?* Figure 7.4 provides an example of the comparison matrix using the physical education example.

FIGURE 7.4

Example of a Comparison Matrix

	Baseball	**Fastpitch Softball**	**Slowpitch Softball**	
Size of Ball	9 inches in circumference	12 inches in circumference	12 inches in circumference	**Similarities and Differences** All three use a round ball. Both types of softball use a ball that is larger in circumference than the one used in baseball.
Baselines	90 feet	60 feet	60 feet	**Similarities and Differences** Baseball uses 90-foot baselines, but both types of softball use 60-foot baselines.
Defensive Players	9 players	9 players	10 players	**Similarities and Differences** Baseball and fastpitch softball use 9 defensive players, but slowpitch softball uses an extra outfielder.

Classifying

When students classify, they group things that are alike into categories based on their characteristics or attributes. At a basic level, students may be given predetermined categories by the teacher and asked to sort content into those categories. To use the process of classification to build deeper student understanding, however, teachers should ask students to generate classification categories and attributes independently. The students should explain the defining features of the categories they have constructed and then defend why each element belongs in a specific category.

Classification Chart

The process of classification requires students to sort elements into categories and to identify attributes for placing items into each category. A classification chart involves a more teacher-directed form of classification. During an introductory poetry unit in which students are first learning about figurative language, for example, the teacher might have students use a classification chart in their academic notebooks to keep track of examples of metaphors, similes, hyperbole, and synecdoche. Periodically, students can pair up with a partner to share their classifications and identify potential errors in their respective understandings. Figure 7.5 provides an example of a classification chart used in a music class. The teacher provides the two broad categories—woodwind and brass. The students then develop the rest of the chart.

FIGURE 7.5
Example of a Classification Chart

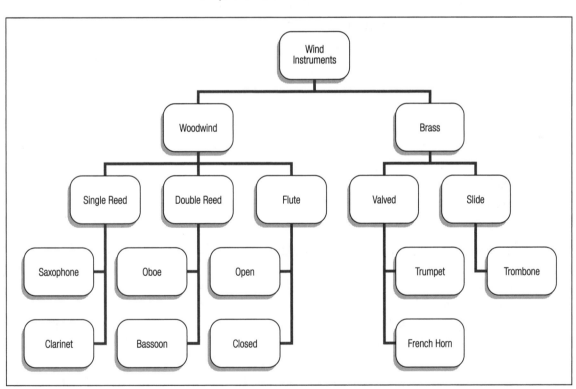

Student-Generated Classification Patterns

To really deepen students' understanding of similarities and differences, teachers should ask them to discover and defend their own classification patterns. Students in a sociology class, for example, might be asked to collect representative problems they have identified in their own community. Their teacher asks them to classify the problems according to conceptual patterns they have studied in the class. At the completion of the process, students are asked to present their conclusions to the entire class or in configurations of small-group teams. At the end of the activity, students can express what they learned in the process—and how peer feedback deepened their understanding.

Creating Similes and Metaphors

An engaging and often underused process for deepening students' understanding involves their creation of metaphors for significant concepts and related ideas. This process has students identify a general or basic pattern that connects information that is not related on the literal or surface level.

Similes

Students can be asked to make direct statements of comparison using the starters *like* or *as*. Third graders studying their community, for example, might be asked to compare it to an object with which they are familiar. "My community is like a stewpot," one of them might declare, "because everybody in it sort of blends together and seems to get along."

Metaphors

Metaphors eliminate the formal grammatical elements of *like* or *as* and consist of direct statements of comparison. "Learning algebra is a thick and difficult forest path," one math student stated. "It always seems challenging, and you always have to expect the unexpected."

Visual Representations of Metaphorical Relationships

To reinforce students' deepening ability to construct formal metaphors, a teacher can provide them with a formal matrix to ensure they include all relevant elements. Students comparing two tragic-hero figures such as Oedipus and Hamlet, for example, might be asked initially to create a chart with the words "Oedipus, Common Abstract Characteristics, Hamlet" written horizontally across it. As they discover parallel elements that unify the two characters and place character-specific descriptions reflecting each element beneath the characters' names, they should begin to discover potential ways in which they can describe metaphorical relationships. For example, Oedipus and Hamlet are both blind men because they are both oblivious to internal character defects that bring about their own fall and eventual demise. Figure 7.6 provides an example from a theater class.

FIGURE 7.6

Metaphor Example—"Life Is a Stage"

Element 1	Common Abstract Characteristics	Element 2
Life		*Stage*
A person is born into life.	Entrance/birth.	A play has an opening scene.
A person dies at the end of his or her life span.	Exit/death.	A play has an ending scene.
A person progresses through life.	Acts/scenes.	A play progresses through acts and scenes.

Creating Analogies

Analogical reasoning can be used as a powerful tool to deepen students' understanding. This process requires students to identify the formal relationship between two sets of items. In effect, students learn to adopt the analogical algorithm of "A is to B as C is to D." Typically, the teacher may choose to exclude one or two elements that students are expected to fill in. Perhaps most significant, students need to support their analogies with reasons and explanations that defend their decision making and justify the relationships they have identified between the two sets of items.

Sentence-Completion Analogies

The sentence-completion analogy is a more formalized structure that presents the analogical relationship directly to the student. For example, "A line is to a stanza as a sentence is to a _____." Sentence-completion activities involving analogies are excellent strategies for modeling the process for students and helping them to move toward more independent work with analogical reasoning.

Visual Prompts for Analogies

A variety of nonlinguistic tools can be used to reinforce students' analogical reasoning. One approach is to use an analogical graphic organizer in which the two items being compared (e.g., people and oxygen) are listed above and below a line that leads to an apex point in the middle of the diagram, in which the "as" structure is added (e.g., in order to survive, need). The analogy is completed with parallel items listed in the analogy line (e.g., plants and carbon dioxide). Once again, such visual prompts can be useful as students begin their work with analogical thinking, with gradual removal of the prompt as students scaffold toward growing levels of independent use of analogies. Figure 7.7 provides another example from science.

FIGURE 7.7

Example of a Visual Prompt for an Analogy

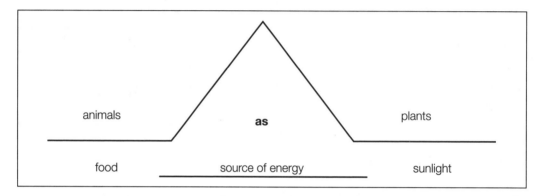

Examples

Elementary Language Arts. Students in class have been reading the book *Tuck Everlasting.* The teacher has provided a few critical-input lessons on the concept of "enduring themes." To help students deepen their understanding of this concept, the teacher assigns a metaphor task in which students must demonstrate the similarities between *Tuck Everlasting* and a story they have read or a movie they have seen that has nothing to do with the plot of living forever (e.g., the plot of *Tuck Everlasting*).

Ninth Grade Mathematics. This teacher has been providing critical-input lessons on the concept of a function. To help students deepen their knowledge, she provides them with a list of 10 types of equations. Each student must classify the 10 equations into two or more categories based on the type of function they represent.

Activity Box

Describe how you have used or could use comparing, classifying, metaphor, or analogy activities in your classroom.

Identifying Errors in Thinking

An important aspect of developing understanding involves providing direct instruction in basic principles of logic and logical fallacies, and then encouraging students to analyze and evaluate faulty logic in themselves and others. To help students be able to identify errors in thinking, it is necessary to introduce them to common errors like those shown in Figure 7.8. As the figure indicates, there are four general categories of errors: (1) faulty logic, (2) attacks, (3) weak references, and (4) misinformation.

FIGURE 7.8

Four Categories of Errors in Thinking

Faulty logic can occur in seven ways:

1. *Contradiction*—presenting conflicting information. If a politician runs on a platform supporting reducing taxes, then states that she would vote for a bill designed to increase taxes, that politician has committed the error of contradiction.

2. *Accident*—failing to recognize that an argument is based on an exception to a rule. For example, if a student concludes that his friend always goes to an amusement park on the first Saturday each summer because he saw his friend go once to celebrate a cousin's graduation, that student has committed the error of accident.

3. *False cause*—confusing a temporal (time) order of events with causality or oversimplifying the reasons behind some event or occurrence. For example, if a person concludes that his favorite team won a game because the game was sold out, he is guilty of ascribing a false cause. The sell-out crowd may have contributed to his team's winning the game, but there were also many other contributing factors.

4. *Begging the question*—making a claim and then arguing for the claim by using statements that are simply the equivalent of the original claim. For example, if a person says that a personal computer he built for himself is better than any other computer being sold and then backs up this statement by simply saying that it is superior to other computers, he is begging the question.

5. *Evading the issue*—changing the topic to avoid addressing the issue. For example, a person is evading the issue if she begins talking about high salaries for professional athletes when asked about her opinions on insurance fraud.

6. *Arguing from ignorance*—arguing that a claim is justified simply because its opposite has not been proven true. For example, if a person argues that there is no life after death because there is no proof of such existence, he is arguing from ignorance.

7. *Composition/division*—asserting something about a whole that is true of only its parts is *composition*; on the flip side, *division* is asserting about all of the parts something that is generally, but not always, true of the whole. For example, if a person asserts that all police officers use excessive force because one police officer is found to have used excessive force, she is committing the error of composition. If a person states that a particular reporter supports liberal causes simply because reporters are generally known for being liberal, he is committing the error of division.

FIGURE 7.8

Four Categories of Errors in Thinking (*Cont.*)

Attacks can occur in three ways:

1. *Poisoning the well*—being so completely committed to a position that you explain away absolutely everything that is offered in opposition to your position. This type of attack represents a person's unwillingness to consider anything that may contradict his or her opinion. For example, if a researcher argues against the findings of 10 studies proposing a contrary position by claiming that each study was based on flawed methodology without offering proof for these claims, she is poisoning the well.

2. *Arguing against the person*—rejecting a claim using derogatory facts (real or alleged) about the person who is making the claim. If a person argues against another person's position on morality by alleging he accepted a bribe, she is arguing against the person.

3. *Appealing to force*—using threats to establish the validity of a claim. If a person threatens to report a lie you told to a person because you disagree with her on a social issue, she is appealing to force.

Weak references occur in five ways:

1. *Sources that reflect biases*—consistently accepting information that supports what we already believe to be true or consistently rejecting information that goes against what we believe to be true. For example, a person is guilty of bias if he rejects evidence supporting claims of faith simply because he does not believe in faith.

2. *Sources that lack credibility*—using a source that is not reputable for a given topic. Determining credibility can be subjective, but there are some characteristics that most people agree damage credibility, such as when a source is known to be biased or has little knowledge of the topic. A person is guilty of using a source that lacks credibility when he supports his claims by citing research from an individual known for questionable methodology.

3. *Appealing to authority*—invoking authority as the last word on an issue. If a person claims that a local government policy is valid and supports this claim by saying the city council said so, she is appealing to authority.

4. *Appealing to the people*—attempting to justify a claim based on its popularity. For example, if a boy tells his parents that he should have a television in his room because all his friends have one, he is appealing to the people.

5. *Appealing to emotion*—using a "sob story" as proof for a claim. For example, if someone uses the story of a tragic illness as a means to convince people to agree with her opinion on health care reform, she is appealing to emotion.

Misinformation occurs in two ways:

1. *Confusing the facts*—using information that seems to be factual but that has been changed in such a way that it is no longer accurate. For example, a person is confusing the facts if he backs up his claim by telling a recent news story with key details missing.

2. *Misapplying a concept or generalization*—misunderstanding or wrongly applying a concept or generalization to support a claim. For example, if someone argues that a person should be arrested after losing a civil case, the person has misunderstood the concept of civil law.

Faulty Logic

Faulty logic includes the following types of errors: contradiction, accident, false cause, begging the question, evading the issue, arguing from ignorance, and composition/

division. Students should be familiar with these terms as part of the academic vocabulary. Increasingly, however, they should be able to identify examples, descriptions, and explanations of how they are applying these terms in examining and critiquing their own reasoning—as well as that of others. During a political campaign, for example, students in a civics class can be asked to revisit the rhetoric and arguments being presented by candidates as they defend their own eligibility and negate that of their opponents.

Attacks

Attacks are commonly found in propaganda, advertising, and other forms of persuasion. Attacks include these types: poisoning the well, arguing against the person, and appealing to force. Becoming increasingly sensitive to these forms of attacks can enrich students' critical reasoning skills and prepare them to be wise and informed consumers of persuasive discourse and literature. Once again, civics students can identify ways in which political candidates subtly or not so subtly use such attacks in their respective campaign speeches and promotional materials.

Weak References

Students can greatly enhance their written and spoken forms of discourse and persuasion by learning to identify, analyze, and evaluate the effect of weak references. Weak references include sources that reflect biases, lack credibility, appeal to authority, appeal to the people, and appeal to emotion. Knowledge of these types of errors provides students with a powerful resource to elaborate and defend their own thesis statements, topic sentences, or hypothesis conclusions.

Misinformation

Misinformation includes confusing the facts and misapplying a concept or generalization. Students in a media class can collect examples of media spots that reflect such fallacies. As they reflect on the examples they discover, they can begin to discern and reinforce patterns of misinformation they encounter in their everyday lives in such arenas as advertising, marketing, product placement, and promotional materials.

Practicing Identifying Errors in Logic

To provide students with practice in identifying errors, we recommend that teachers generate practice activities like the one presented in Figure 7.9. The exercise deals with one of the categories of logical errors—faulty logic. Before assigning this exercise, the teacher would have gone through the seven errors of faulty logic, discussing and providing examples of each. Once students understand the type of errors in reasoning people commonly

(con't on pg. 99)

FIGURE 7.9

Practice Exercise for Faulty Logic

Directions: In this exercise you are asked to identify errors referred to as "faulty logic." There are seven types of faulty logic errors:

- Contradiction
- Accident
- False cause
- Begging the question
- Evading the issue
- Arguing from ignorance
- Composition and division

1. Following the corporate scandal at Enron, the U.S. economy experienced an economic slump, and Phil was laid off from his job. Phil says Enron caused him to lose his job.

   This is an example of _____

2. Jana argues that Santa is real because Santa exists.

   This is an example of _____

3. After observing an ambulance with its siren blaring speed through a red light, Merle concludes it is OK to drive through red lights.

   This is an example of _____

4. Susan tells her friends in the school cafeteria that she hates broccoli. That same evening at dinner, Susan thanks her mom for making broccoli because it's one of her favorite foods.

   This is an example of _____

5. Miss Jones argues that there is no cure for cancer because scientists have not discovered one yet.

   This is an example of _____

6. President Lincoln was assassinated as the American Civil War came to an end. Mark concludes that the Civil War's end caused President Lincoln's assassination.

   This is an example of _____

7. Because Colorado has a Republican governor, Julie concludes that all residents of Colorado are Republicans.

   This is an example of _____

8. When Walter's teacher asks him where his book report is, Walter tells his teacher that he admires the sweater she's wearing.

   This is an example of _____

9. Because water is wet, Rick concludes that the elements that make up water—hydrogen and oxygen—must also be wet.

   This is an example of _____

10. Ann tells her parents that she never drives over the speed limit in the family car. On her way to school, Ann drives 50 m.p.h. in a 40 m.p.h. zone because she's late for school.

    This is an example of _____

make, they can use this knowledge as a tool to deepen their understanding of content that has been addressed in critical-input lessons. For examples of exercises that address other types of reasoning errors, see *The Pathfinder Project: The Power of One* (Marzano, Paynter, & Doty, 2003).

Examples

High School Science. Students in this general science class have been studying various theories of global warming. After presenting students with various types of reasoning errors, the teacher organizes students in teams of five and provides them with two current but contradictory articles on global warming. The teams analyze the articles for errors and present their findings to the entire class.

Elementary Social Studies. In this class students have been examining the positions of the two major presidential candidates on how best to help the economy. The teacher has spent some time introducing a few of the more common errors in reasoning. Once students have a general understanding of these errors, the teacher plays a videotape of the last presidential debate. At strategic points in the debate, the teacher stops the tape and asks students to record any errors they observed. The whole class then discusses what they saw.

Activity Box

Describe how you have used or could use a specific type of error to help students better understand the content you teach.

Checking for Understanding

Use the following rating scale to assess your current understanding and comfort level regarding key strategies and processes presented in this module:

4 = I understand and already fully implement this strategy in my classroom.

3 = I understand this strategy, but I need to practice using it in my classroom.

2 = I can explain this strategy, but I am not fully confident that I can use it.

1 = I do not understand this strategy, and I do not currently use it in my classroom.

___ 1. Using comparing activities
Based on my rating, I may need to revisit the following:

___ 2. Using classifying activities
Based on my rating, I may need to revisit the following:

___ 3. Using activities involving similes and metaphors
Based on my rating, I may need to revisit the following:

___ 4. Using analogy activities
Based on my rating, I may need to revisit the following:

___ 5. Using activities involving identification of errors in thinking
Based on my rating, I may need to revisit the following:

Module 8

Helping Students Practice Skills, Strategies, and Processes

When reading this module, it is important to remember the distinctions between declarative and procedural knowledge. In the former, students extend and refine their understanding of key information such as facts, generalizations, and principles by constructing personal meaning and integrating new information into their existing cognitive schema. The activities described in Module 7 can be used with both declarative and procedural knowledge. However, they don't address advanced development of procedural knowledge.

In contrast, this module emphasizes ways to maximize students' complete learning of procedural knowledge. As students become fluent and independent in their use of procedures, they move toward a condition of automaticity in which they are able to retrieve and use the procedure as an essential part of their cognitive toolkit. When they achieve the level of automatic retrieval and independent application, they can be said to have truly "learned" a new procedure.

Reflecting on Your Current Beliefs and Practices

Before examining the strategies in this module, take some time to examine your current beliefs and practices by answering the following questions:

1. How do you typically help students acquire and integrate new procedural knowledge?

_____

_____

_____

_____

2. How do you ensure that students develop effective models for procedural knowledge, internalizing the models' key attributes and behaviors?

_____

_____

_____

_____

3. How do you use massed and distributed practice to help students shape their use and understanding of key skills, strategies, and processes? For example, to what extent do you design initial massed, structured practice sessions and gradually distribute and vary the nature of practice sessions?

_____

_____

_____

_____

4. How do you help students progress toward conceptual understanding and independent transfer of procedural knowledge? For example, how do you design practice sessions that enhance students' fluency—that is, their growing capacity to use procedural knowledge independently?

_____

_____

_____

_____

5. To what extent do you incorporate a variety of cooperative learning structures and tasks to reinforce students' modeling, shaping, and internalizing of procedural knowledge?

_____

_____

_____

_____

Recommendations for Classroom Practice

This module addresses the following strategies for Design Question 3:

- Providing opportunities for students to practice skills, strategies, and processes
- Determining the extent to which cooperative learning groups will be used

Providing Opportunities for Students to Practice Skills, Strategies, and Processes

The opportunities for students to practice skills, strategies, and processes should be organized so that they progress along a predictable and certifiable continuum. Initial practice sessions should be highly structured, spaced closely together, and heavily monitored by the teacher for purposes of on-the-spot coaching. As students begin to shape their use of skills, strategies, or processes, however, they will begin to move toward growing levels of fluency and independent use. At this point, practice sessions should become gradually less structured and more varied. Throughout this developmental process, students should be encouraged to monitor their growing competency, their evolving efficiency, and their movement toward automatic retrieval and use of the skill, strategy, or process.

Structured Practice Sessions Spaced Closely Together

At the beginning of the process of acquiring new procedural knowledge, students benefit from critical-input experiences that provide a clearly articulated model of the procedure. Such activities should allow students an opportunity or two to try out the procedural knowledge, with careful monitoring and coaching by the teacher. After the initial input experience, students should participate in a series of practice sessions spaced closely together. Initial massed practice sessions should reinforce students' success rates and concentrate on a small part of an overall strategy or procedure. A dance instructor, for example, may work with students to learn a new and perhaps complicated dance. She begins by modeling initial steps and movements, and then has her students model them in controlled sessions that allow her to coach and monitor their behaviors. The well-crafted modeling of initial steps and procedures ensures that all students acquire and integrate the basics of the dance before attempting more complicated or intricate movements and interactions with a partner.

Practice Sessions That Are Gradually Less Structured and More Varied

As students progress from initial modeling toward shaping of a procedure, practice sessions can be designed to allow students to practice increasingly complex and interrelated steps and elements. Students learning to use a specific computer application, for example, might begin by modeling and replicating essential elements of the strategy. As they progress toward the shaping phase of acquiring procedural knowledge, however, their teacher designs activities and tasks that allow them to apply their strategies in more complex situations. At this point the teacher may also choose to incorporate opportunities for cooperative learning interactions such as a pair-share or peer-coaching exercise. Throughout this process, the teacher is also careful to revisit with students the criteria for effective execution of the procedure.

Practice Sessions That Help Students Develop Fluency

The final phase of learning procedural knowledge is to develop it to a level of fluency or automatic independent transfer. Fluency is necessary for procedural knowledge that students will need in later life in their education or in their careers. Fluency evolves as students participate in exercises and tasks that replicate how the strategy or procedure might be used in real life.

Students' accuracy and speed in using procedural knowledge can be emphasized during this phase of knowledge acquisition by asking students to keep track of their progress in their academic notebooks. To practice speed and accuracy, students must be able to execute a skill, a strategy, or a process independently. At this level, practice can be assigned as homework when appropriate. When trying to develop speed and accuracy, it is useful to have students record their progress as depicted in Figure 8.1. Here a student has kept track of her speed and accuracy in typing over four practice sessions. She recorded speed in total words typed over a two-minute interval. She recorded accuracy as percent of errors.

FIGURE 8.1

Chart Showing Typing Speed and Accuracy

Practice Session	Speed (Total Words Typed)	Accuracy (% of Errors)
1	75	10%
2	83	12%
3	80	8%
4	101	8%

Teachers should work with students to determine when they may be ready for a culminating performance task or project that requires their application of procedural knowledge to authentic, real-world tasks and settings. Regarding the computer application mentioned previously, for example, a teacher might ask students to work with a partner to use the application for a simulated business or educational presentation. Part of their presentation might include a debriefing on how they have progressed in their understanding and independent transfer of the procedures they have learned during the unit.

Examples

Elementary Physical Education. This physical education teacher is focusing on teaching the overhand baseball throw. At first, she models the procedure for students and engages them in highly structured practice activities. Students spend some time practicing the procedure every day for the first three days. After that, the practice sessions are spaced further and further apart.

Secondary Science. This science teacher has provided students with a safety procedure they will be using in all their science experiments. To ensure that students can perform the procedure with fluency, she has them chart their speed and accuracy once they obtain a level of skill at which they can perform the procedure without help.

Activity Box

Identify a skill, a strategy, or a process you have taught or will teach. Describe how you could use the types of practice described in this section.

Determining the Extent to Which Cooperative Learning Groups Will Be Used

The authentic, real-world use of procedural knowledge frequently involves working with others in collaborative, interactive ways. Therefore, as students move toward fluency, they should have opportunities to participate in a range of cooperative learning activities and structures. Cooperative learning activities involving procedural knowledge can be as simple as a pair-check or listen-think-pair-share. After individual students have worked through a practice activity, for example, they can meet in small groups to check their work for accuracy and describe their personal approaches to the exercises.

However, more complex cooperative learning structures such as a jigsaw (with students forming base and expert groups and helping to coach one another in variations for use of the procedural knowledge) and student tournaments (in which informal competitions encourage students to display high levels of accuracy and speed in their use of procedural knowledge) allow for more varied roles as well as both individual and group accountability. These more complex structures also simulate more natural settings in which the procedural knowledge is used in real-world, authentic ways. Ideally, cornerstone activities involving procedural knowledge can be designed to help students gain experience that replicates professional applications of the procedures they are learning.

Comparison Activities

While learning procedural knowledge, students might be asked to participate in a variety of small and highly structured cooperative learning tasks involving variations on the process of comparison: for example, comparing and contrasting, classifying, and creating metaphors and analogies. Such activities can deepen students' ability to explain the procedural knowledge they are acquiring and monitor their own progress via peer coaching and feedback. Paired partners might answer such questions as the following: *How does our progress now compare to when we first started learning these strategies and processes? How might we classify techniques for improving our work with these strategies and processes? If we were to coach other students in using this knowledge, what metaphors or analogies might we use to help them?*

Error Analysis Activities and Opportunities for Cooperative Practice

After students move from initial massed practice toward more distributed applications of procedural knowledge, they can work with partners or in small teams to assess their progress using clearly articulated evaluation criteria. In pairs or triads, for example, they can compare their individual progress, including data concerning their increasing speed and accuracy in using the procedural knowledge. Peers can also coach one another in identifying errors or missteps in using the skill, strategy, or procedure. Variations on this process can include paired practice sessions in which one partner tries out or applies the procedure while the other provides coaching feedback and advice. After each partner practices and receives feedback, pairs can make observations about areas of strength and areas in need of improvement.

Authentic, Real-World Cooperative Learning Tasks and Peer Critiques

As suggested previously, a major goal for teaching procedural knowledge is to help every student achieve a level of fluent, automatic use of the procedure. Cooperative learning tasks and projects are ideal venues for helping students demonstrate independent use and internalization of key procedural knowledge. The dance instructor mentioned previously, for example, might ask her students to move from modeling to shaping toward independent application of what she has taught them by ending a unit with authentic class performances. These culminating performances might require students working in pairs or quartets to create and present to the rest of the class an original version of the dance they have been studying. At the conclusion of their performance, peer review activities might occur, with other students giving praise, asking questions, and ending with any suggestions for improvement they may have identified.

Examples

Elementary Mathematics. While having students practice estimation strategies, this teacher organizes them into triads and assigns them a real-world task that requires them to solve a series of estimation problems. As the teams work on these tasks, they identify strengths and weaknesses in their estimation skills.

Secondary Geography. This teacher has been working with students on the skill of reading a contour map. To provide a real-life context for this skill, she provides students with a contour map of the area around the school. Students interpret the map and then evaluate its accuracy via a field trip to specific locations they have examined.

Activity Box

Describe how you have used or could use cooperative learning strategies when teaching procedural knowledge.

Checking for Understanding

Use the following rating scale to assess your current understanding and comfort level regarding key strategies and processes presented in this module:

4 = I understand and already fully implement this strategy in my classroom.

3 = I understand this strategy, but I need to practice using it in my classroom.

2 = I can explain this strategy, but I am not fully confident that I can use it.

1 = I do not understand this strategy, and I do not currently use it in my classroom.

___ 1. Spacing practice sessions
Based on my rating, I may need to revisit the following:

___ 2. Having students chart their speed and accuracy
Based on my rating, I may need to revisit the following:

___ 3. Using cooperative groups to enhance the development of procedural knowledge
Based on my rating, I may need to revisit the following:

Design Question 3

What Will I Do to Help Students Practice and Deepen Their Understanding of New Knowledge?

Module 9

Using Homework and Academic Notebooks to Deepen Student Understanding

Homework and academic notebooks are the final consideration related to Design Question 3. Both of these types of strategies should be done thoughtfully. Effective homework should have reasonable time requirements, a clear purpose, and clear alignment with identified learning goals. It should also allow opportunities for independent performance at key points during the student's learning cycle. Academic notebooks can also become powerful catalysts for helping students deepen their understanding when teachers encourage students to use their notebooks as interactive and organic resources for monitoring their own learning.

Reflecting on Your Current Beliefs and Practices

Before examining the strategies in this module, take some time to examine your current beliefs and practices by answering the following questions:

1. How do you use homework to deepen students' understanding?

_____

_____

_____

_____

2. What do you think are the pitfalls and misuses of homework?

_____

_____

_____

_____

3. To what extent do academic notebooks reinforce students' understanding of the content you are teaching them?

_____

_____

_____

_____

4. How do you ask students to revisit and revise their thinking as part of their work with academic notebooks?

_____

_____

_____

_____

Recommendations for Classroom Practice

This module addresses the following strategies for Design Question 3:

• Assigning purposeful homework that involves appropriate participation from the home

• Having students systematically revise and make corrections in their academic notebooks

Assigning Purposeful Homework That Involves Appropriate Participation from the Home

Homework is purposeful when it reinforces student learning. When students are first encountering new knowledge, for example, homework can be designed as an engaging and interesting previewing activity. Similarly, homework can be used to help students extend and refine their learning. When students are working with important declarative knowledge (facts, generalizations, and principles), homework can be designed to deepen their understanding of that information. For example, students might be assigned tasks involving comparison, classification, creating metaphors or analogies, or various forms of error analysis. Homework can also enhance students' growing fluency with procedural knowledge. Exercises and tasks that require students to apply procedural knowledge can form the basis for this approach to homework. Likewise, parents or family members can be asked to help students monitor accuracy and speed as they try out or apply key strategies, skills, or procedures.

Homework That Introduces New Content

Teachers can introduce new content to students before the students work directly with it in class. This approach to homework can become, in effect, a previewing activity for a critical-input experience for students, focusing students' understanding of the new content and its connections to prior learning. Students might be asked to read an introduction to new material or watch a media-based overview of it. When beginning an exploration of one of Shakespeare's tragedies and its relationship to the canon of Shakespeare's work, for example, students might be asked to read an excerpt on the Elizabethan era and the role of the Globe Theatre for homework. They might be asked to consider such questions as these: *What is the significance of Shakespeare within the history of world literature? Why is he such an enduring and powerful force? How did his involvement with the Globe Theatre influence his work and the theater of his day?* Students also might be asked to reflect on previous experiences they have had with Shakespearean tragedy, including any other plays of his they may have read or watched.

Homework That Helps Students Deepen Their Knowledge

Homework can be an effective way for students to extend and refine their understanding of essential declarative knowledge, particularly when it involves the strategies addressed in Module 7: comparison, classification, creating similes and metaphors, creating analogies, and error analysis. Students in a U.S. government class studying the American presidency, for example, might be assigned homework requiring them to reflect on the enduring legacy of a president they consider to have made lasting and significant contributions. Another assignment might ask them to compare their choice with another president. Students might also be asked to classify various presidents according to roles or categories of behavior they consider to be positive and negative elements of the presidency. They might create a metaphor or an analogy to describe a contemporary American president as they perceive that person. Similarly, their teacher might have them identify fallacies in reasoning and errors in logic in a specific president's campaign literature or in the various written or oral presidential addresses to various constituencies.

Homework That Enhances Students' Fluency with Procedural Knowledge

This approach to homework involves assigning exercises, activities, or performance tasks designed to enhance students' fluency in using specific skills, strategies, or processes. A foreign language teacher, for example, might assign a series of activities in which students are asked to complete translations of short excerpts within an identified amount of time with a specified level of accuracy. The next day, students compare their results and apply the key linguistic elements from their work in whole-class and one-on-one conversations. Similarly, elementary students might be assigned to solve addition and subtraction problems quickly and without making a great number of errors. Their teacher may also ask them to monitor the amount of time they devote to each problem—and report on their speed and accuracy when they return to class and discuss their answers.

Encouraging Appropriate Participation from the Home

An interesting aspect of the research on homework is appropriate participation from parents and family members. We recommend that teachers send home suggestions or directions to parents about ways in which they can support their children's successful completion of assignments without undue interference or control. The teacher, for example, might give suggestions for types of questions family members might pose if the homework involves declarative knowledge. For example, in a homework assignment involving students' study of the American Civil War, family members might be encouraged to ask questions such as these: *What led to that particular battle? What were the lasting effects of that battle? How did that battle compare to others you've studied?* Family members can ask students to summarize or paraphrase what they have read if they are being exposed to new content. Similarly, if students do timed exercises involving their application of procedural knowledge, a family member might help by timing them in accordance with homework directions.

Examples

Elementary Mathematics. This teacher is planning her instructional activities and assignments for the week for her unit on fractions and decimals. She plans to start the week with structured practice sessions on converting fractions to decimals. By Wednesday, students should be skilled enough to do the procedure at home. To this end, she develops directions for parents or guardians describing how they can help monitor their children's speed and accuracy.

Secondary Civics. This teacher will present an important critical-input lesson on criminal versus civil law on Wednesday. On Tuesday she assigns homework as a preview activity.

She asks students to read the first eight pages of the textbook chapter on this topic and be prepared to summarize what they have read.

Activity Box

For each of the following areas, describe how you have used or could use the suggestions presented in this section.

1. Homework that introduces new content:

2. Homework that helps students deepen their knowledge:

3. Homework that enhances students' fluency with procedural knowledge:

4. Homework that involves participation from the home:

Having Students Systematically Revise and Make Corrections in Their Academic Notebooks

Students should periodically reexamine their understanding of content by making new entries in their notebooks after homework has been corrected and discussed. Students can also reexamine the entries in their notebooks at any time, identifying areas that they may have initially misunderstood or incorporated inaccurately. These activities can be done independently or as part of a cooperative learning structure such as a pair-share activity.

Making Academic Notebooks Interactive

A key purpose for using academic notebooks is to have students revisit and revise their notebooks. This formal process of systematic revision can involve a variety of strategies. For example, students might make new entries in their notebooks after homework has been corrected and discussed. At any time during a unit or over several related units, students should be encouraged to reexamine notebook entries, identifying those things about which they were accurate initially and those things about which they may have been inaccurate or incomplete. Systematic revision can also involve cooperative learning pairs or triads in which students compare notebook entries, discover areas of agreement and disagreement, and revise areas that they discover are incomplete or inaccurate.

Using Academic Notebooks for Review

The process of systematic revision described in the previous section can become a useful technique for helping students study for exams and quizzes. In partnership with other students, learners can use their academic notebooks to determine the terms, concepts, big ideas, and understandings they need to commit to long-term memory. They can also partner with other students to reach consensus about significant information they need to retain, including coaching one another to ensure that they can explain that information accurately and completely. Either independently or with one or more partners, students can use their academic notebooks to generate questions for their teacher or the entire class. In particular, students can deepen their understanding of essential content by using material from their academic notebooks to generate higher-order questions related to the topics, issues, and skills and strategies they are studying.

Examples

Elementary Science. At the end of each week this teacher has students review the entries in their academic notebooks for the week. Students add to their notes and also correct previous misconceptions. Students then meet in small groups to compare the changes they have made.

Secondary Social Studies. Periodically this teacher has students pair up and compare the entries in their academic notebooks. Pairs of students identify common areas of confusion and common areas of agreement. They also generate questions to be asked of the teacher.

Activity Box

Compare your use of academic notebooks with the recommendations described in this section.

Checking for Understanding

Use the following rating scale to assess your current understanding and comfort level regarding key strategies and processes presented in this module:

4 = I understand and already fully implement this strategy in my classroom.
3 = I understand this strategy, but I need to practice using it in my classroom.

2 = I can explain this strategy, but I am not fully confident that I can use it.

1 = I do not understand this strategy, and I do not currently use it in my classroom.

___ 1. Homework that introduces new content
Based on my rating, I may need to revisit the following:

___ 2. Homework that helps deepen students' knowledge
Based on my rating, I may need to revisit the following:

___ 3. Homework designed to enhance fluency
Based on my rating, I may need to revisit the following:

___ 4. Effective parent participation in homework
Based on my rating, I may need to revisit the following:

___ 5. Students' review of academic notebooks
Based on my rating, I may need to revisit the following:

Design Question 4

What Will I Do to Help Students Generate and
Test Hypotheses About New Knowledge?

Module 10

Teaching Students to Support
Claims and Assertions with Evidence

Module 11

Hypothesis Testing and
Higher-Order Thinking

Module 12

Engaging Students in Task Design,
Cooperative Learning, and Self-
Evaluation

Module 10

Teaching Students to Support Claims and Assertions with Evidence

True understanding requires students to move beyond initial acquisition and integration of new knowledge toward growing levels of refinement and use. Design Question 4 deals with strategies to help students progress beyond basic levels of knowing by engaging them in tasks that require experimentation with the new knowledge—that is, generating and testing hypotheses about it. The next module—Module 11—addresses four specific types of tasks that can be used to this end: experimental-inquiry tasks, problem-solving tasks, decision-making tasks, and investigation tasks. Module 12 deals with engaging students in designing their own tasks and using cooperative groups. However, to effectively use tasks for generating and testing hypotheses, students must understand the nature of support. Specifically, they must understand the following:

• Valid claims must be supported through the development of *grounds*—supporting assertions and declarations.

• The support should be explained and discussed via *backing*, which establishes the validity of grounds and discusses the grounds in depth.

• Exceptions to the claims should be identified through *qualifiers*, which state the degree of certainty for the claim and exceptions to the claim.

• Statistical information should be used and analyzed with an understanding of its limitations.

This module—Module 10—addresses strategies for enhancing students' understanding of and ability to use these elements.

Reflecting on Your Current Beliefs and Practices

Before examining the strategies in this module, take some time to examine your current beliefs and practices by answering the following questions:

1. How do you ensure that students deepen their understanding of knowledge by forming claims and assertions?

_____

_____

_____

_____

2. How do you teach students to understand the importance of supporting claims and assertions with evidence?

_____

_____

_____

_____

3. How do you encourage students to identify levels of certainty regarding their claims?

_____

_____

_____

_____

4. What do you do to enhance students' understanding of the proper use of statistical information?

_____

_____

_____

_____

Recommendations for Classroom Practice

This module addresses the following strategies for Design Question 4:

- Establishing grounds to support valid claims
- Providing backing to establish the validity of grounds
- Framing qualifiers to analyze levels of certainty and exceptions for claims
- Addressing the limits of statistical information

Establishing Grounds to Support Valid Claims

Simply stated, grounds are the initial evidence provided for a claim. If politicians make the claim "I am the best candidate for this office," we naturally expect them to provide supporting evidence. This initial evidence constitutes the grounds supporting the claim.

Grounds can assume a variety of formats, including (1) matters of common knowledge (building upon consensus-driven facts, examples, and related information universally acknowledged to be true and accurate); (2) expert opinion (direct and indirect quotes from recognized authorities within a field or discipline, especially well-respected experts specializing in areas being defended by the student); (3) experimental evidence (evidence generated via professional scientific experimentation or via student-generated experiments designed to test and confirm a specific hypothesis); and (4) other factual information related to the field or content being studied, investigated, and tested.

With students at the elementary level, the concept of grounds to support a claim can be addressed in a rudimentary but powerful manner. We recommend using the term "my new idea" to represent a claim. For example, after observing and talking about the behavior of classroom pets, students might be asked to think of "my new idea"—something about pets they haven't thought of before. This is tantamount to a claim. To introduce the concept of grounds supporting claims, the teacher would simply ask students to explain why they think their new idea is true.

At the secondary level, a much more sophisticated approach can be taken. To illustrate, let us consider how grounds might be approached in English/language arts, social studies, science, and mathematics.

In English/language arts, grounds can be developed by asking students to read extensively in a field they are investigating. Students would then synthesize the information gleaned from this reading to determine what is considered common knowledge regarding the subject of investigation. Students should also be made aware of the importance of reflecting the latest critical stances and points of view concerning a topic of investigation. This type of information is typically considered expert opinion.

In social studies, "common knowledge" for a given topic can be ascertained by asking students to compare and contrast historical, political, economic, and cultural perspectives and points of view regarding the issue under investigation. Students can explain how this knowledge base has been formed and how it has been modified or transformed via primary and secondary sources available in recent eras. Social studies is an ideal venue in which students can research and debate contrasting expert opinions on a subject, a process, or an era. For example, students might address questions like these: *How does ideological bias or political stance affect a theorist's analysis of an issue or process? To what extent are facts today different from facts in previous eras concerning key historical events and situations? What accounts for shifts in what we consider to be valid factual evidence?*

Science is the perfect venue to examine the power of experimental evidence. Students need help in understanding the significance of experimental inquiry and scientific investigation as the heart of formulating scientific grounds. Students might address questions like these: *How exactly do scientists formulate scientific knowledge and factual evidence? To what extent does the paradigm of a particular scientific discipline or content area shape and influence how scientists study specific scientific phenomena? What constitutes valid and reliable scientific evidence? How can we, as students, generate and analyze scientific data to support claims and assertions?*

Mathematics and its range of academic disciplines provide an interesting context for students to examine the nature of grounds in supporting claims and assertions. Students can examine issues like these: *Why do scientists consider mathematics the universal language of science? How do we express scientific assertions and claims via mathematical evidence? What is the role of mathematics in generating and supporting scientific hypotheses, claims, and assertions?*

Examples

Elementary Science. This elementary science teacher has involved students in a unit on weather. After studying various aspects of local weather patterns, the teacher asks students to write down their "new ideas" and explain why they think their new idea is true.

High School Social Studies. After studying the backgrounds of the Democratic and Republican presidential candidates, students in this 10th grade social studies class are asked to develop a claim regarding which candidate is the best person for the job and to provide grounds supporting their claims.

Activity Box

What are some ways you might help students understand and develop the concept of grounds regarding a topic you have had or will have students investigate?

Providing Backing to Establish the Validity of Grounds

Just as grounds provide the support for a claim, backing establishes the validity of grounds. It is one thing for students to present grounds for their arguments. It is quite another for them to provide sufficient and coherent backing to ensure that their grounds are both convincing and valid.

Again, at the elementary level, the idea of backing for grounds can be approached in a rudimentary fashion. Once students have stated their new idea (their claim) and presented the reasons why they think their new idea is true (their grounds), the teacher can introduce the concept that reasons must themselves be supported. Again, the terms *claims*, *grounds*, and *backing* do not have to be used (although we suggest that these terms be introduced as early as possible). To illustrate, students' new ideas and their reasons why their new ideas are true can be recorded on the board or on chart paper. One student might have written the following:

> My new idea is that hamsters like to help each other. I think this is true because I saw them take turns running on the wheel and I saw them share the food dish.

Using this as an example, the teacher would ask the student to explain what she actually saw that looked like the hamsters were taking turns running on the wheel. The student might respond that she saw "one hamster would get on for a while, and then the other would try to get on and the one on the wheel would get off to make room." Over time, such interactions would reinforce the notion that new ideas and the support for these ideas should have a basic structure like that depicted in Figure 10.1.

FIGURE 10.1
Framework for New Ideas

New Idea:
Reason #1 why I think it is true:
What I actually observed:
Reason #2 why I think it is true:
What I actually observed:

The concept of backing would be approached in a much more sophisticated fashion at the secondary level. To illustrate, we again consider four subject areas: English/language arts, social studies, science, and mathematics.

In English/language arts, the concept of backing and its relationship to grounds fits quite well with the concept of topic sentence and supporting details. In fact, the relationship among a claim, grounds, and backing for grounds can be represented as shown in Figure 10.2. In the figure, a claim is analogous to a thesis statement (e.g., "The movie *The Matrix* should be considered a classic"). Grounds statements are analogous to topic sentences supporting a thesis statement (e.g., "The movie has a large following, and the following continues to grow"; "The movie portrays archetypal characters"; "The movie has a plot that is similar to many of those from Shakespearean tragedies"). Each of these topic sentences would be validated by supporting details (backing statements). Language arts teachers can help students make these connections and then examine argumentative essays to determine how well they follow this pattern.

FIGURE 10.2

Framework for Claim with Grounds and Backing

Claim (Thesis Statement)
> Grounds 1 (Topic Sentence 1)
>> Backing 1a (Support 1a)
>> Backing 1b (Support 1b)
>> Backing 1c (Support 1c)
> Grounds 2 (Topic Sentence 2)
>> Backing 2a (Support 2a)
>> Backing 2b (Support 2b)
>> Backing 2c (Support 2c)

Social studies can be used to reinforce the concept of backing from the perspective of primary sources as the ultimate type of valid information. Too often secondary sources are used as backing when, in fact, they are interpretations of primary sources. Social studies classes are also ideal contexts for examining what constitutes valid—versus biased or illogical—backing and support for assertions, claims, and hypotheses.

In science classes, students should have extensive opportunities to explore the concept of backing from the perspective of raw observational data. Such data are foundational to scientific conclusions just as primary sources are foundational to conclusions drawn in the social sciences. Additionally, science students can be encouraged to read, discuss, and evaluate the substantiality of scientific evidence presented in articles and other professional scientific writings. Does the author/scientist, for example, present sufficient backing to fully support his grounds for scientific conclusion? To what extent were the scientific protocols and processes used to formulate backing for arguments appropriate, valid, and extensive enough to defend the ideas presented in the particular writing or set of writings?

In mathematics, a range of mathematical disciplines can enhance students' understanding of the significance of backing as an essential building block of effective arguments and hypothesis-testing processes. Mathematical models are typically the basis of backing statements. A question to consider when addressing backing from the perspective of mathematics is this: *Does the mathematical model presented by an author sufficiently and appropriately reinforce and defend the major grounds that are being used to defend a claim?*

Examples

Elementary Science. After students have described their new ideas about what makes plants grow and provided their reasons why they believe their new ideas to be true, their teacher asks them to select one of their reasons and explain what they actually observed that led them to their stated reason.

Secondary Composition. This high school composition teacher uses claims, grounds, and backing as the framework for writing argumentation essays. Students are encouraged to think of backing as the bedrock on which effective arguments are developed.

Activity Box

Which of the approaches to developing the concept of backing most closely relates to your subject area? Explain why.

Framing Qualifiers to Analyze Levels of Certainty and Exceptions for Claims

A major part of students' becoming effective critical thinkers is their growing recognition that not all arguments can be made with the same degree of certainty. Therefore, they need to understand the concept of *qualifiers* as part of a well-balanced argument. Specifically, qualifiers are statements and related evidence that qualify or characterize the degree of certainty for claims being presented. Qualifiers can also be used to assess the degree of certainty regarding exceptions and counterarguments being presented against a particular claim or assertion.

We suggest that students' understanding of the concept of qualifiers can extend and refine their understanding of the four categories of errors we presented in Design

Question 3: *What will I do to help students practice and deepen their understanding of new knowledge?* The four categories are faulty logic, attacks, weak references, and misinformation.

With elementary students, the concept of qualifiers might be addressed by explaining that new ideas describe things we are learning. However, something we have seen happen one time might not always happen the same way every time. Therefore, it is useful for them to think about "things that might change my new idea." To illustrate, when asked, the student who generated the new idea that hamsters like to help each other might add the qualifying idea that "they might not help each other if there isn't enough food for both of them." This effectively illustrates the notion of a qualifier.

At the secondary level, qualifiers can be addressed in a much more rigorous way. Again, we consider four subject areas.

English/language arts is wide open for students to examine the power of alternative perspectives and points of view. In expository and argumentative/persuasive writing activities, for example, students should be encouraged to anticipate how critics or individuals advocating counterarguments might respond to the ideas, grounds, and backing they are presenting. A similar process can be used in many forms of oral discussion and debate, especially when students are discussing and investigating controversial issues and ideas. Literature provides another ideal context for students to examine the concept of qualifier ideas and evidence. How, for example, do different literary characters view the same events, processes, and conflicts? What accounts for differing perspectives and points of view about the same events?

In social studies, debates and alternative perspectives represent one of the great motivating components of any class. Students should be encouraged to formulate qualifiers and counterarguments for ideas, theories, and historical interpretations they are studying in a particular unit or lesson. Why would there be controversy or debate about a particular historical event, economic trend, or political, social, or cultural process? What specific grounds, backing, and qualifiers do theorists present about specific historical events and trends? Once again, students should be encouraged to examine the role of ideological and values-driven perspectives and points of view in shaping individuals' and groups' interpretations of events, trends, and processes.

In science, the various disciplines offer a wide range of opportunities for students to explore and discuss the nature of qualifiers in hypothesis testing and scientific argumentation. Conflicting theories and interpretations regarding scientific processes and phenomena provide ideal venues to illustrate qualifiers. For example, what accounts for changes in scientific paradigms such as the movement away from a Ptolemaic view of the universe toward the Copernican revolution? Similarly, how does Newtonian physics differ from subatomic physics' depiction of natural processes and the structure of the universe? Students can also investigate the concept of qualifiers as they share their conclusions about a particular science lab in which they participated.

In mathematics, students can benefit from discussing and investigating the role of math in the support of scientific claims and assertions. To what extent, for example, can we identify qualifiers related to a particular scientific article or related publication? Is there mathematical or statistical evidence presented as a key component of a qualifier? Whenever possible, students should be encouraged to appreciate both the inherent value of mathematics and its universal applications to all scientific fields and endeavors. As the next section of this module will reinforce, however, they also need to appreciate the limitations and potential errors in the use of statistical information.

Examples

Elementary Science. After her students have stated their new ideas, the reasons for their new ideas, and the observations that led to their reasons, this elementary teacher always has students list at least one thing or one situation that might change their new idea.

Secondary Social Studies. After students have presented their arguments regarding a specific claim, this secondary teacher asks them to examine an alternative point of view that would negate their claim or support a rival claim.

Activity Box

Which approach to the concept of qualifiers most closely fits your subject area? Explain how you might use the concept of qualifiers.

Addressing the Limits of Statistical Information

Students' understanding of qualifiers also rests on their appreciation of the power—and limitations—of statistical evidence. Here we emphasize five major types of statistical limitations students should be made aware of:

• Regression toward the mean—being aware that an extreme score on a measure is most commonly followed by a more moderate score that is closer to the mean.

• Errors of conjunction—being aware that is it less likely that two or more independent events will occur simultaneously than that they will occur in isolation.

• Keeping aware of base rates—using the general or typical patterns of occurrences in a category of events as the basis on which to predict what will happen in a specific situation.

• Understanding the limits of extrapolation—realizing that using trends to make predictions—extrapolating—is a useful practice as long as the prediction does not extend beyond the data for which trends have been observed.

• Adjusting estimates of risk to account for the cumulative nature of probabilistic events—realizing that even though the probability of a risky event might be highly unlikely, the probability of the event occurring increases with time and the number of events.

At the elementary level, teachers can approach the notion of the limits of statistical information by having students make rudimentary judgments about how likely something is. A simple scale like that in Figure 10.3 might be employed. Using this scale, students can be asked to judge the probability of events. For example, during an elementary science unit on weather, students might be asked to estimate the chance that it will rain on a given afternoon. As students make probability guesses regarding this event, the teacher would ask them to explain the reasoning behind their guesses, keeping in mind the limits of statistical information. The class would then discuss the reasonableness of logic underlying the student guesses.

FIGURE 10.3

Probability Scale

3 = It's going to happen for sure.

2 = Very good chance it will happen.

1 = It might happen, but it's not very likely.

0 = It won't happen for sure.

At the secondary level, the limits of statistical information can be addressed in greater depth. Again, we consider four subject areas.

In English/language arts, when students are working on formal research projects or more informal types of investigation (for oral and written products and performances), teachers can encourage them to consider the statistical evidence used by one or more authors. Internet sites frequently present conclusions that go well beyond the original evidence. This is a form of extrapolating beyond known trends.

Social studies and its wide range of disciplines (e.g., history, economics, anthropology, and sociology) offer multiple opportunities for students to examine and critique the statistical evidence presented in primary and secondary sources, as well as in their textbooks. To what extent do any of the errors or fallacies associated with statistical information appear to weaken a particular argument, case, grounds, or backing presented in a social science publication?

In science, one of the key aspects of scientific literacy involves students' ability to analyze and draw inferences about statistical data generated via scientific experimentation and in scientific publications. All science classrooms can and should reinforce the five major limits for statistical information identified earlier. Students should be encouraged to understand these concepts and apply them as they examine their own data conclusions as well as those presented by scientific writers and authorities.

In mathematics, probability and statistics should be a fundamental component of students' education. In particular, students should be made aware of the fact that probability plays a big part in how cultures form conclusions and make decisions. This can be exemplified by examining the probabilities associated with projected phenomena like global warming, the earth being struck by an asteroid, and so on.

Examples

Elementary Health. This teacher presents students with statistical information about how unlikely it is that a person will be struck by lightning. She then has students examine how this probability increases if one makes a habit of standing outside during lightning storms. Students come to the common conclusion that just because a dangerous event doesn't happen very often, you still increase your risk by continuing to ignore or seeking out that danger.

Secondary Mathematics. This secondary mathematics teacher has students examine various projections for global warming from the perspective of the five major types of statistical errors. Students conclude that many of these projections have extrapolated beyond known trends.

Activity Box

Describe how you have used or could use the concept of statistical probability in your class.

Checking for Understanding

Use the following rating scale to assess your current understanding and comfort level regarding the key strategies and processes presented in this module:

4 = I understand and already fully implement this strategy in my classroom.

3 = I understand this strategy, but I need to practice using it in my classroom.

2 = I can explain this strategy, but I am not fully confident that I can use it.

1 = I do not understand this strategy, and I do not currently use it in my classroom.

___ 1. Grounds

Based on my rating, I may need to revisit the following:

___ 2. Backing

Based on my rating, I may need to revisit the following:

___ 3. Qualifiers

Based on my rating, I may need to revisit the following:

___ 4. The limits of statistical information

Based on my rating, I may need to revisit the following:

Design Question 4

What Will I Do to Help Students Generate and Test Hypotheses About
New Knowledge?

Module 11

Hypothesis Testing and Higher-Order Thinking

All students benefit from participating in authentic, real-world tasks that allow them to use academic knowledge in purposeful and reality-based ways. Specifically, students' ability to deepen their understanding of key declarative and procedural knowledge depends upon their experiences using it in conjunction with a variety of higher-order reasoning processes—specifically with the cognitive process of generating and testing hypotheses. This module, therefore, addresses the following types of real-world tasks that can be taught in a way that fosters hypothesis generation and testing: experimental inquiry, problem solving, decision making, and investigation.

Reflecting on Your Current Beliefs and Practices

Before examining the strategies in this module, take some time to examine your beliefs and practices by answering the following questions:

1. How do you typically help students to experiment with new knowledge?

_____

_____

_____

_____

2. How do you encourage your students to generate and test hypotheses about the knowledge they are learning?

_____

_____

_____

_____

3. How do you incorporate problem-solving tasks and learning activities into your units and lessons?

_____

_____

_____

_____

4. How do your units and lessons incorporate opportunities for students to engage in decision making?

_____

_____

_____

_____

5. To what extent do students in your class engage in a variety of investigation activities related to the knowledge they are learning?

_____

_____

_____

_____

Recommendations for Classroom Practice

This module addresses the following strategies for Design Question 4:

- Experimental-inquiry tasks
- Problem-solving tasks
- Decision-making tasks
- Investigation tasks

Experimental Inquiry: It's Not Just for Science!

Although experimental inquiry is a fundamental building block of science instruction, it can become a tool for promoting students' generation and testing of hypotheses in a variety of content areas. Students should be taught to make predictions based on observations and to design ways (e.g., experiments, surveys, questionnaires, interviews, observations) to test those predictions—and then examine the results in light of the original prediction. Here we present some examples of experimental-inquiry tasks that occur outside the domain of science instruction.

In English/language arts, teachers can ask students to use experimental-inquiry strategies to formulate and test hypotheses as part of their research and composition activities. For example, students might predict how their fellow students would respond to a particular topical question of interest (e.g., *Should we be required to wear uniforms in this school?*) Next, students would collect data to test their hypothesis using interviews, questionnaires, or surveys. After polling a sufficient sampling of students, they would analyze their data and present an oral or written analysis of its meaning. As part of this process they would compare their original prediction against the results evident in the data they collected.

Social studies teachers can engage students in formulating and testing hypotheses about attitudinal changes evident in the contemporary era across different generations. For example, students might interview or survey members of different generations about such issues as their attitudes about the economy, war, cultural norms, or other issues of interest based upon content studied. At the conclusion of their investigation, they would test their initial predictions about attitudinal differences and similarities against patterns revealed through their data collection and analysis. A variation of this approach would involve students in updating historical, sociological, economic, or political surveys from prior eras compared to the current era.

To help reinforce the process of generating and testing hypotheses within the framework of experimental inquiry, we recommend teachers use the stimulus questions shown in Figure 11.1. These questions highlight the basic elements of the experimental-inquiry process.

FIGURE 11.1

Questions to Stimulate Experimental Inquiry

- What's my prediction?
- How will I test my prediction?
- What do I expect to see if my prediction is accurate?
- What actually happened?
- Did my prediction come true?
- How has my thinking changed about the situation?

Examples

Elementary Mathematics. Students in this elementary classroom have been practicing three-column addition. After students have developed some fluency with the procedure, the teacher assigns them the task of changing some of the steps to determine the effects of the changes on the ease or difficulty with which they can perform the procedure.

Secondary Physical Education. Students have been studying various ways to hit a ground stroke in tennis. Once they have some of the basics, the teacher has them experiment by making slight changes in their hand position or stance.

Activity Box

Describe a possible experimental-inquiry task you might use in your class.

Purposeful and Authentic Problem Solving

Problem-solving tasks require students to use knowledge they are learning in order to generate and defend solutions to situations involving an unusual context or constraint. Such tasks challenge students to determine what must be done differently given the unusual context or constraint. Before engaging in a problem-solving task, students should be asked to predict how the unusual context or constraint affects the situation. At the conclusion of a problem-solving task, students should restate their predictions and then contrast their initial predictions with what actually occurred in a particular context. They should describe their conclusions with well-structured support.

In English/language arts, for example, a teacher might ask students to take the role of a character in a literary work they are reading and develop a strategy for solving a problem. To illustrate, consider *Hamlet*. Before finishing the play, students might be asked to address Hamlet's problems with his Uncle Claudius. Similarly, students might be asked to address the moral crisis faced by Huckleberry Finn. How would they resolve this issue? In each case, students would generate a set of alternatives and select the one they feel is best. After completing the story, they would then contrast their solutions with those used by the fictional character.

A history teacher might ask students to develop a problem-solving strategy or intervention related to a major economic problem in contemporary society or in a historical context. For example, had they been president of the United States during the Great Depression, how might they have addressed one of the social or economic problems facing the nation?

If they were elected president in the 21st century, how would they address a recurrent problem such as funding Social Security or eliminating economic recessions? Again, students would be asked to contrast their proposed solutions with those actually taken.

To help reinforce the process of generating and testing hypotheses within the framework of problem solving, we recommend the use of the stimulus questions shown in Figure 11.2.

In some cases students will not be able to actually try out the possible solutions they have generated. For example, students would not be able to actually try out the solution they would recommend to Hamlet, nor would they be able to try out their solutions to issues during the Great Depression. In such cases, students would build a logical case for the solution they believe would be the most viable and contrast their solutions with those actually used. Their logical cases should include claims, grounds, backing, and qualifiers as described in Module 10.

FIGURE 11.2

Questions to Stimulate Problem Solving

- What's the goal?
- What obstacle or unusual situation makes it difficult to accomplish the goal?
- What are some ways one might overcome the obstacle or the unusual situation?
- Which solution do I predict will work best and why?
- What actually happened?
- Do the results fit with my original prediction?
- If not, how should my thinking change regarding the problem?

Copyright ©2008. Marzano & Associates. Reprinted with permission.

Examples

Elementary Language Arts. A language arts teacher asks students to write a brief composition without any initial drafts. That is, they must generate their final draft without writing any preliminary drafts. Also, they cannot erase anything they have written. Before students begin writing, they must generate a strategy for overcoming this obstacle. Although students don't have much success at writing effective compositions, the activity provides them with a keen awareness of the importance of the revising and editing phases of the writing process.

Secondary Health. This health teacher asks students to develop a 1,800-calorie-per-day diet that alternates between high carbs and high protein from day to day. Although the task is a fabricated one, the constraints they have to work under increase students' understanding of dietary requirements.

Activity Box

Design a problem-solving task you might use in class.

Promoting Students' Decision-Making Prowess

Well-designed decision-making tasks should require students to select among equally appealing alternatives. Students begin by identifying alternatives to be considered. Next, they address the criteria by which alternatives will be judged. With alternatives and criteria identified, students examine alternatives in light of the criteria that will be used to make a selection.

As with problem-solving tasks, English/language arts teachers can ask students to identify and describe significant decisions faced by characters in both fiction and nonfiction. Students then analyze the decision-making process used by a particular literary figure and compare that process to alternative approaches they would recommend.

In social studies classes, students can use decision making to examine events in history. They can continuously compare how individuals and groups in certain eras arrived at particular social, cultural, economic, and political decisions versus how we might approach the same decision-making task today. At key juncture points throughout the academic year, students can engage in more formal research involving decision-making processes related to a content focus area in which they have special interest. For example, students might examine the process used to make a decision to engage in a war with Iraq.

To facilitate the decision-making process, it is helpful to use a decision-making matrix like that shown in Figure 11.3. It is set up to determine which story among a set of six (alternatives A through F) would be the best to recommend to a student who doesn't like to read much.

Decision-making tasks require a fair amount of structuring by the teacher. The first step in designing a decision-making task is to identify or have students identify the alternatives to be considered. In the case of the sample task in Figure 11.3, six alternatives (books) are provided for students. An option is for the teacher to provide three of the titles and ask students to supply three titles of their own. The next step involves the criteria by which the alternatives will be judged. In the case of the sample task, three criteria have been provided for students. Again, an option would be to have students generate the criteria or to provide some criteria for students and have them generate some on their own.

FIGURE 11.3

Yes/No Decision-Making Matrix

Alternatives						
Criteria	A	B	C	D	E	F
1	X	X	X	0	?	X
2	X	0	X	X	X	?
3	X	0	?	0	0	0

Alternatives: A = *Holes*

B = *The Hobbit*

C = *A Girl Named Disaster*

D = *The Outsiders*

E = *Izzy, Will–Nilly*

F = *Island of the Blue Dolphins*

Criteria: 1 = A story that is easy to follow

2 = A story that has a message that relates to the lives of students

3 = A story that is written in a way that engages the reader

With alternatives and criteria identified, students can complete the decision-making matrix. Note that three symbols have been used in Figure 11.3: an *X* indicates that the alternative possesses the criterion, a *0* means that it does not possess the criterion, and a question mark (?) indicates that the student is not sure. When students count up the number of *X*s for each alternative, they have a rank ordering of the alternatives in terms of the criteria. In the case of Figure 11.3, *Holes* (Alternative A) has the most *X*s.

Figure 11.3 uses a yes/no approach to criteria (a book either meets the criterion or does not meet the criterion). Another approach is more quantitative in nature and also more precise. In this system, each criterion is given a score indicating how important it is, using the following scale: 3 is "critically important," 2 is "important but not critical," 1 is "not very important." Similarly, each alternative is assigned a score indicating the extent to which it possesses each criterion, using the following scale: 3 is "completely possesses the criterion," 2 is "possesses the criterion to a great extent but not completely," 1 is "possesses the criterion a little bit," and 0 is "does not possess the criterion at all." This is depicted in Figure 11.4.

FIGURE 11.4

Quantitative Method

Criteria	Alternatives					
	A	B	C	D	E	F
1 (2)	(2) × 3 = 6	(2) × 2 = 4	(2) × 3 = 6	(2) × 1 = 2	(2) × 2 = 4	(2) × 3 = 6
2 (1)	(1) × 2 = 2	(1) × 1 = 1	(1) × 3 = 3	(1) × 3 = 3	(1) × 3 = 3	(1) × 1 = 1
3 (3)	(3) × 2 = 6	(3) × 1 = 3	(3) × 2 = 6	(3) × 0 = 0	(3) × 1 = 3	(3) × 3 = 9
Total	14	8	15	5	10	16

Note that each cell has two scores that are multiplied, and the product is displayed. The score in parentheses is the score of the criterion. The first criterion (*is easy to follow*) was assigned a weight of 2 by the student or students who completed this matrix. Every cell in the first row has the score of 2 in parentheses. The score it is multiplied by is the score the student or students have assigned for a given alternative relative to the criterion. Alternative A (*Holes*) has received a score of 3 for this criterion, indicating that *Holes* completely possess the criterion. The product score is 6. Also notice that the product scores are summed for each alternative. When these products are summed, the alternatives can again be rank ordered in terms of the extent to which they possess the criterion.

As before, to make decision-making tasks reap the benefits of generating and testing hypotheses, students must contrast their initial predictions with the actual outcomes of the activity. In this case, students would explain how the decision-making task confirmed or denied their original opinions. They would state their conclusions using proper support.

To help facilitate the decision-making process, we recommend the use of the stimulus questions depicted in Figure 11.5.

FIGURE 11.5

Questions to Stimulate Decision Making

- What alternatives am I considering?
- What criteria am I using to select among alternatives?
- What do I predict will be the best alternative?
- Which alternative came out on top?
- Do the results fit with my original prediction? If not, how should my thinking change?

Examples

Elementary Physical Education. This physical education teacher asks students to use data from their most recent fitness assessment to decide what aspects of their personal fitness might need attention.

Secondary Technology. This high school technology teacher provides students with the following decision-making task:

> You've just discovered that the data you imported into a spreadsheet have a significant flaw: all the data have been shifted by one column, so that the variable names identify the wrong data. Determine how you will restore or reimport the data, and explain your reasoning. Consider at least two methods for accomplishing this task and at least two criteria by which you will make your decision.

Activity Box

Design a decision-making task you might use in your class.

Exploring Different Forms of Investigation

Investigation tasks involve testing hypotheses about past, present, or future events. The rich opportunities and range of assessment and teaching-learning options inherent in the investigation process make this type of task a particularly significant one for teachers designing curriculum. There are three interrelated forms of investigation a teacher might use:

- *Historical investigation* involves answering questions about what really happened, or why "X" happened?
- *Projective investigation* involves answering questions such as "What would happen if _____?"
- *Definitional investigation* involves answering questions such as "What are the important features of _____?" or "What are the defining characteristics of _____?"

It is important to keep in mind that the three types of investigation share a common set of steps, which might be described as in Figure 11.6. The common steps for all three types of investigation are determining what is already known, identifying confusions or contradictions in that knowledge base, and developing a plausible resolution to the confusion or contradiction. Preceding these common steps, the first step differentiates the focus of the process—a concept to be defined, a past event to be explained, or a future or hypothetical event to be defined or explained. The following examples describe how investigation might be used in different subject areas.

FIGURE 11.6

A Common Process for Investigation Tasks

- Clearly identify . . .

    a. The concept to be defined (definitional investigation), or
    b. The past event to be explained (historical investigation), or
    c. The future or hypothetical event (projective investigation) to be defined or explained.

- Identify what is already known or agreed upon.
- Identify any confusions or contradictions.
- Develop a plausible resolution to the confusion or contradiction.

In an English/language arts class, students can engage in historical investigations as part of their study of literary eras as well as in integrated curriculum designs involving social studies and English. For example, students might be asked to address questions like these: *What political, social, and cultural events and processes gave rise to the romantic era? What are the historical origins of the modern novel?* Relative to projective investigation, students might be asked to answer questions like these: *How would contemporary American literature have been different without the contributions of (e.g., Hemingway, Fitzgerald, Faulkner)?* Definitional investigation can provide a rich venue for students to deepen their understanding of key language arts concepts. For example, they might investigate changing concepts of such genres as the epic or the tragedy across literary and historical eras.

In social studies classes, students can be asked to complete a wide variety of investigational tasks as part of their study of history, economics, political science, and geography. For example, history students can complete historical research as well as projective investigations speculating about how history might be different had certain major historical outcomes been different (e.g., *What if the South had won the Civil War?*). Similarly, definitional investigations can guide and inform students' evolving perceptions about key course or grade-level concepts. For example, students could be asked to consider questions such as this: *Over historical eras and across civilizations, what changes have occurred in our understanding of such concepts as the following: leadership, law and public policy, citizenship, rights and responsibilities, democracy?*

To help reinforce the process of investigation, we recommend the use of the stimulus questions depicted in Figure 11.7.

FIGURE 11.7

Questions to Stimulate Investigation

- Am I focusing on something that has to be defined better, something that happened in the past, or something that might possibly happen?
- What do I predict I will find out?
- What is known about my subject?
- What are some confusions or contradictions in what is known about the topic?
- What do I predict to be the resolution to these confusions or contradictions?
- Did my findings fit with my original prediction? If not, how should my thinking change?

Examples

Elementary Social Studies. This elementary social studies teacher provides students with the following investigation task:

Select three kinds of basic foods that you eat every day, such as bread, milk, and vegetables. How did a family in early America obtain the same kinds of food? Did this affect how they spent their time?

Secondary Art. This secondary art teacher presents students with the following investigation task:

Investigate the process for creating an oil painting during the Renaissance and compare it with how artists create them today. What techniques have remained the same over the centuries, and why do they continue to be in use today?

Activity Box

Design an investigation task you might use in school.

Checking for Understanding

Use the following rating scale to assess your current understanding and comfort level regarding the strategies and practices presented in this module:

4 = I understand and already fully implement this strategy in my classroom.

3 = I understand this strategy, but I need to practice using it in my classroom.

2 = I can explain this strategy, but I am not fully confident that I can use it.

1 = I do not understand this strategy, and I do not currently use it in my classroom.

___ 1.   Experimental-inquiry tasks

Based on my rating, I may need to revisit the following:

___ 2.   Problem-solving tasks

Based on my rating, I may need to revisit the following:

___ 3.   Decision-making tasks

Based on my rating, I may need to revisit the following:

___ 4.   Investigation tasks

Based on my rating, I may need to revisit the following:

Module 12

Engaging Students in Task Design, Cooperative Learning, and Self-Evaluation

This module emphasizes the power of having students design their own tasks for the generation and testing of hypotheses. When students participate in designing the kinds of project-based tasks described in the previous module, they reap many benefits. Specifically, students develop a heightened sense of motivation and efficacy when they are allowed to engage in self-designed authentic tasks that require them to transfer knowledge to the world beyond the classroom. The more learning and assessment tasks are reality based, the more students understand curriculum content at higher levels. A fundamental condition for higher levels of understanding is that students engage in self-monitoring, self-evaluation, and self-regulation. This module will also revisit a recurring theme in *The Art and Science of Teaching*—the power of shared experience and cooperative learning as essential building blocks of the teaching-learning process.

Reflecting on Your Current Beliefs and Practices

Before examining the strategies in this module, take some time to reflect on your current beliefs and practices by answering the following questions:

1. How do you ensure that students take a direct role in task design, when appropriate?

_____

_____

_____

_____

2. To what extent do you attempt to incorporate student interests into task design?

_____

_____

_____

3. How do you encourage students to engage in ongoing processes of self-monitoring, self-regulation, and self-evaluation?

_____

_____

_____

_____

4. How do you encourage students to engage in cooperative learning processes and structures to reinforce their understanding and higher-order thinking?

_____

_____

_____

_____

Recommendations for Classroom Practice

This module addresses the following strategies for Design Question 4:

- Engaging students in task design
- Using cooperative learning to enhance students' work with performance tasks and projects
- Encouraging metacognition and self-regulation

Engaging Students in Task Design

When students design their own tasks, it is important for the teacher to work closely with them so that the tasks and projects are not simply interesting things to do but represent genuine contributions to the students' learning. We suggest that as students progress from initial knowledge and skills acquisition toward growing levels of proficiency and independence, they should be asked to address the following question:

What are your initial questions and predictions about this (content/information)?

This initial question helps students focus on a topic of personal interest within the framework of the unit.

Next, students would try to determine which type of task would best address their questions and predictions. The following stimulus questions can be used to help students identify the type of task they will design:

Relative to my questions and predictions, is there an important . . .
- Hypothesis I want to test?
- Problem I want to study?
- Decision I want to examine?
- Concept I want to examine?
- Event I want to study?
- Hypothetical or future event I want to examine?

As the following examples will confirm, this process can be used in a wide variety of subject areas.

English/language arts lends itself to student-generated problem-solving and decision-making tasks. For example, students might independently identify a specific problem or decision encountered in a work of literature they have studied and develop a presentation or performance that models how they have addressed the identified issue. Students can also enhance their oral, written, and media-based communication skills via experimental-inquiry tasks they design to test a hypothesis they have generated about key issues confronting them, their school, or their community (e.g., ways to improve school spirit, ways to improve cafeteria food selections, strategies for eliminating neighborhood violence).

Social studies is particularly well suited to student-generated investigation tasks. For example, some learners might choose to investigate the historical developments associated with a major event or process they have encountered. Others might want to learn more about an intriguing concept or a big idea such as democracy, the rule of law, individual liberties, or competing concepts of government. Adventurous students can be encouraged to work either independently or collaboratively on projective investigations. In a history class, for example, students can reflect upon such questions as these: *How would our world be different if X had not happened? What might have happened if the British had won the American Revolutionary War? How will current economic trends play out for future generations?*

Students in a wide range of science classes can apply their developing knowledge and expertise to authentic, real-world decision-making and problem-solving activities, especially ones that reflect their personal interests, values, and priorities. In biology, for example, students might generate and test hypotheses about local ecosystems and develop an action plan for evaluating the quality of living systems and resources within that ecosystem.

Students' experiences in world language courses can be enhanced through opportunities for independent investigations into aspects of the culture, history, and current events of the world regions that use the language they are studying. How, for example, do teenagers who speak the language being studied experience adolescence in their particular regions or cultures? What accounts for idiomatic expressions and slang unique to a culture—or universal across cultural and linguistic lines? Students' literary experiences can also be augmented by allowing them to choose independent reading selections, with accompanying research and written analyses of a particular work or genre of literature. Finally, problem-solving and decision-making scenarios can be enriched by allowing students to choose the particular issue they wish to present on or respond to using the foreign language they are studying.

Culminating projects and performance tasks involving technology offer a wonderful context to allow students to formulate and test hypotheses. Such projects and tasks also allow students to use one or more of the complex reasoning tasks (experimental inquiry, problem solving, decision making, investigation) to complete products and performances involving the technology. Potential is also rich for integrated or interdisciplinary projects involving technology applied to a particular content area. Students investigating a historical event, individual, or trend, for example, might use PowerPoint and related presentation technology to present their conclusions. Whole-class projects can also use technology, including the creation of class Web sites showcasing individual contributions by each student in that classroom.

In health and physical education, teachers might encourage students to understand the applications and personal implications of health and physical fitness strategies and concepts via independent projects of their own design. Students might formulate personal hypotheses about how a change in diet or physical activity might affect them or members of their family. In turn, they can design ways to implement the identified changes and share their effects with the rest of the class. A wonderful independent project in this area might involve students' development of a personal fitness plan that can be modified throughout the academic year. As students learn diet, health, and fitness information and skills, they can adjust the plan and collect personal performance and health data to monitor its effect.

Visual and performing arts allow for a wide range of student choice concerning end products and performances. Arts showcases are invaluable settings for students to display and explain individual artistic artifacts or performances that reflect independent choice, vision, and sensibilities. The entire range of visual arts, for example, can become an ideal venue for students to experiment with media and methods for expressing their personal insights and observations. Similarly, student-created individual performances involving knowledge and skills taught in a performing arts class (e.g., a personal musical performance, dance, multimedia or dramatic presentation) always involve elements of decision making and problem solving.

Examples

Elementary Mathematics. At the end of a unit on computing the area of irregular shapes, this elementary mathematics teacher asks students to solve a problem of their own design using the techniques addressed in class, particularly those involving nonstandard units of measure.

Secondary Technology. After addressing advances in personal computers over the last 10 years, this secondary technology teacher invites students to identify and research some aspect of the history of computers (historical investigation), the future use of computers (projective investigation), or the current use of computers (definitional investigation).

Activity Box

Imagine you are a student in your class going through a specific unit you have taught. Describe an authentic task you would design.

Using Cooperative Learning to Enhance Students' Work with Performance Tasks and Projects

Student-designed tasks are ideal for group interactions. Culminating performance tasks and projects—especially those that allow for student choice and expression of personal interests—can use a range of cooperative learning structures and processes. Groups can easily collaborate on gathering issues-related information, organizing that information, taking a shared position regarding its meaning, and finding ways to express conclusions to the entire class.

Culminating performance tasks and projects can involve a combination of independent and cooperative learning activities. Cooperative groups can gather information and organize it for related topics. As a follow-up, however, students can perform all other components of a task (e.g., an investigation, an experiment, a problem-solving scenario, a decision-making process) individually. Given that all tasks related to hypothesis generation and testing involve prediction, each student can generate a personal initial prediction and contrast final conclusions with the initial prediction generated by the group.

As teachers engage students in cooperative tasks, they should keep in mind the following important tenets of cooperative learning:

- The capacity of cooperative learning to promote positive interdependence among learners within a classroom.
- The critical need for any cooperative learning structure or group to be grounded in both individual and group accountability—that is, avoiding the phenomenon of one or two group members doing the bulk of the work.
- The need to review with students and provide ongoing coaching on their use of such interpersonal and group skills as active listening, conflict resolution, restraint of impulsivity, summarizing and paraphrasing, and time management.
- The imperative of ensuring that roles and responsibilities be shared and varied at different times; for example, a group facilitator one day might assume the role of the group recorder the next.
- The need to use a range of cooperative learning structures and practices, including (1) using a variety of criteria for grouping students; (2) establishing base groups as well as informal and formal work groups; and (3) using cooperative learning to complement overall class learning practices (i.e., in combination with whole-group and independent learning processes), not as an exclusive instructional practice.

As the following examples suggest, cooperative structures can be used in a variety of subject areas in the context of student-designed tasks.

In English/language arts, cooperative learning can be easily integrated into a variety of teacher- or student-designed tasks and projects. For example, students might work in jigsaw cooperative learning groups to form expertise on a particular topic or subject area concentration. After teaching the rest of the class what they have learned as a cohort, the groups can then disband and allow for individual investigation. Such investigations might involve discovering the solution to a problem or making a key decision related to a theme or specific work of literature studied. Cooperative learning structures are ideal for allowing students to share information and expertise, particularly what they may have learned about a particular author, literary era, genre, or trend.

In history, students can form pairs, triads, and larger cooperative learning groups to research and report back on key aspects of history that are not presented in detail in the course textbook. Similarly, cooperative learning groups can become experts in a particular body of information needed for a problem-solving or decision-making scenario or case study. A cooperative learning group can also be useful in implementing curriculum tiering and compacting. For example, a group of students might have a shared interest in music. This group might investigate the music of each era studied during a course, reporting to the entire class throughout the year as part of class discussion and study. Similar expert groups might investigate painting, architecture, or practical arts from various eras.

In science, whenever students are working on experimental-inquiry tasks conducted in lab settings, they must be able to work collaboratively to frame hypotheses, make observations, collect and analyze data, and report results. Cooperative learning processes are especially useful tools for enhancing students' engagement in performance tasks and projects involving case studies and authentic, real-world scenarios. In a science WebQuest involving students' exploration of biomes around the world, for example, members of a cooperative learning group can assume various roles (e.g., explorer, scientist, statistician, regional inhabitant), each contributing to the group's observations, data monitoring, and final presentation of conclusions. Science fair projects can also involve cooperative learning processes, including paired or team-based projects that allow students to expand their access to resources, data sources, texts, and technologies.

In foreign language classes, group-oriented cooperative learning projects are ideal settings for students to enhance their communication skills in the language they are studying. Student-designed projects involving cooperative learning cohorts can range from a cohort study of a historical era involving a region or country speaking the studied language to group performances and presentations focusing on a variety of issues, such as the following: a cultural phenomenon, a comparison of lifestyles in two regions or countries, or a dramatization of a visit to a region or country. Ideally, cooperative learning groups can be established at the beginning of an instructional cycle (e.g., at the beginning of a semester), with the same group spiraling their language skills throughout that cycle. Initially, groups can engage in small dialogues and spontaneous scenario reactions using the language. At key juncture points throughout the semester or year, they can design original ways to synthesize key learnings (e.g., group-generated performances, debates, dramatizations, and presentations) and use the language with growing levels of spontaneity and fluency.

Examples

Elementary Composition. This elementary composition teacher organizes students in cooperative groups to write a composition of their own design. Students in each group must be prepared to show how they took on a variety of roles throughout the project (e.g., proofreader, fact checker, information gatherer).

Secondary Health. Students in this middle school health class are formed into cooperative groups to identify and carry out a project that applies key concepts addressed in class to real-life health issues the students face.

Activity Box

Using the task you designed for the previous activity box, describe how cooperative grouping might be used to help you complete the task.

Encouraging Metacognition and Self-Regulation

Student-designed tasks present ideal venues for students to improve their use of such life-long metaskills as self-regulation, time management, and goal setting. The following are specific techniques teachers can use to enhance students' self-regulation, self-monitoring, and self-evaluation. Although these strategies can be used for a variety of tasks, they are particularly useful in culminating performance tasks and projects, especially when students have a role in their design and development.

Use of Scoring Scales (Rubrics)

As suggested in Modules 2 and 3, students benefit from using scoring scales. For long-term performance tasks and projects, each evaluation criterion should be assigned a scale as described in those modules. Ideally, students should work with the scales throughout the time they are completing a performance task, monitoring how they are progressing from Basic to Proficient to Advanced levels on the scales.

Academic Notebooks for Data Collection and Analysis

Throughout an academic year, students can collect and analyze data reflecting their levels of proficiency and competency in relationship to key evaluation criteria. An entire section of their class notebook can be devoted to charts, graphs, or other visual representations of their progress toward learning goals that have been addressed in different units (see Module 4). When students are completing independent performance tasks and projects—especially those they have helped to design—teachers need to coach and to support their ability to self-monitor relative to the learning goals associated with the task. This process can help students see how successful they have been in moving from initial acquisition of knowledge and skills toward growing levels of independent use and understanding.

Journals and Think Logs

These metacognitive tools can greatly assist students in reflecting on what they are learning, why they are learning it, and barriers or problems that may be impeding their progress. Journal activities, for example, can be effective for lesson closure. Generally, these activities are open-ended written reflections, usually taking no more than three to five minutes at the end of a lesson segment or class. These activities provide students with opportunities to comment and reflect on lessons and their reactions to them. The teacher may choose to pose specific questions for particular journal items: *What was the purpose of today's lesson? To what extent did it enhance your achievement of our unit's learning goals? What questions did it raise? What problems, if any, did you encounter?*

A variation of the reflective journal is the think log. This approach requires a more focused response from students, asking them to assess and evaluate their use of specific thinking skills, processes, and habits of mind during a particular lesson, using questions such as these: *How effectively did you use the skill of classification in today's lesson? To what extent did you incorporate the elements of the decision-making matrix in your work today? How well did you apply one or more of the following habits of mind during this lesson: self-regulation, critical thinking, creativity?*

Interviews with Students

Students can benefit from periodically engaging in formal and informal interviews conducted by their teacher. As they work on culminating performance tasks and projects, for example, the teacher can take one or two students aside and ask them how they are progressing toward achieving their long-range goals. Such informal interview strategies are especially useful during visits to the media center or when students are using technology independently (e.g., online searches, WebQuests). At key juncture points throughout the time students are working on independent projects, however, a more formal interview process might prove useful. Such interviews should be preceded and accompanied by a checklist or other scoring tool. Students should be clear about the kinds of interview questions the teacher may pose and how they relate to the purpose and goals of the project. It is also useful to incorporate the project's scale (rubric) as part of the discussion.

Peer-Response Groups

Peer coaching is always a useful process to enhance student learning, especially during the development of independent performance tasks and projects. Formal peer-response groups can be conducted periodically to allow students to share drafts of their work in progress, eliciting peer feedback and coaching advice on maintaining strengths and eliminating possible weaknesses. The Bay Area Writing Project's "P-Q-P" protocol is a useful tool for students' work with peer-response groups. Students should receive modeling and shaping opportunities to (1) present *praise*, followed by (2) *questions* they would like answered about the work in progress and (3) *polish* suggestions—recommendations for possible modifications of the work in progress before it is submitted in final form. This approach can also enhance students' overall ability to provide objective, formal feedback. It also creates a sense of safety and community within the peer-response group, ensuring that students receive praise first and objectively framed questions second, with any critique or suggestions for modification as a final part of the process.

Formal Self-Evaluations

After students complete significant projects or performance tasks, it is useful to give them the opportunity to complete a more formal self-evaluation. Ideally, this self-assessment will be tied to the evaluation criteria articulated in the scale used throughout the project. Students should also be encouraged to use data from their academic notebooks to justify their self-evaluations and suggested grades (if appropriate). The more opportunities students have to become self-evaluative, the greater their understanding of the learning goals and related evaluation criteria for which they are accountable.

Examples

Elementary Language Arts. While students are working on their projects during class, this language arts teacher periodically calls each student up to her desk. She asks the students to evaluate their level of effort and progress on their projects. The teacher records students' responses and then uses these responses as the basis for subsequent conversations with them.

Secondary Science. Periodically, this science teacher collects students' academic notebooks and makes comments about each student's progress. She conferences with each student by going over her comments and eliciting student input regarding the accuracy of those comments.

Activity Box

Which of the suggestions in this section most closely resembles what you have done in your class to enhance students' metacognitive skills? Describe how it is similar to the activities you have used.

Checking for Understanding

Use the following rating scale to assess your current level of understanding of key strategies and processes presented in this module:

4 = I understand and already fully implement this strategy in my classroom.

3 = I understand this strategy, but I need to practice using it in my classroom.

2 = I can explain this strategy, but I am not fully confident that I can use it.

1 = I do not understand this strategy, and I do not currently use it in my classroom.

___ 1.   Engaging students in task design
Based on my rating, I may need to revisit the following:

___ 2.   Using cooperative learning to enhance students' work with performance tasks and projects
Based on my rating, I may need to revisit the following:

___ 3.   Encouraging metacognition and self-regulation
Based on my rating, I may need to revisit the following:

Design Question 5

What Will I Do to Engage Students?

Module 13

Using Games and Inconsequential Competition to Promote Student Engagement

Module 14

Rules of Engagement: Questioning, Physical Movement, and Pacing

Module 15

Additional Cognitive, Affective, and Social Interaction Strategies for Promoting Student Engagement

Module 13

Using Games and Inconsequential Competition to Promote Student Engagement

A key component in promoting high levels of student achievement is ensuring that all students are intellectually, emotionally, and socially engaged with the content they are learning and the tasks they are assigned. *The Art and Science of Teaching* identifies five general factors related to student engagement:

• *High Energy*—Teachers can use physical activity, appropriate pacing, and communication of enthusiasm and intensity in working with students to promote engagement and motivation.

• *Missing Information*—Teachers can capitalize on the innate human need for closure by asking students to discover and supply missing information.

• *The Self-System*—Effective engagement of students also involves incorporating topics, ideas, and processes that students find inherently interesting and valuable to them.

• *Mild Pressure*—When students experience mild pressure while engaging in such activities as questioning, games, and competitions, they tend to focus their attention on key elements of the learning process.

• *Mild Controversy and Competition*—Teachers can structure and manage nonthreatening forms of controversy and competition through such processes as debates, tournaments, and related forms of team-based activities.

This module (Module 13) and the next two (Modules 14 and 15) present strategies based on these five factors that teachers can use to engage students. This module focuses on the use of games and other forms of nonthreatening competition as catalysts for promoting student engagement.

Reflecting on Your Current Beliefs and Practices

Before examining the strategies in this module, take some time to examine your current beliefs and practices by answering the following questions:

1. To what extent does your unit and lesson planning incorporate strategies designed to promote and enhance student engagement?

_____

_____

_____

_____

2. How do you use games to reinforce student retention of key information and skills?

_____

_____

_____

_____

3. How do you use various types of inconsequential competition to help students extend and refine their learning?

_____

_____

_____

_____

4. How do you try to engage in "flow" activities—challenging activities that are compelling but not threatening to learners?

_____

_____

_____

_____

Recommendations for Classroom Practice

This module addresses the following strategies for Design Question 5:

- Using games that focus on academic content
- Using inconsequential competition

Using Games That Focus on Academic Content

At first glance, some educators may view games as interesting but superficial additions to curriculum practice. However, the research associated with student engagement suggests that game-based learning tasks and activities can help students deepen their understanding of core curriculum content. Additionally, they can expand students' motivation and energy levels.

We believe games can stimulate students' attention because they require students to access and supply missing information, one of the key building blocks of engagement. We recommend that classroom games focus on key academic content, such as important concepts and vocabulary terms. The following examples represent four game structures that can easily be used to engage students in a brief review of academic content.

What Is the Question?

This game is modeled on the television game show *Jeopardy!* As depicted in Figure 13.1, the teacher creates a matrix with relevant categories (e.g., Science, Math, Language Arts) and point categories (generally 100, 200, 300, 400, and 500). The matrix can be constructed using PowerPoint, an overhead transparency, or a bulletin board display. Clues in the form of words, pictures, or a combination of the two are included in each of the matrix cells. For example, assume that the answer that was being sought was "plate tectonics." The clue might be "The study of the large plates that form the surface of the earth." Likewise, the clue might be a picture or diagram that depicts the movement of these plates. As the teacher reveals the clues, students signal their understanding by stating a question for which that concept would be the answer. In this case, the "answer" would be "What is plate tectonics?" The teacher decides if a student's question represents an adequate understanding of the term. If a student or team of students correctly answer an item, the respondent can call for an item in any category at any level. For example, if members of a team correctly answer "Math for 100 points," they can request Language Arts for 400 points. Team members keep answering until they miss an item.

FIGURE 13.1

Matrix for "What Is the Question?"

	Science	Math	Language Arts	Sports/Arts	General
100					
200					
300					
400					
500					

Name That Category

In this game, modeled on the television game show *The $100,000 Pyramid*, students try to determine what the terms in a list have in common. Students are organized in teams composed of one "clue giver" and one or more "guessers." A game board like that depicted in Figure 13.2 shows names of various categories. The object of the game is for the clue giver to list words that fit the category until teammates correctly identify the category name. At the beginning of each round, the teacher hides the category names. Only the clue giver on each team is able to see the game board. As the teacher reveals the first category, clue givers begin to list terms that pertain to that category. For example, clues for the first category in Figure 13.2 might be "water, orange juice, tea," and so on. The teacher reveals the next category as soon as she sees that a team has correctly identified the first category and is ready to move on to the next.

FIGURE 13.2
Game Board for "Name That Category"

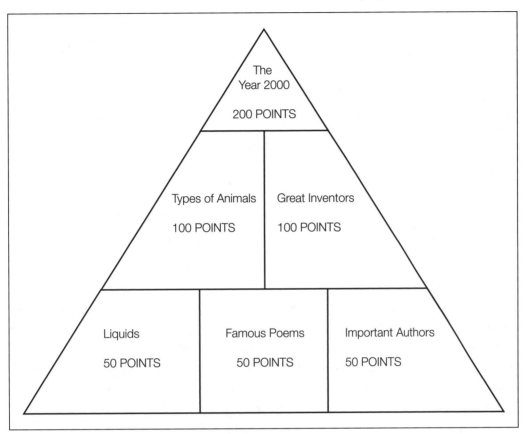

Talk a Mile a Minute

In this game, students are given a list of seven related terms such as *square, circle, rectangle, triangle, right triangle, oval,* and *diamond*. These terms are related because they are all shapes. To play each round, each team designates someone as the talker. The talker tries to get the team to say each of the words by quickly describing them. The talker is allowed to say anything about the terms while "talking a mile a minute" but may not use any words in the category title or any rhyming words. For example, the talker could not say "these are all shapes," nor could she say "this word rhymes with bare." The talker keeps talking until the team members identify all terms in the category. If members of the team are having difficulty with a particular term, the talker skips it and comes back to it later. The first few teams to identify all the terms receive points. Figure 13.3 shows a list that might be used in an English/language arts class.

FIGURE 13.3

List for "Talk a Mile a Minute"

Types of Literature

Fiction

Nonfiction

Mystery

Romance

Biography

Autobiography

Science Fiction

Fantasy

Classroom Feud

This game is modeled after the television quiz show *Family Feud*. To prepare for the game, the teacher constructs at least one question for every student in the class. Questions can be multiple choice, fill in the blank, and short answer. One student from each team serves as the responder for the group. Students on each team take turns being responders via some systematic process. The teacher presents a question to the responder for a team, who turns to her team members and shares with them the answer she thinks is correct— or tells her team that she does not know the answer. Team members either agree with the responder or offer suggestions regarding the correct answer. The responder has 15 seconds to decide which answer to offer as the correct one. When the answer is offered, the teacher determines if it is correct or acceptable. Correct answers receive a point. Incorrect answers result in the opposing team having the opportunity to answer. The most recent responder for that team again acts as responder for the group. He or she has 15 seconds to come up with an alternative response, again taking suggestions from the team. If the answer is incorrect, the other team gets the point and is asked the next question. If a correct answer is not offered by the challenging team, no point is awarded. When every student on both teams has functioned as the responder, the team with the most points wins.

Examples

Elementary Language Arts. This elementary language arts teacher uses games as a way to briefly review content. Once or twice a week she engages students in games that include the critical concepts that have been addressed during the unit. She extends the game by asking students which concepts were the hardest to guess or to provide clues for. As students discuss these difficult concepts, they review the concepts' defining characteristics.

Secondary Civics. Once or twice a week this teacher organizes students into impromptu groups and has them play games that use key civics concepts. Those examples that were most difficult for students are discussed and reviewed after the game. Additionally, after each game the teacher gives students time to make additions to their academic notebooks based on new insights they gained as a result of the game and the subsequent discussion.

Activity Box

Describe how you have used or could use games using academic content you teach.

Using Inconsequential Competition

When students compete in the spirit of fun, their engagement increases in response to a combination of mild pressure, high energy, and activation of the self-system. Since competitive games inevitably involve placement of students into small groups, well-designed tasks involving inconsequential competition also require teachers to be sensitive to key elements of cooperative learning: mutual interdependence, clear role delineation, and modification of groups and responsibilities during different assignments. For example, group membership can be systematically changed so that students who exhibit a high degree of content mastery are paired with those who do not. As games are played, the top team or teams can be assigned team points. At the end of a unit, team points are totaled, with two or more teams with the highest number of points singled out for some form of tangible reward. Games apply nicely to a variety of subject areas.

In English/language arts classes, students can benefit from inconsequential-competition tasks focusing on their review of such areas as vocabulary, spelling, and literary terms and elements. Teachers can use the range of games described earlier to create various types of inconsequential competitions that help students remember vocabulary, spelling, and literary terms due to the heightened emotions generated during competition. In social studies, in addition to using various games and tournaments designed to help students review key content, teachers can use competition to help students investigate and debate competing perspectives and points of view regarding important content. Informal competitions integrated into review activities greatly enhance students' understanding of what information is worth retaining, and what information may be secondary in its importance.

In addition to using small-group tasks that promote inconsequential competition to help students retain key unit terms, science teachers might also use informal competition as a catalyst for students to explore competing theories and hypotheses. When answers to some questions are equivocal, students can debate the relative merits of potential answers.

The benefits of inconsequential competition described previously apply equally well to all mathematics content areas and grade levels. Additionally, mathematics teachers can enhance learning by using small-group competition to encourage student insights into alternative approaches to solving specific types of problems. Which team, for example, can solve a specific mathematical problem in the most efficient yet elegant manner? Which team can propose the greatest number of accurate and appropriate ways to solve a word problem?

Examples

Elementary Physical Education. This physical education teacher organizes students into new groups of three or four in each unit. Points are assigned to each team for each game. At the end of the unit, the three teams with the highest number of points receive some inconsequential reward such as coupons to buy juice in the cafeteria.

Secondary Mathematics. This mathematics teacher uses games to review content. Completion is always an aspect of the games. However, because the teacher reorganizes the groups in each unit, every student gets a chance to be on winning teams throughout the year.

Activity Box

Describe one possible positive consequence of inconsequential competition in your classroom.

Checking for Understanding

Use the following rating scale to assess your current understanding and comfort level regarding key strategies and processes presented in this module:

4 = I understand and already fully implement this strategy in my classroom.

3 = I understand this strategy, but I need to practice using it in my classroom.

2 = I can explain this strategy, but I am not fully confident that I can use it.

1 = I do not understand this strategy, and I do not currently use it in my classroom.

___ 1. Using games that focus on academic content
Based on my rating, I may need to revisit the following:

___ 2. Using inconsequential competition
Based on my rating, I may need to revisit the following:

Module 14

Rules of Engagement: Questioning, Physical Movement, and Pacing

How can teachers ensure that all students are engaged and motivated? Rather than being single faceted, engagement displays itself in a variety of ways. For example, students can demonstrate that they are engaged in the learning process through on-task behavior. They can also show that they are engaged through their emotional reactions, expressing positive emotions and feelings that reflect their sense of authenticity and purpose during the learning process. Finally, engagement can manifest cognitively when students appear genuinely invested in understanding and retaining what they are being asked to learn and willing to persevere in overcoming obstacles and misconceptions.

This module continues our exploration of strategies for engaging students, with special emphasis on response rates, providing opportunities for physical movement, and appropriately pacing lessons and units. Each of these three strategies uses the five factors associated with high levels of student engagement:

- High energy
- Missing information
- The self-system
- Mild pressure
- Mild controversy and competition

Reflecting on Your Current Beliefs and Practices

Before examining the strategies in this module, take some time to examine your current beliefs and practices by answering the following questions:

1. How does your approach to questioning students and engaging in follow-up probes influence your students' achievement? To what extent do you help students respond to various types of questions with appropriate evidence and supporting details?

_____

_____

_____

_____

2. How do you make certain that all your students are participating and engaged when responding to higher-order questions?

_____

_____

_____

_____

3. To what extent do you incorporate opportunities for physical movement into your lessons? How does this physical movement and activity enhance student learning, motivation, and engagement?

_____

_____

_____

_____

4. How do you pace lessons and units? To what extent does your pacing support—or work against—student learning?

_____

_____

_____

_____

Recommendations for Classroom Practice

This module addresses the following strategies for Design Question 5:

- Using a variety of question structures
- Using wait-time strategies

- Using follow-up questioning and response strategies
- Using physical movement
- Promoting engagement through pacing

Using a Variety of Question Structures

Questions can activate student engagement through two pathways: (1) encouraging the learner to investigate missing information and (2) providing mild pressure for the learner. Effective questioning ensures that the students understand what they are being asked and why. Question structures teachers can use include the following:

- *Retrieval*—Requiring students to recognize, recall, and execute knowledge as it was explicitly taught
- *Analytical*—Requiring students to take apart information and determine how parts relate to the whole
- *Predictive*—Asking students to form conjectures and hypotheses about what will happen next in a narrative or a sequence of information or actions
- *Interpretive*—Requiring students to make and defend inferences about the intentions of an author
- *Evaluative*—Engaging students in using identified criteria to make judgments and assessments of something

Recall that in Module 6 we discussed two types of inferential questions: general inferential questions and elaborative interrogations. Whereas retrieval questions are typically not inferential in nature, analytical, predictive, interpretive, and evaluative questions are almost always inferential. Thus, except for retrieval, the question types discussed here can be thought of as expansions of our discussion in Module 6 on general inferential questions and elaborative interrogations.

Retrieval Questions

Retrieval questions ask students to recognize, recall, and execute knowledge that was directly taught. Although some educators may consider such questions to be "lower order," they have an important place in the teaching-learning process. Specifically, they help students acquire and integrate new declarative knowledge (i.e., information such as vocabulary terms, facts, generalizations, and principles) or new procedural knowledge (i.e., skills, strategies, and processes). Retrieval questions can help students (1) construct meaning about new knowledge, (2) revisit and store that knowledge, and (3) discover connections and patterns relating that new knowledge to previously learned content. Here are examples from language arts and social studies, respectively:

We've been studying compound sentences and how you can use them in your compositions. What are the key elements of a compound sentence? Can you give examples of compound sentences that use those elements?

As we finish this first section of our unit on the American Civil War, how would you summarize the major economic, political, and social conflicts that gave rise to it?

Analytical Questions

Analytical questions require students to take apart information and determine how parts relate to the whole. They are most effective when students are asked about complex content they have just read, heard, observed through demonstration, or experienced in some other way. Here are examples from social studies and science, respectively:

How did the social and cultural conflicts we have been studying give rise to imbalance and unrest within the region?

How does the symbiotic relationship between these organisms aid in the survival of this ecosystem?

Predictive Questions

Predictive questions ask students to form conjectures and hypotheses about what will happen next in a narrative or a sequence of information or actions. Such questions are most effective when students are required to explain and defend their predictions. Here are examples from geography and literature, respectively:

Based on the history of this region over the last 20 years, what do you predict will happen next to its economy? Explain what you are basing your prediction(s) on.

How do you predict the story will end? Why do you think this will happen? Use statements right from the story to explain how you came up with your prediction(s).

Interpretive Questions

Interpretive questions require students to make and defend inferences about the intentions of an author. They can often elicit a range of viable responses. Therefore, as students respond to them, they need to present textual support and related evidence to confirm their conclusions. Here are examples from literature and statistics, respectively:

What do you think the speaker in the poem means when he says, "I have miles to go before I sleep"? Use information from the poem to back up your answer.

Why do you think the author of our mathematics textbook decided to provide two different types of graphs to demonstrate the concept of the mean?

Evaluative Questions

Evaluative questions ask students to use identified criteria to make judgments and assessments of something. Effective responses to evaluative questions require students to provide evidence to justify their conclusions based upon clearly articulated evaluation standards. Here are examples from mathematics and science, respectively:

In your opinion, which of the solutions we have generated as a class are the most elegant and appropriate solutions to this problem? Why? What are the characteristics of an elegant and appropriate solution?

In your opinion, how effective was the argument that was presented in this article about global warming? Explain the criteria you are using as the basis for your evaluation.

Activity Box

Which of the types of questions described in this section do you use or might you use? What are some specific examples?

Using Wait-Time Strategies

The power of wait-time strategies as a catalyst for student engagement has been recognized for a number of years. By allowing at least three seconds for students to respond to a question, for example, teachers greatly expand the number of students who both hear the question and cognitively process it.

Similarly, giving students time to pause and reflect on what they have said in response to a question—as well as what another student may have said—encourages learners to process ideas and formulate follow-up questions. Teachers can also take advantage of "pause time" when presenting new information and skills, allowing students to formulate thoughts and questions and creating a sense of anticipation as to what may occur next in the teaching-learning sequence. In the following sections we consider five types of wait-time strategies.

Post-Teacher-Question Wait Time

When posing a question, teachers should allow at least three seconds for students to respond. Here are some examples.

Art. An art teacher asks the following question: "What are some of the critical things to remember when applying oil-based paints?" The teacher pauses for a few seconds before calling on students to answer. As she does so, she scans the classroom, trying to make eye contact with as many students as possible.

Physical Education. After demonstrating proper versus improper form for shooting a free throw, a physical education teacher asks the following question: "What were the major errors I made when I showed you an incorrect way to shoot a free throw?" Even though some students immediately raise their hands, the teacher waits for a while before calling for an answer.

Within-Student Pause Time

The teacher should allow time for students to think during pauses while they are answering or asking a question. Once again, three seconds is ideal. This strategy also gives students processing time to formulate or reformulate self-initiated questions. Here are some examples.

World History. This instructor is committed to helping students see connections and patterns involving earlier eras in world history and the world of the 21st century. After observing that her students have a particularly difficult time seeing connections between ancient civilizations and the modern era, she formulates questions that might help them "uncover" and reveal possible relationships between early world civilizations (e.g., Meso-potamia, the Indus River Valley, Egypt) and our world today (e.g., "What is the enduring legacy of this civilization?" "Why do we still study this particular civilization?" "What connections and patterns can you observe between this ancient civilization and issues we confront today?"). As students respond, the teacher takes advantage of pauses in their responses. She emphasizes that everyone in the class should respect the need for "pause time" while students are responding. She finds that this encourages students to think more deeply about their answers.

Geometry. Students in this geometry class seem to be struggling with the application of the Pythagorean theorem. The teacher proposes that they "start from the very beginning." She poses questions that were supposedly addressed at the very beginning of the unit. She warns students not to answer too quickly but to think over their responses. While students are addressing her questions, she sometimes asks them to pause and think more deeply before responding further.

Post-Student-Response Wait Time

It is advisable to pause a few seconds between the time a student has completed a response and other students are allowed to respond. This process helps to focus student attention and sharpen students' thinking processes. Here are some examples.

Art History. Students in a high school art class are asked to respond to classic works of art reflective of the genre or medium in which they are currently working. In many cases, students have never seen the specific paintings, sculptures, or other genres to which they are responding. "What do you observe?" the teacher asks. "How does the artist use the medium to present the subject of the work or communicate the theme?" As students respond to these questions and to the works of art themselves, the teacher consistently pauses after each answer, allowing the student and the other members of the class to reflect upon what has been said. The teacher is pleased to observe that as students become more comfortable with the process of post-student-response wait time, they appear more engaged in the questioning process. They also seem more eager to comment on and share their reactions to both the works of art they are studying and their peers' reactions to these works.

Economics. A high school economics teacher decides that she has been spending too much time lecturing on economic theory and too little time focusing students' investigation of the connections between economics and their own lives and experiences. In presenting her latest unit on "Economic Ideologies," she encourages her students to pose their own questions about the theories and theorists they are studying. "What does each economist appear to be telling us about the role of money within an economy?" she asks. As students respond to her questions and pose questions of their own, the teacher consciously imposes a three-second moratorium on immediate responses to questions. "We need to spend a few seconds reflecting on what we are all saying before we react," she says. Her use of post-student-response wait time encourages her students to become more reflective and sensitive to the nuances of what they are studying and learning.

Teacher Pause Time

While presenting content, teachers should pause to allow students time to process and formulate thoughts and questions regarding new information. This strategy is especially useful when students are studying difficult or complex information for the first time. Here are some examples.

Measurement. Students in an elementary mathematics classroom are encountering the metric system for the first time. Their teacher knows that every time she teaches this system of measurement, students experience retroactive inhibition as they attempt to internalize an entirely new system for measuring solids and liquids. As they begin their study, she reinforces the importance of learning the new system—especially in light of its almost universal use in many world regions and economies—and why she will be using pause time as students ask questions and share their reactions. Throughout this unit, she makes a concerted effort to slow down and allow students time to process and formulate their thoughts and questions. Often she simply pauses briefly while presenting information. Students grow to respect the value of this pause time.

Biology. Students are investigating interdependency within ecosystems. Their teacher is especially interested in encouraging them to understand the complexity and fragility of such systems. Throughout this unit, therefore, students are asked to formulate their thoughts and questions about each system, writing their responses in their academic notebooks. At key juncture points throughout the unit, the teacher asks students to share their written reflections in paired, small-group, and whole-group discussion sessions. As students present their thoughts, the teacher pauses two to three seconds, allowing everyone in the class to reflect on what has been said. As students learn to model and apply this pause time, they appear to be more interested in learning new information about each of the ecosystems being investigated.

Impact Pause Time

Uninterrupted silence creates a sense of anticipation about what will occur next. This anticipation contributes to students' interest in the material studied and augments their engagement in the learning process. Here are some examples.

American Literature. An English teacher has discovered that her students seem particularly engaged and interested in works of literature involving mystery and the supernatural. She takes advantage of this interest by actively encouraging them to anticipate what will happen next in narratives they are discussing: "What do you predict will happen to the protagonist? Do you think he'll make it out of this situation—or will something awful happen to him? Let's find out." These are questions for which the teacher does not want an oral answer. She is simply pausing to provide a dramatic punch to the content. This strategy enhances students' anticipation about discovering how the plot unfolds as well as the accuracy of their predictions.

Chemistry. Students in this chemistry class are always entertained when their teacher demonstrates "mystery chemical reactions." After asking students to brainstorm everything they know about specific chemicals and their composition, the teacher encourages them to predict what may happen when two or more chemicals are combined. He says, "Get a picture in your mind about what will happen." After a brief pause, he says, "Let's see if you're right." His continuing use of impact pause time helps students experience chemistry as engaging and involving, not as something abstract or theoretical.

Activity Box

Which of the wait-time strategies described in this section has the greatest potential to enhance student engagement in your classroom? Explain why.

Using Follow-Up Questioning and Response Strategies

In addition to wait-time techniques, teachers can enhance student engagement by using a variety of follow-up questioning and student-response strategies. Follow-up probes require students to justify or defend their responses to questions with evidence from text or personal knowledge. As students construct support for their responses and points of view, at least four factors involved in engagement are activated: high energy, the self-system, mild pressure, and the potential for mild controversy and competition (as students debate contrasting ideas and perspectives). Additional question-based response strategies that promote engagement include response cards, choral responses, response chaining, and hand signals.

Response Cards

Response cards require some type of reusable material, such as a 12-by-12-inch whiteboard. When a question is asked, students record their answers on individual response cards. Forced-choice items like true-false or multiple-choice questions work nicely with response cards. The teacher asks the true-false question. Each student then writes "true" or "false" on the response card. Questions requiring one-word answers, phrases, and even short sentences can also be used. When the teacher gives a signal, the students hold up their response cards so the teacher can see. The teacher uses this feedback to guide subsequent interactions with students. Here are some examples.

Arithmetic. As students review their knowledge of multiplication facts, their teacher asks them to record their answers to various problems and exercises on their whiteboards. As students hold up their answers to each multiplication problem, the teacher begins to discern patterns among students, including which multiplication facts are clear to everyone and which ones appear to be presenting difficulties to some or all.

History. This teacher uses response cards to help students review for an important test on the origins of World War II. In reviewing key historical figures associated with the war, the teacher holds up a set of photographs. Students are challenged to write down on their whiteboards the correct name and correct spelling for each figure.

Choral Responses

Choral responses can be used to engage students in reviewing and repeating key information, especially content that students are finding difficult. When it becomes clear that students are having trouble with specific information, the teacher provides them with the target information and asks students to repeat the information as a group. The intent with choral response is not that all students are to learn content in a verbatim fashion; rather, the intent is to provide an "imprint" of important information that all students are finding difficult. Here are some examples.

Elementary Geography. While discussing an important geography generalization, the teacher realizes that students simply are not making the connection between the development of a specific region they have studied and the generalization that the geography of a region can have an effect on its development and its future. She stops the discussion and says, "Let's go back to how this unit started. We talked about the fact that the geography of a region can have an effect on its development and its future. Since then we have seen example after example of this generalization in the region where we live. But I think we've forgotten where we started. So I want everyone to say the following along with me: *The geography of a region can have an effect on its development and its future.* OK. Let's all say that. Again. Again. One more time. Now let's go back and review some of the examples we've seen."

High School Literature. Students appear to be having a great deal of difficulty distinguishing among various types of figurative language used in poetry. Observing their confusion, the teacher decides to stop the lesson and engage students in a choral-response review session. She begins: "Let's stop for a second here. It seems as if we're having troubling keeping straight the differences between various types of figurative devices used by the poets we're studying. Why don't we start with a definition? *Figurative language involves symbolic language in which words and phrases represent something abstract and implied rather than literal and directly stated.* Now, everyone, let's repeat that definition together . . . ." The instructor reviews key figurative terms (e.g., metaphor, simile, synecdoche) and their definitions, encouraging students to repeat them using this choral-response technique. At the conclusion of this brief review, students seem more engaged and comfortable with finding examples in the poems they are reading.

Response Chaining

Response chaining involves linking or chaining students' responses, beginning with asking a question to which a specific student responds, with the class then voting on the accuracy of that response, using three options: the answer was correct, partially correct, or incorrect. Follow-up responses and discussion are aligned with the option chosen. When a student contends that a previous student's response was correct, the teacher asks the student to explain why it was correct or to add to the previous student's answer. When a student contends that a previous student's response was partially correct, the teacher asks the student to explain which part of the response was correct and which part was incorrect. When a student contends that a previous student's response was incorrect, the teacher asks the student to explain what was wrong and to provide the correct response. Here are some examples.

Mathematics. Maria has worked a problem on the whiteboard involving the calculation of the mean, the median, and the mode. The teacher calls on Debra and asks her if she agrees with the answers. Debra says the answers provided by Maria were partially correct. The teacher asks Debra to explain which part of the answer was correct and which was incorrect. Debra notes that the mean and mode were correctly computed, but the median is off. The teacher then calls on Jose and asks him to agree or disagree with Debra's analysis. After Jose's response, the teacher reviews the various opinions offered by Maria, Debra, and Jose and points out which responses are the most accurate.

Civics. Joe has responded to the following question: "What are the major steps involved in a bill becoming a law in our state legislature?" The teacher calls on Sally and asks her if she agrees with Joe's response. Sally says that she agrees with Joe's general response, but that he left out one important step. The teacher asks Sally to explain which part of the answer was correct and which step needs to be added to ensure that the description of the process is complete. Sally notes that a bill needs to be reviewed by the appropriate legislative subcommittees before it can be submitted for a vote. The teacher then calls on Joe and asks him to agree or disagree with Sally's analysis. After this interaction, the teacher comments on both students' responses, clarifying any incomplete answers and misunderstandings.

Hand Signals

Hand signals can be used to indicate how well students understand key content. A common set of hand signals is thumbs-up, palm flat, thumbs-down. Thumbs-up indicates that a student understands the content addressed in a lesson; thumbs-down indicates that a student does not understand the content; and palm flat indicates that a student understands some of the content but is also confused about some of the content. Here are some examples.

Chemistry. Throughout the academic year, this instructor revisits key terminology and concepts significant to the core curriculum of chemistry. As an informal check for understanding, the teacher says, "Give me feedback on how clear you are about each of the following terms. Give me a thumbs-up if you clearly understand it and can explain it to someone else. Give me a flat palm if you have a basic knowledge of the term's definition, but you have trouble using or applying that term. Give me a thumbs-down if you do not understand the term at all and need to revisit it." The teacher then poses a series of significant concepts and critical terminology (e.g., the Law of Conservation of Matter, chemical composition, compounds, chemical reactions) and uses students' application of these hand signals to determine which terms need further instruction and student coaching.

English/Language Arts. Students are preparing to write their junior-year research paper during their high school English class. As the teacher presents the project to students, she is interested in seeing how familiar students are with conventions for documenting sources identified in various style manuals. Students are asked to use the "thumbs-up, palm flat, thumbs-down" feedback process to indicate to the teacher their level of understanding and experience with various manuals. The teacher says, "Use our hand-gesture process to describe your comfort level with and understanding of each of the following: *The Modern Language Association Handbook*; *The Chicago Manual of Style*; Turabian; the *Publication Manual of the American Psychological Association*."

Activity Box

Describe a specific situation for which you could use one of the strategies described in this section.

Using Physical Movement

Research on brain-based teaching and learning reinforces the importance of incorporating physical activity and movement in the classroom. Physical movement is especially important because it increases students' energy and ability to concentrate, two key factors in active engagement in learning. As the following suggestions illustrate, productive physical movement in the classroom can take a variety of forms.

Stand Up and Stretch

Periodically students can be asked to stand up and stretch, especially when there appears to be a need to change focus, concentration, or engagement. Here are some examples.

Fourth Grade Science. The teacher notices that when she presents complex or challenging science content immediately after lunch, students seem less engaged or interested. They also seem to struggle more in acquiring and retaining key concepts. To address this issue, she has students stand up and stretch as a change of pace every time she shifts her content focus or begins to introduce a challenging new term or idea. Whenever possible, she encourages the students to stand by their desks and reflect on what they have just learned and assess how comfortable they are with that content.

High School Algebra. Students in this class appear to lack energy and interest in this instructor's algebra classroom as they struggle to understand how to solve quadratic equations. As a change of pace, the teacher revisits with them the concept of the mind-body connection, including the value of physical exercise and movement to keep the mind alert and focused. The class and the teacher agree to stand and stretch every 15 minutes or so, producing more active student engagement, concentration, and anticipation.

Body Representations

To enhance engagement and increase the energy level of students, teachers can have students create body representations in which they act out important content (e.g., forming cause-effect chains; physically acting out key sequence elements). Here are some examples.

Elementary Mathematics. Right before lunch, this 5th grade mathematics teacher notices that students are a little lethargic. She asks her students to stand and practice some "body math." She begins by asking all students to demonstrate *radius*. Many of the students raise one hand and move it around the perimeter of an imaginary circle. The teacher then asks students to demonstrate *diameter*. Many students position both hands to form a straight line. The teacher uses body math periodically throughout the unit to get students up and moving around for a few moments. It also serves as a brief review of important content.

Secondary Life Science. Students are being asked to investigate the diversity of living organisms and how they can be compared scientifically. As they explore the scientific system for classifying organisms using the six-kingdom system (archaebacteria, eubacteria, protists, fungi, plants, and animals), students are asked to break into teams. Each team is responsible for presenting to the rest of the class a body representation for each of the six kingdoms. At the conclusion of their presentations, the teacher asks the students to identify from the entire set presented what they consider the most effective body representation for each kingdom. At key points in the unit, the teacher reviews the six-kingdom system, with students using the body representations they selected.

Give One, Get One

Give One, Get One is a process in which pairs of students stand together (or sit together) and use their academic notebooks to compare notes with a partner, identifying shared information and information that they don't have in common. Each student compares his notes with those of his partner. Each student tries to get new information from his partner and give information to his partner. Pairs can also identify questions they have as a team. As a whole-class activity, the teacher then responds to questions posed by student pairs. Here are some examples.

Secondary Comparative Government. Students are asked to pair up and review the entries in their academic notebooks, helping their partners reexamine information from class lectures and media presentations on governmental structures throughout the world. The teacher emphasizes: "Use these opportunities to get new information from your partner as well as to give information to your partner that he or she may not have recorded or considered important." At the conclusion of each Give One, Get One session, the whole class discusses the terms, concepts, and generalizations they would like to revisit in order to develop a deeper understanding of the content.

Elementary Reading. In an elementary unit on folk literature, students are asked to keep a running summary of the key features and characteristics associated with each genre they study (e.g., fable, folk tale, legend, myth, fairy tale, tall tale). As students complete their reading and discussion of each genre, they are asked to pair up with a new partner. Each team revisits the summaries in their academic notebooks, sharing information to ensure that each partner has a complete description of the genre's major characteristics and recurrent features.

Vote with Your Feet

Voting with your feet involves students moving to corners with signs identifying answers to a question (true-false, multiple choice) or reactions to answers to a question (incorrect, partially correct, totally correct). Here are some examples.

Elementary Weather Unit. Students appear highly engaged in this unit on "Clouds and the Weather," but the teacher notices that many of them have difficulty when asked to distinguish among various types of cloud formations. To address this issue, the teacher has students "vote with their feet." She posts the names of important cloud formations on signs throughout the room. As she holds up a photograph of a particular formation, students move to the sign they think identifies the correct name of the formation. When large numbers of students choose an incorrect sign, the instructor uses this as an opportunity to review with the whole class the specific characteristics of that formation. She also asks, "For those of you who identified this formation correctly, what clues did you see in the photograph that helped you?"

High School Computer Applications. During their initial investigation of each computer application, students get to see how much of the content they have retained and understood by "voting with their feet." In reviewing a word processing application, for example, the teacher has posted signs throughout the room identifying such menu choices as File, Edit, View, Insert, Format, Tools, Table, and Help. She then describes a particular task, and students move to the section of the room with the sign they believe names the component they would most likely use to address the task. This process allows the teacher to see immediately which students have a clear understanding of key application elements, and which students may need review.

Corners Activities

During corners activities students assemble in different sections of the classroom to discuss a relevant question related to key content. Each corner of the room deals with a different question relative to a specific topic. Here are some examples.

Social Studies Unit on State Government. Students in this 8th grade social studies class are studying the state court system and how it treats juvenile offenders. Throughout the lesson, the teacher asks students to rotate through four different corners, each of which contains a different question related to these issues: "What are the differences between delinquent behavior and unruly behavior? What are the legal consequences for each?" "What are the rights of juveniles when taken into custody?" "How would you describe and explain the juvenile justice system to a citizen new to our state?" "Which delinquent behaviors can subject juvenile offenders to the adult criminal justice process?" At the end of each rotation, the teacher asks students to share their reactions and insights with the whole class. When the lesson concludes, students are asked to select one of the questions they found especially interesting and, for homework, develop a short essay summarizing their conclusions.

Earth and Space Science. At the beginning of class, students are asked to consider the following question: "How does the physical geography of a region affect the economy and living conditions of that region?" After writing their initial reactions in their academic notebooks, students then participate in a series of corners activities involving brainstorming responses to questions about different regions of the United States:

- What are the major physical and economic characteristics of states in the Pacific Northwest?
- What are the major physical and economic characteristics of states in the Southwest?
- What are the major physical and economic characteristics of states in the South?
- What are the major physical and economic characteristics of states in the Midwest?
- What are the major physical and economic characteristics of states in the Northeast?

As students finish formulating their insights and conclusions about various regions, they reassemble in their original table groups to revisit their initial reactions to the question: "How does the physical geography of a region affect the economy and living conditions of that region?" They complete the lesson by revising their initial written response, identifying areas in which their thinking remained the same and areas in which it changed significantly.

Stand and Be Counted

Teachers can end classes by having students "stand and be counted," based on their self-assessment of how well they understood the key ideas and concepts presented in the lesson. For example, self-assessment options might be the following: (1) *I clearly understand all of the major ideas and concepts presented today;* (2) *I understand most of the ideas and concepts presented today;* (3) *I need help understanding many of the ideas and concepts presented today;* and (4) *I didn't get any of the ideas and concepts presented today.* Here are some examples.

Trigonometry. This teacher realizes the challenge of teaching students to understand higher-level forms of mathematics. Therefore, he ends many classes with a closure activity in which he asks students to "stand and be counted." He asks them to assess and declare how clearly they understood the major ideas and concepts presented in that lesson. The teacher uses this informal polling process to prepare the do-now/anticipatory set for his next day's lesson as well as to identify students who may need individual or small-group coaching.

Mathematics Unit on Equivalent Fractions. Third graders are working to understand the differences between unequal and equivalent fractions. Their teacher uses periodic "stand and be counted" activities to elicit feedback from students on different aspects of this unit. At one point, for example, she may ask them to stand and identify their level of knowledge of key unit concepts. At another point, she may ask them to identify their level of understanding about key issues and processes presented in the unit. She is particularly alert about identifying students who may need additional coaching and direct instruction, especially those who stand when the following statements are posted: *I need help understanding many of the ideas and concepts presented today; I didn't get any of the ideas and concepts presented today.*

Activity Box

How have you used physical movement to enhance student engagement in your class? What are some new ideas you have about use of physical movement?

Promoting Engagement Through Pacing

Pacing and flow are essential ingredients in promoting high levels of student engagement. Effective pacing requires effective classroom management, including clearly articulated and understood administrative practices for classroom activities such as handing in assignments and distributing materials. Another important pacing issue involves transitioning from one activity to another, manifesting an overall logic to the manner in which a lesson proceeds. Engaged learning occurs when students are actively aware of and engaged in following the flow and sequence of teaching-learning activities.

Procedures for Administrative Tasks

Teachers should develop and clearly communicate well-established procedures for common administrative tasks (e.g., handing in assignments, distributing materials, storing materials after an activity, getting organized into groups). Here are some examples.

Biology. Students appear eager to participate in various labs, especially those involving hands-on work analyzing the physical structures of different organisms. However, the teacher understands the value of ensuring a safe, orderly, and inviting learning environment during lab experiences. Therefore, she revisits at the beginning of each lab the procedures for distributing specimen trays and equipment, including microscopes. She appoints different students on different days to oversee distribution of materials, including collecting and storing resources at the end of each lab. She is also very consistent in revisiting with students safety procedures and protocols for working with lab partners.

Second Grade Arts and Crafts. These 2nd grade students really enjoy opportunities to express themselves artistically. Their teacher makes certain that regular opportunities are provided for students to work in different media in response to different artistic challenges by asking questions such as these: "How would you feel if you were one of the animals we learned about in our story today?" "How would you show how these characters are connected?" "How would you have solved this problem?" To ensure that each art experience is a positive one, the teacher revisits and discusses with students such issues as the following: "How will we distribute our materials?" "What rules should we follow to ensure that everyone enjoys our art experience today?" "What will we need to do when we have finished this assignment?"

Transitions

One key component of pacing is effective transitions between activities. Effective transitions involve at least three components: (1) signaling the end of the previous activity, (2) announcing the next activity, and (3) moving quickly to the next activity. Here are some examples.

Secondary Family and Consumer Science. In this lesson students are expected to complete a series of challenging but timed cooking activities, all of which will culminate in a final class activity in which students will eat the meal they prepared together. To ensure a smooth transition from one activity to the next, the teacher posts key time markers (e.g., "We have 10 minutes until we change stations"); clearly announces the need to transition to the next activity; and appoints different classroom monitors for different activities, with the monitors responsible for identifying potential trouble spots or logistical issues that need to be addressed.

Middle School Physical Education. Students in this physical education class are encouraged to try out as many different forms of aerobic exercise as they can within the time provided. The teacher clearly models each form of exercise and provides clear time limits for students to rehearse and shape their use of the exercise. Students are then given time limits to complete each exercise independently as well as clear instructions for moving to the next activity. At the conclusion of the class, the teacher gives students 10 minutes for independent practice, encouraging them to review and extend their use of the aerobic exercises they found the most enjoyable or beneficial. Clear time markers and strategies for transitioning are reinforced throughout the lesson. The class concludes with students completing written reflections on their experiences in their academic notebooks.

Understanding the Purpose of Lesson Segments

One way to enhance effective pacing is to make sure students understand which of the following types of lesson segments are occurring at any point in time: (1) administrative segments, (2) segments that introduce students to new knowledge via critical-input experiences, (3) segments that help students practice and deepen their understanding of key knowledge and skills, and (4) segments designed to help students deepen their understanding via complex reasoning processes (e.g., problem solving, decision making, investigation, experimental inquiry, systems analysis, and hypothesis testing). Here are some examples.

Language Arts Unit on Argumentative/Persuasive Writing. This middle school English teacher understands that every time he teaches this unit, students have difficulty presenting and defending an argument with solid evidence and sufficient elaboration. Therefore, he has decided to provide students with an advance organizer for the unit, clearly laying out its key elements and the purpose for each lesson. After discussing the purpose of the unit and the lessons within it, the teacher makes a concerted effort to revisit key administrative procedures and rules, including deadlines, time management issues, and his overall design rationale. He also improves student understanding and engagement by balancing written and spoken techniques for argumentation and debate, coaching students to acquire and integrate basic information and skills before moving on to more complex assignments. In addition, for every new rhetorical device or strategy, he engages students in critical-input experiences that help them to see what they are learning, why they are learning it, and how it connects to them and their world. At key juncture points, students deepen their understanding by using complex reasoning processes—including problem solving, decision making, investigation, and hypothesis testing—to present, defend, and counter arguments. During each type of lesson, the teacher reminds students of the purpose of the lesson and the expected behaviors that go along with it. The unit culminates in students' participation in an authentic project involving their use of argumentation and persuasion strategies and processes in a real-world application of their choice.

Business. This high school business teacher is committed to ensuring that everything her students learn in class has an authentic application in the modern world of work. Therefore, every lesson and unit segment has a clearly articulated and authentic purpose that students are asked to reflect on and revisit. The overall unit is effectively paced, with students receiving ongoing coaching as they acquire and integrate key information and job-related skills. Each new segment begins with some form of simulation, ensuring that critical-input experiences help students to see the connection of curriculum content to their chosen career field or pathway. Modeling and shaping of skills and procedures inevitably lead to students' development of a capacity for automaticity—spontaneous and immediate retrieval and independent application of procedural knowledge. Throughout this unit, students participate in business-related scenarios, tasks, and situations involving on-the-spot problem solving, decision making, systems analysis, and hypothesis testing. Students maintain a business portfolio that includes work-related artifacts as well as self-reflections and self-evaluations involving their use of scoring rubrics.

Activity Box

How well do you think you use effective pacing strategies as described in this section? What are your strengths? What are your weaknesses?

Checking for Understanding

Use the following rating scale to assess your understanding and current comfort level regarding key strategies and processes presented in this module:

4 = I understand and already fully implement this strategy in my classroom.
3 = I understand this strategy, but I need to practice using it in my classroom.
2 = I can explain this strategy, but I am not fully confident that I can use it.
1 = I do not understand this strategy, and I do not currently use it in my classroom.

___1.   Using a variety of question structures
Based on my rating, I may need to revisit the following:

___ 2.   Using wait-time structures
Based on my rating, I may need to revisit the following:

___ 3.   Using follow-up questions and response strategies
Based on my rating, I may need to revisit the following:

___ 4.   Using physical movement
Based on my rating, I may need to revisit the following:

___ 5.   Using appropriate pacing
Based on my rating, I may need to revisit the following:

Module 15

Additional Cognitive, Affective, and Social Interaction Strategies for Promoting Student Engagement

In this module we continue to address Design Question 5: *What will I do to engage students?* Here we investigate how teacher enthusiasm and intensity affect students' commitment to learning and motivation. We also explore the psychological rationale for periodically including friendly controversy in classroom discussion to enliven and enrich students' experience of instruction. From there we present a variety of strategies to encourage students to talk about themselves, sharing their personal experiences and background knowledge to extend their interest in the content they are studying. Finally, we investigate how students' love of unusual facts and anomalies can be used to enhance engagement.

As in the previous two modules, the strategies and processes presented in this module are grounded in the five areas identified as necessary elements for promoting student engagement:

- High energy
- Missing information
- The self-system
- Mild pressure
- Mild controversy and competition

Reflecting on Your Current Beliefs and Practices

Before examining the strategies in this module, take some time to examine your current beliefs and practices by answering the following questions:

1. How do you demonstrate enthusiasm for the content you are teaching? To what extent do all your students pick up on and internalize that enthusiasm?

_____

_____

_____

_____

2. To what extent do you build a sense of academic trust with your students, ensuring that all learners see the value and authentic purpose of learning what you are teaching them?

_____

_____

_____

_____

3. When appropriate, how do you engage students in activities emphasizing friendly controversy?

_____

_____

_____

_____

4. Do you provide opportunities for students to talk about themselves? If so, how do you align academic content with student interests?

_____

_____

_____

_____

5. In what areas of your curriculum might you include unusual information to spark students' curiosity and interest?

_____

_____

_____

_____

Recommendations for Classroom Practice

This module addresses the following strategies for Design Question 5:

- Demonstrating intensity and enthusiasm for content
- Engaging students in friendly controversy
- Providing opportunities for students to talk about themselves
- Presenting unusual information

Demonstrating Intensity and Enthusiasm for Content

There are many ways to promote student engagement by demonstrating teacher intensity and enthusiasm for the content being taught. In situations that are critical for learning, teacher intensity and enthusiasm should be clearly evident. In addition to the words being spoken, everything about the teacher's tone and manner should communicate to students that the content is important and they should give it their full attention. Behaviors that demonstrate intensity and enthusiasm include the following:

- Directly stating to students why they are expected to learn what they will be studying, including direct connections to both their personal interests and the world beyond the classroom
- Using a variety of verbal and nonverbal signals—including gestures, vocal inflections, eye contact, and pacing—to reinforce students' understanding of what they are learning and why they are learning it
- Using a variety of nonlinguistic representations—from visual organizers to pictographs to flow charts—to help students see the big-picture connections and patterns in what they are learning
- Making direct statements about the relevance and importance of the content
- Describing personal anecdotes about the content

Examples

High School Chemistry. Students in this teacher's class are demonstrating confusion and difficulty in understanding many of the new concepts being introduced on the topic of chemical equilibrium. They also are periodically expressing doubts about the value or need to learn what the teacher is presenting. He decides to modify his approach by adding a variety of strategies to express his own enthusiasm and interest. Throughout each class, he revisits the reason students are being asked to learn the concepts. He stresses the connection between chemical equilibrium and real-world situations and settings, including stories about ways in which chemists have used key unit concepts in producing products and resources that are familiar to students. At key juncture points in his lessons, he asks students to make overt connections between their home, community, and the concepts being taught and learned. Finally, he punctuates every lesson with stories about his own struggles and insight. He sees a marked increase in student engagement and motivation as a result of adding these strategies to his repertoire.

First Grade Reading. This teacher incorporates into her reading lessons many of the strategies proven effective in demonstrating intensity and enthusiasm for content. She makes a deliberate effort to use vocal inflections, gestures, eye contact, and proxemics (i.e., closeness and physical connectivity such as a pat on the shoulder or a "high-five") to build enthusiasm in her students for what they are reading and discussing. At key points in her lesson, she also asks students to summarize why they are learning a particular sound-symbol combination or using a particular reading strategy. In spite of the maturity levels of her students, she is able to engage them in all aspects of the reading process and sees them becoming more enthusiastic about being good readers and text-based informa-tion processors. In fact, one of the homework assignments she gives her 1st graders is to share their own enthusiasm for reading with family members. Students are then asked to report to the rest of the class what they said about why they enjoy reading and how their family reacted to their ideas.

Activity Box

How well do you think you show enthusiasm in the classroom? What are your strengths? How might you use some of the strategies presented in this section?

Engaging Students in Friendly Controversy

The more students debate and challenge one another over content studied and varying perspectives that are associated with it, the more active and engaged they become in the learning process. For example, teachers can have students participate in dialogue about topics about which they have differing opinions. As much as possible, teachers should engage students in friendly debate, including both formal and informal debates, seminars, and perspective-driven discussions.

Teachers can also use movement to enhance interesting and friendly discussions of controversial content issues. Students who take one position can move to one side of the classroom and those with the opposite position to the other side. Those not attached to either position stand in the middle. Selected students from each group "present their case." At the conclusion of this debate or discussion, students are given a final opportunity to reposition themselves in relationship to the perspectives presented.

There are numerous ways to involve students in friendly controversy. They include the following strategies:

1. *Debating*. Teach students the basics of formal debating, including such concepts as supporting evidence and assuming the affirmative or negative position relative to a stated idea or assertion. Periodically ask students to assume a particular point of view, present evidence to support it, and debrief on the extent to which their opinions changed as they listened to other students' perspectives.

2. *O-P-V*. Use a variation of Edward DeBono's famous O-P-V strategy in which students are asked to defend the "opposite point of view" from the one they agree with or support. This strategy is especially useful in getting students with overly dogmatic or rigid attitudes to explore the nuances of a particular topic or issue. It is also especially useful in reinforcing students' need to provide supporting evidence to back up their claims and assertions.

3. *Seminars*. Use seminar formats in which students explore a text, video, or other resource that expresses highly charged or opinionated perspectives about a key issue or topic related to curriculum content. The seminar groups should contain three to five members, with each member assuming a specific role in the seminar. One student serves as moderator/facilitator. Another serves as recorder, keeping notes about what is said, questions that arise, and areas of agreement and disagreement among group members. Another student serves as sergeant-at-arms to keep everyone on task. Others can take turns as synthesizers and group representatives during whole-class debriefings.

4. *Varying perspectives*. Incorporate topics and content that allow students to explore, discuss, and debate varying perspectives on the same issue, event, or process. For example, what were the various political perspectives associated with the United States' entry into World War II? Students can be asked to assume the point of view of an individual or group advocating one position versus another. Part of the lesson can involve a whole-group or small-group debriefing using a Venn diagram that compares the various perspectives discussed and areas of congruence and disagreement.

5. *Expert opinions*. Engage students in researching the opinions of experts who hold contrasting perspectives and points of view about a particular issue or topic. A cooperative learning jigsaw, for example, might engage students in exploring a particular researcher or thought leader and reporting back to the whole group about what they discovered in that individual's writings and related presentations. The class then debates the merits of the varying perspectives and the validity—or lack of validity—of particular thinkers' ideas, positions, and evidence.

Examples

World History. Students enliven their study of ancient civilizations by assuming a variety of roles and vantage points as they explore conflicting worldviews and belief systems. As they study the Indus River Valley civilization, for example, they assume different vantage points to discuss the origins and merits of—and inherent problems associated with—the caste system. One student might defend the ideas and philosophy of a religious leader while another assumes the role of an untouchable. The teacher encourages students to research the enduring legacy of the perspectives and institutions encountered in various ancient civilizations, debating how justifiable they may have been then and how defensible they may or may not be now.

American Literature. Every year this instructor encourages students to become enthusiastic about reading complex works of American literature by asking them to participate in debates and mock trials extending from specific novels and plays. As they read and discuss Hawthorne's *The Scarlet Letter*, for example, they all become New England town members engaged in Hester Prynne's trial. Similarly, when they read Thoreau's *Walden* and "Civil Disobedience," they discuss and debate the implications of the author's transcendental ideals and their relevance for the world of the 21st century: *Is civil disobedience ever justified? Under what circumstances might you be willing—or unwilling—to engage in an act of civil disobedience?*

Activity Box

Why do you think friendly controversy has the effect of enhancing engagement? How have you used it in the past? What are some new ideas you have?

Providing Opportunities for Students to Talk About Themselves

Strategies that engage affective and social aspects of students' personalities can also be used to enhance students' engagement. When students are encouraged to see themselves in the content they study, for example, they experience a greater level of ownership for their own learning. Consequently, they should have numerous opportunities—where appropriate and feasible—to talk about themselves, their interests, and their personal learning goals in connection with the curriculum and learning goals they are required to learn.

In classrooms that are genuinely student-centered communities of learning, everyone has regular opportunities to share personal experiences, insights, and points of view. Teachers need to create situations in which students can talk about themselves and incorporate their personal interests in significant classroom tasks. These activities commonly involve students in making connections between their own lives and the content addressed in class.

Strategies related to this engagement technique include the following:

1. *Interest surveys.* At the beginning of the year and at the beginning of each unit, ask students to identify what they wish to explore and investigate regarding the content in each part of the curriculum. Whenever feasible, incorporate particular student interests and goals into the design of lessons and units.

2. *Student learning profiles.* This process can range from formal inventories of student learning profiles to more informal discussions and surveys in which students reflect on such issues as the following: *Under what circumstances and conditions do you learn best? Which of the following types of learning activities and assignments do you prefer—creative, analytical, practical, or a combination? How do you prefer to express yourself—through writing, oral communication, physical expression, artistic media, or other?* The more students are asked to reflect on their learning profiles and preferences, the more teachers can incorporate options for students to have choice as to approach, format, and process for demonstrating their achievement of key learning goals.

3. *Making explicit connections between content and student interests.* At relevant points within the curriculum, stop formal instruction and give students opportunities to share their observations and insights about key content. Ask students to identify connections and patterns involving their personal experiences and interests in relationship to key content being explored. At a more formal level, ask students to create metaphors, analogies, graphic organizers, or other forms of nonlinguistic representations to illustrate how specific content relates to them and their personal interests.

Examples

Health and Nutrition. In this 4th grade classroom, students are encouraged to relate everything they study and learn to themselves and their own physical, emotional, and social development. They keep a fitness journal as part of their academic notebooks. This journal includes personal fitness goals, periodic written reflections about how they are doing in achieving those goals, and action steps for improving their personal eating habits, exercise habits, and social and emotional responses. At key points in various units, the teacher asks students to engage in think-pair-share activities and small-group discussions in which they celebrate their successes and receive advice and support from peers about realizing specific fitness targets related to health and nutrition.

Geometry. This award-winning teacher knows that the abstractions and conceptual complexity of geometry always present challenges to her students. Therefore, in every unit, students are asked to become "geometry investigators," answering these questions: *Where in your life do you see evidence of the concepts, principles, and theorems we have studied in this unit being used in your world? How do professionals in the world of work use these geometric principles? How would our world be different if there were no geometry?* At significant and relevant points in each unit—including closure activities at the end of units—students are asked to share their insights and personal reflections about the relevance of what they have studied to them, their homes, and their community.

Activity Box

Other than the ways described in this section, what other situations can you think of for providing students with opportunities to talk about themselves?

Presenting Unusual Information

To engage students' interest and imagination, teachers can periodically interject unusual or "out of the mainstream" information related to content being studied. Engaging students in exploring little-known facts can capture their attention and make academic content come alive.

Strategies for acquiring and sharing unusual content-based information include the following:

1. *WebQuests*. Use the Internet and WebQuest format to have students find a range of obscure but interesting facts and ideas associated with the content being studied at a particular point in the curriculum. Each student can be given a "one-minute headline" opportunity to share the most unusual (but factual) information discovered.

2. *A class-generated "Ripley's Believe It or Not."* Ask students to compile an electronic database of unusual or little-known information about content being studied. This database can become a kind of in-class Wikipedia, with students adding to and (where appropriate) correcting misconceptions or inaccuracies. Each class can transmit a "legacy" of arcane but interesting information about the content for other classes and future students to study and reflect upon.

3. *History files*. It can be especially entertaining and enlightening for students to research differences among various historical eras' perceptions of "facts" related to specific content being studied. For example, astronomy students can investigate differences among astronomical facts in such eras as the medieval era, the European Renaissance, and the 21st century. How, for example, did Ptolemy view the cosmos versus Galileo and Stephen Hawking?

4. *Guest speakers and "first-hand" consultants*. Whenever possible, invite individuals to the classroom who can share direct experience with students. As students study the Vietnam War, for example, it might be feasible to have a veteran from that war share his experiences with the class. The more students can interact with such experts—and discover new

and unusual information to complement the textbook version of topics—the more engaged and motivated they become.

Examples

Second Grade Social Studies. As students in this classroom explore the theme of "Me and My Community," their teacher makes a point of periodically asking community representatives to visit the classroom and share their experiences and points of view. She encourages them to share little-known but interesting facts about their roles and contributions. During a lesson on the role of fire and police services in the community, for example, actual representatives of the fire and police departments visit with students and answer their questions about what it is really like to be in their profession. Each representative shares insights into what it means to be part of the community and expresses hopes for how the students can make a contribution as citizens of that same community.

Middle School Life Science. As students study interdependence within ecological systems, they are encouraged to visit and observe patterns in local ecosystems of their choice. Each of them is responsible for bringing back to class a list of unusual or interesting phenomena observed when visiting the ecosystem or biome. The teacher engages students' interest even further by asking them to create an in-class guidebook with chapters devoted to each of the ecosystems visited. At the conclusion of students' investigation of interconnections and interdependency within such systems, they invite to class a representative from the school system's nature center. Students donate their class guidebook (emphasizing little known or rarely observed aspects of local ecosystems) to the nature center as part of its permanent collection of resources.

Activity Box

What are some ways you might use the strategies described in this section?

Checking for Understanding

Use the following rating scale to assess your current understanding and comfort level regarding the strategies and processes presented in this module:

4 = I understand and already fully implement this strategy in my classroom.

3 = I understand this strategy, but I need to practice using it in my classroom.

2 = I can explain this strategy, but I am not fully confident that I can use it.

1 = I do not understand this strategy, and I do not currently use it in my classroom.

____ 1.   Demonstrating intensity and enthusiasm for content

Based on my rating, I may need to revisit the following:

____ 2.   Engaging students in friendly controversy

Based on my rating, I may need to revisit the following:

____ 3.   Providing opportunities for students to talk about themselves

Based on my rating, I may need to revisit the following:

____ 4.   Providing unusual information

Based on my rating, I may need to revisit the following:

Design Question 6

What Will I Do to Establish or Maintain
Classroom Rules and Procedures?

Module 16
Effective Classroom Organization

Module 17
Establishing and Maintaining
Classroom Rules and Procedures

Design Question 6

What Will I Do to Establish or Maintain Classroom Rules and Procedures?

Module 16

Effective Classroom Organization

A key component of *The Art and Science of Teaching* is a teacher's approach to establishing and maintaining classroom rules and procedures. This module and the next (Module 17) address these issues in the context of Design Question 6: *What will I do to establish or maintain classroom rules and procedures?*

At the beginning of each academic year, effective teachers ensure that their students are clear about what they are expected to do and how they are expected to do it. Throughout the year, teachers also need to revisit with students the rules and procedures for which they are responsible. It is especially important to have ongoing discussions with students to ensure that appropriate modifications are made in a timely manner, including additions and alterations to reinforce the classroom as a community of collaborative learning.

An essential but often overlooked part of this process involves the organization of the physical classroom itself. In fact, the way teachers organize their classrooms communicates to the student both consciously and unconsciously how they will manage instruction and facilitate student learning. This module deals with this important aspect of classroom management. Key aspects of room organization include how a teacher organizes physical space, promotes effective traffic flow, and structures various components of the room, especially students' access to learning centers, materials, technology, and equipment.

Reflecting on Your Current Beliefs and Practices

Before exploring the strategies in this module, take some time to examine your current beliefs and practices by answering the following questions:

1. In your opinion, what is the relationship between student achievement and the physical organization of your classroom?

_____

_____

_____

_____

2. To what extent do you use explicit strategies for organizing your classroom to maximize student learning and on-task behavior?

_____

_____

_____

_____

3. How do you make certain that all students have easy access to you—and you to them?

_____

_____

_____

_____

4. To what extent are you sensitive to the organization and storage of material resources in your classroom?

_____

_____

_____

_____

5. How do you ensure flexibility in organizing students to maximize their learning process?

_____

_____

_____

_____

Recommendations for Classroom Practice

This module addresses the following strategies for Design Question 6:

- Ensuring student access to learning centers, technology, and equipment
- Decorating the room to reinforce learning
- Preparing and organizing materials
- Arranging students' desks and chairs and the teacher's work area

Ensuring Student Access to Learning Centers, Technology, and Equipment

The building blocks of differentiated instruction include flexible grouping and students' ease of access to educational resources. Individual and small-group learning is also enhanced through placement of computers, printers, and related forms of electronic technology. Effective teachers think about materials and equipment that may require special locations for safety reasons (e.g., living and preserved animal and plant specimens, chemicals, and lab equipment). Finally, it is important to consider how bookshelves and conference tables should be placed so that traffic patterns are enhanced to support—rather than distract from—students' individual, small-group, and whole-group learning activities. Figure 16.1 contains a list of things to consider regarding access to learning centers, technology, and equipment.

FIGURE 16.1

Things to Consider Regarding Access to Learning Centers, Technology, and Equipment

- How many centers are needed?
- What are the primary patterns of movement around the class?
- Should some centers be close to particular books, materials, or other resources?
- What is the best placement for computers and printers?
- Do certain materials and equipment require special placement for safety reasons (for example, chemicals, lab equipment)?
- Where might bookshelves be easily accessed but not create traffic jams?

Source: From *A Handbook for Classroom Management That Works* (p. 139), by R. J. Marzano, B. B. Gaddy, M. C. Foseid, M. P. Foseid, & J. S. Marzano, 2005, Alexandria, VA: ASCD. Copyright © 2005 by ASCD. Adapted with permission.

Examples

Grade 10 English Language Arts. Students in this classroom are improving their writing and self-expression skills by using word processing applications when they are drafting compositions. However, their teacher notices that the physical placement of the in-class computer minilab is causing both traffic congestion and discipline problems as students jockey for access. After consulting the district technology specialist, this English teacher reconfigures the lab into a series of separate stations distributed throughout the classroom. The result is that students have easier access to computers as they draft their compositions. In addition, unnecessary talking and student conflicts are greatly diminished.

Middle School Family and Consumer Science. This class is designed to help middle school students apply a range of practical, real-world concepts and processes to everything from nutrition to sewing. Over the course of the semester, students are expected to complete a series of projects involving a range of curriculum topics. Given the scope of content and logistical challenges in this class, the instructor arranges the physical space of the classroom so that students can easily access the class computers and group workspace. She makes an ongoing effort to help students avoid traffic jams and complete projects in a timely and efficient manner. At least once a week, she begins her classes with a 10-minute "town meeting" during which students reflect on what they have accomplished and how the classroom supports—or sometimes works against—their achievement. When problems surface, the class collaborates on finding solutions and making recommendations for changes in spatial arrangements and logistics.

Activity Box

Briefly describe the organization of your room. How can it be changed to enhance traffic patterns?

Decorating the Room to Reinforce Learning

The way a classroom is decorated communicates a powerful message to students. As they enter and exit a room, for example, they receive conscious and unconscious messages about what the teacher considers important in terms of current teaching-learning activities and projects. When wall space and the overall appearance of the classroom are aligned with learning goals and instructional priorities, students receive reinforcement for the value of what they are learning and why they are learning it.

Consider, for example, the overall physical organization of a classroom and how its components reflect instructional priorities. It is important to use bulletin boards, calendars, and visual displays that highlight current learning goals, assignment time lines, and announcements. Perhaps most important is determining how examples of student work will be displayed. It is important for students to see themselves in their classroom and to benefit from samples of effective student work and visual artifacts that are personalized in various ways. Figure 16.2 contains a list of things to consider regarding room decoration.

FIGURE 16.2

Things to Consider Regarding Room Decoration

- Where is the door to the classroom? What do you want students to see as they enter and leave the room?
- Are wall spaces available for bulletin boards, calendars, and displays to post learning goals, assignments, special announcements, and student work? What is the best placement for these things?
- Will you be creating a poster with pockets for each student?
- How much empty space should you leave for later use?
- What else might need to be displayed—for example, the alphabet, poems, vocabulary lists, classroom rules, the daily timeline, standards or learning goals?

Source: From *A Handbook for Classroom Management That Works* (p. 139), by R. J. Marzano, B. B. Gaddy, M. C. Foseid, M. P. Foseid, & J. S. Marzano, 2005, Alexandria, VA: ASCD. Copyright © 2005 by ASCD. Adapted with permission.

Examples

Fifth Grade Science. Elementary school teachers in this school are concerned that the time they are required to spend on test preparation in language arts and mathematics sometimes shortchanges opportunities for science instruction. They decide to address this issue by using the wall space and related visual displays in their classrooms to help students see the value of science, as well as its connections to reading and mathematics. Each teacher regularly changes classroom displays to align with the science curriculum for a particular unit. They use posters, photographs, and interactive game activities to help students see the relationship between what they are reading in language and key science facts and concepts. They also use these displays to encourage students to apply mathematical concepts and processes of statistical analysis to key scientific concepts and issues (e.g., *What do you predict will happen to the ecosystem presented here if the following scientific data remain constant? What will happen if they increase exponentially?*). The presence of these visual displays and artifacts makes it easier for teachers to engage students in immediate applications of reading and mathematical concepts as they relate to the science curriculum.

Senior Humanities Classroom. This teacher makes a concerted effort to use the classroom as a kind of humanities gallery for his students. In fact, every time he transitions from one unit to another, he changes his bulletin boards and display areas to reflect the new content. When students study the European Renaissance, for example, he uses a range of photographs and art posters to highlight key examples of Renaissance sculpture, architecture, and paintings. He also encourages students to view these displays as interactive, with reaction sheets posted at key points so that students can write their initial responses to the art works and revise those reactions as they become more familiar with the era or the aesthetic principles they are studying. Having these visual displays so easily accessible encourages students to perceive themselves as actively involved in processing and critiquing significant artistic works.

Activity Box

Contrast how you decorate your room with the examples described in this section. What are some ways you might change your classroom?

Preparing and Organizing Materials

The more teachers pay attention to ensuring that required learning materials are prepared and organized in their classrooms, the greater are the chances their classrooms will effectively promote learning for all students. The range of materials teachers should consider can include something as seemingly simple as the availability of writing paper to the availability of the latest technology-driven resources. These materials are especially important when teachers consider the different types of lesson segments that will occur throughout a unit.

For example, in lesson segments devoted to routine activities and related student behaviors, teachers should make certain that students have easy access to required materials (e.g., pens, pencils, paper, attendance and seating charts). In lesson segments devoted to content, teachers should ensure that print, nonprint, and technology-based materials are available and carefully organized to support critical-input lessons, lessons devoted to practicing and deepening knowledge, and lessons devoted to generating and testing hypotheses. Finally, teachers should make certain that necessary materials are available for on-the-spot activities, including activities that (1) promote engagement, (2) articulate consequences for rules and procedures, (3) reinforce positive relationships, and (4) communicate high expectations for the success of all learners. Figure 16.3 contains a list of things to consider regarding preparation and organization of materials.

FIGURE 16.3

Things to Consider Regarding Preparation and Organization of Materials

It is extremely helpful to have most of the necessary materials ready before students arrive on the first day of school. Depending on students' grade level, the content area, and the types of lessons and units that have been planned, teachers might want to have the following materials prepared and organized:

- Pens, pencils, and paper
- Paper clips, staplers, and staples
- Music and a CD player
- Band-Aids, tissues, and any other first-aid equipment your school requires
- Attendance materials, class sheets, and seating charts
- In/out boxes for collected papers and transparencies
- Extra bulb for the overhead projector
- Sticky notes and name tags

In addition, teachers should think about the following questions:

- What materials will be needed for the lessons and units planned for the first few weeks of school?
- What materials and resources may need to be ordered now for later use?

Source: From *A Handbook for Classroom Management That Works* (p. 140), by R. J. Marzano, B. B. Gaddy, M. C. Foseid, M. P. Foseid, & J. S. Marzano, 2005, Alexandria, VA: ASCD. Copyright © 2005 by ASCD. Adapted with permission.

Examples

Third Grade Mathematics. A recent policy decision from the board of education has mandated that elementary mathematics teachers in this district use a variety of manipulative materials to help students understand complex concepts. Although teachers support the decision, they are complaining that the new math manipulatives are difficult to keep organized. One new teacher uses this change as an opportunity to improve the organization of her classroom and how she stores and distributes hands-on materials. Instead of keeping the manipulatives in cabinets and storage spaces throughout her classroom, she designates a single cabinet for their storage. She also appoints table-specific materials managers who are responsible for picking up lesson-specific manipulatives, distributing them at their tables, and ensuring that they are replaced appropriately. Students change this role weekly to ensure that everyone contributes to the management and distribution of materials.

Biology. An interesting ethical issue has surfaced in this classroom, resulting in the teacher's reexamination of how he prepares and organizes laboratory materials. Some students are objecting to labs that use biological specimens for dissection. Although the instructor respects their desire to express their conscience, he recognizes that their understanding of biological structures and processes will be limited without their participation in the labs. After conferring with his supervisor, the teacher gets permission to allow these students to use computer software simulations to study lab-related specimens. He places three computer terminals in one section of the classroom for use by this group, with a small table for follow-up discussion and comparison of observation notes. This alternative learning approach—complemented by the arrangement of materials and physical space—reduces students' concerns and leaves them feeling acknowledged for their ethical choices.

Activity Box

Considering the ways you prepare and organize materials, what do you do that enhances student learning and what do you do that might detract from student learning?

Arranging Students' Desks and Chairs and the Teacher's Work Area

How teachers organize desks and chairs in their classroom can inhibit or facilitate student learning. Depending on how many students are in the class, careful consideration should be given to the connection between a room's layout and potential safety issues. The effectiveness of grouping arrangements (e.g., whole-group, small-group, and one-on-one instruction) also depends on this element. For example, how does the arrangement of classroom desks, chairs, and the teacher's work area ensure students ease of access and ability to hear instructions? How does the placement of storage areas and boards enhance learning—or impede it?

Seating arrangements are also closely linked to students' ability to see overhead projector and related technology-based presentations. Seating arrangements can encourage or discourage student discussions and productive interaction. Finally, the effective placement of desks, chairs, and work areas enhances students' ability to perceive and interpret nonverbal communication patterns, including eye contact, gestures, and related body language. Figure 16.4 contains a list of things to consider regarding arranging students' desks and chairs and the teacher's work area.

Examples

First Grade Reading. During a time of larger class sizes resulting from enrollment increases, teachers responsible for 1st grade reading in this school collaborate to maximize student achievement. In addition to more rigorous attention to data analysis and flexible

FIGURE 16.4

**Things to Consider Regarding Arrangement of Students'
Desks and Chairs and Teacher's Work Area**

- How many students will be in the class?
- Does the room's layout present any safety issues?
- Where will whole-group instruction take place?
- Will all students be able to easily see you during whole-group instruction or see other students who are making presentations?
- Where is the storage area for materials you will use most frequently for whole-group instruction?
- Where is the blackboard or whiteboard located?
- If you will use an overhead projector, what is the best placement for that?
- To what extent will you be pairing students or creating small groups for learning?
- What seating arrangement will best encourage student discussion and productive interaction?
- Should you place your desk at the front of the room or at the back of the room?
- Regardless of where you place your desk, can you easily see all students and make eye contact with them as needed?

Source: From *A Handbook for Classroom Management That Works* (p. 139), by R. J. Marzano, B. B. Gaddy, M. C. Foseid, M. P. Foseid, & J. S. Marzano, 2005, Alexandria, VA: ASCD. Copyright © 2005 by ASCD. Adapted with permission.

grouping, these instructors examine how they can use the physical arrangement of desks, chairs, and teacher work areas to support students' reading progress. They all decide to rearrange these resources into distinct room areas with clearly designated reading-related purposes. The first area, located in the center of their classrooms, is reserved for whole-class instruction, with student desks separated to support this approach. Another section is used for small-group instruction, including opportunities for teachers and support personnel to meet one-on-one with students experiencing difficulty or needing extra coaching. A third area becomes a more open spot, with pillows and rugs to encourage students' independent exploration of big books and other high-interest materials. Finally, all classrooms are reconfigured to include a section for learning centers that engage students in tasks that reinforce key phonetic-analysis and word-recognition skills.

Middle School U.S. History. Social studies teachers at this school are concerned that their approach to teaching history has overemphasized facts and details to the exclusion of deep-level understanding. In particular, they recognize that a majority of their students seem passive in the face of studying history and generally disinterested in the work of historians. Eighth grade instructors decide to turn their classrooms into history workshops. They restructure seating arrangements into cooperative learning cohorts with four desks and chairs per group. Students are encouraged to vary self-assigned roles (e.g., facilitator, materials manager, recorder, synthesizer) and work collaboratively to solve history-related problems and investigations. Part of each United States history classroom is reorganized to contain a history library, with scholarly articles, books, artifacts, and reproductions of primary source materials such as letters, journals, and newspaper articles. Another section of the classroom is devoted to a small computer lab with Internet access, allowing individuals and small groups to conduct online investigations. At the end of the first semester, this reconfigured classroom arrangement and a greater instructional emphasis upon project-based learning result in increased student motivation and understanding of what historians actually do. Students also appear much more aware of the enduring issues, processes, and patterns that have shaped and defined the American experience.

Activity Box

If you had total freedom in regard to how to arrange desks and chairs in your classroom, what would it look like?

Checking for Understanding

Use the following rating scale to assess your current understanding and comfort level regarding the strategies and processes presented in this module:

4 = I understand and already fully implement this strategy in my classroom.

3 = I understand this strategy, but I need to practice using it in my classroom.

2 = I can explain this strategy, but I am not fully confident that I can use it.

1 = I do not understand this strategy, and I do not currently use it in my classroom.

_____ 1.   Ensuring student access to learning centers, technology, and equipment
Based on my rating, I may need to revisit the following:

_____ 2.   Decorating the room to reinforce learning
Based on my rating, I may need to revisit the following:

___3.   Preparing and organizing materials

Based on my rating, I may need to revisit the following:

___4.   Arranging students' desks and chairs and the teacher's work area

Based on my rating, I may need to revisit the following:

Design Question 6

What Will I Do to Establish or Maintain Classroom Rules and Procedures?

Module 17

Establishing and Maintaining Classroom Rules and Procedures

This module continues to explore Design Question 6: *What will I do to establish or maintain classroom rules and procedures?* Classroom rules and procedures are fundamental and essential to building a productive learning community within the classroom. An essential goal for teachers should be to promote student understanding and ownership of the rules and procedures necessary to maximize learning. In addition, students should be encouraged to periodically revisit classroom operating principles, providing input about how those principles might be changed and how the class as a whole might improve their attention to classroom rules and procedures.

We suggest that teachers minimize the number of rules and procedures to ensure student understanding, adherence, and buy-in. Teachers should begin by establishing general classroom rules and then work toward procedures for more specific areas such as the beginning and end of the school day or period, transitions, and the efficient use of materials and equipment. The following generalizations should guide the design and implementation of classroom rules and procedures:

• Although rules and procedures should be established at the beginning of the school year, students need reminders of when rules and procedures must be added or altered.

• Rules establish general expectations or standards regarding student behavior.

• Procedures describe those behaviors that will help students realize the rules.

• The utility of rules and procedures is enhanced if students have input into their design, especially if the teacher facilitates periodic discussions via classroom meetings.

Reflecting on Your Current Beliefs and Practices

Before examining the strategies in this module, take some time to examine your current beliefs and practices by answering the following questions:

1. In your opinion, what is the relationship between student achievement and the type and quality of interactions with students about classroom rules and procedures?

_____

_____

_____

2. To what extent do you use specific strategies to ensure that students adhere to rules and procedures?

_____

_____

_____

3. How do you make certain that all students understand their rights and responsibilities?

_____

_____

_____

4. To what extent do you periodically review with students key classroom rules and procedures?

_____

_____

_____

5. How do you use classroom meetings to promote students' understanding of and adherence to rules and procedures?

_____

_____

_____

Recommendations for Classroom Practice

This module addresses the following strategies for Design Question 6:

- Establishing a small set of rules and procedures
- Interacting with students about classroom rules and procedures
- Periodically reviewing rules and procedures and making changes as necessary
- Using classroom meetings to design and maintain rules and procedures

Establishing a Small Set of Rules and Procedures

There are a number of areas for which a teacher might establish rules and procedures. One of them is general classroom behavior. Figure 17.1 depicts sample rules in this area.

FIGURE 17.1

Sample Rules for General Behavior

Classroom Rules (1st Grade)

1. Be safe.
2. Be kind.
3. Be polite.

Classroom Rules (2nd Grade)

1. Listen carefully.
2. Follow directions.
3. Work quietly. Do not disturb others who are working.
4. Respect others. Be kind with your words and actions.
5. Respect school and personal property.
6. Work and play safely.

Classroom Rules (3rd Grade)

1. Be kind and respectful to others and yourself.
2. Listen when others are speaking.
3. Use your manners and be safe.
4. Keep your hands and mean words to yourself.
5. Have fun.

Rules for Classroom Behavior (Secondary)

1. Respect one another at all times.
2. Maintain eye contact when communicating with others or when someone—a teacher or a classmate—is speaking.

FIGURE 17.1

Sample Rules for General Behavior (*Cont.*)

---

3. Use "6-inch voices" when working in small groups or in pairs.
4. When working in groups say "please" and "thank you"; praise each other and use good manners.
5. Remember: only one person speaks at a time.

Making Our Classroom a Place for Learning (Secondary)

1. Respect others—when someone is speaking, listen.
2. Follow directions.
3. Keep hands, feet, objects, and unkind remarks to yourself.
4. Bring required materials to class.
5. Be in your seat when the bell rings.
6. Raise your hand.
7. Remember the rules we set for leaving your seat or leaving the classroom: maintain respect and quiet, think before you act, and minimize disruptions to the learning process.

Source: From *A Handbook for Classroom Management That Works* (p. 12), by R. J. Marzano, B. B. Gaddy, M. C. Foseid, M. P. Foseid, & J. S. Marzano, 2005, Alexandria, VA: ASCD. Copyright © 2005 by ASCD. Reprinted with permission.

Another area for which rules and procedures are commonly established is beginning and ending the period or school day. Figure 17.2 provides sample rules for preparing for homework at the end of class.

FIGURE 17.2

Sample Rules for Preparing for Homework at the End of Class

---

1. Plan a daily homework time.
2. Take home everything you'll need.
3. Choose a quiet study place.
4. Read and follow all directions.
5. Do your work neatly and carefully.
6. Ask for help if you need it, but do the work yourself.
7. Keep your homework in a special place.
8. Return your homework on time.

Source: From *A Handbook for Classroom Management That Works* (p. 17), by R. J. Marzano, B. B. Gaddy, M. C. Foseid, M. P. Foseid, & J. S. Marzano, 2005, Alexandria, VA: ASCD. Copyright © 2005 by ASCD. Adapted with permission.

Transitions and potential interruptions frequently require explicit rules and proce-dures. As an illustration, Figure 17.3 provides an example of rules for use of the bathroom.

FIGURE 17.3

Sample Rules for Use of the Bathroom

1. No talking in the bathroom.
2. You have only three minutes of bathroom time.
3. Do your job and don't mess around.
4. Go to the bathroom only during group bathroom breaks, recess, or independent work time.

We promise to follow the bathroom rules. (Each student in the class signs the rules sheet.)

Source: From *A Handbook for Classroom Management That Works* (p. 19), by R. J. Marzano, B. B. Gaddy, M. C. Foseid, M. P. Foseid, & J. S. Marzano, 2005, Alexandria, VA: ASCD. Copyright © 2005 by ASCD. Reprinted with permission.

Group work is commonly the subject of rules and procedures. Figure 17.4 provides some examples.

FIGURE 17.4

Sample Rules for Group Work

1. Take turns talking quietly.
2. Listen to each other's ideas.
3. Praise each other's ideas.
4. Help each other when asked.
5. Stay together until everyone is finished.
6. Talk about how you worked well together and how you might improve.

Source: From *A Handbook for Classroom Management That Works* (p. 25), by R. J. Marzano, B. B. Gaddy, M. C. Foseid, M. P. Foseid, & J. S. Marzano, 2005, Alexandria, VA: ASCD. Copyright © 2005 by ASCD. Adapted with permission.

Seat work and teacher-led activities are other topics for which rules and procedures are frequently established. Figure 17.5 provides some examples.

FIGURE 17.5

Sample Rules for Seat Work

1. You may talk quietly with a classmate if you have a question.
2. If you need further help, raise your hand and the teacher will come to your desk.
3. When you complete the assignment, start one of the enrichment activities posted on the board.

Copyright © 2008. Marzano & Associates. Reprinted with permission.

Finally, use of common materials and supplies is also a subject for rules and procedures. Figure 17.6 provides some examples.

FIGURE 17.6

Sample Rules for Common Materials and Supplies

Be Prepared Every Day

1. Bring a pencil or pen to class.
2. Bring a spiral notebook for note taking and other work.
3. Bring your textbook to class each day.
4. If you forget your materials, remember the Borrowing Rules we set:
   - Try to borrow what you need from a classmate. OR . . .
   - You may borrow up to five times from the community shelf.
   - Put a checkmark next to your name each time you borrow something.
   - Don't forget to return what you have borrowed at the end of class.

Source: From *A Handbook for Classroom Management That Works* (p. 22), by R. J. Marzano, B. B. Gaddy, M. C. Foseid, M. P. Foseid, & J. S. Marzano, 2005, Alexandria, VA: ASCD. Copyright © 2005 by ASCD. Adapted with permission.

The examples in Figures 17.1 to 17.6 are rules—general statements of expectations. A teacher might find that for some of these rules explicit procedures must be developed.

A procedure describes the specific actions a student must take to follow the rule. To illustrate, consider Figure 17.7, which illustrates a procedure for beginning the school day in an elementary classroom. Providing students with steps like those in Figure 17.7 gives them clear guidance (i.e., a clear procedure) regarding how each day will begin.

Obviously it would be counterproductive to establish procedures for every classroom rule. Consequently, it is important to identify a small set of rules and then develop procedures only for those rules for which students need specific guidelines regarding how

FIGURE 17.7

Sample Procedure for Beginning the Day

1. I will greet each student individually at the door.
2. You should read silently for a short time while I quickly take attendance. Then I will stop by each student's desk to provide feedback about individual behavior or academic performance.
3. As a class, we will stand and recite the Pledge of Allegiance and then listen to a recording of "God Bless America."

to behave. Limiting the number of rules and procedures in a classroom will help ensure that students understand and adhere to them.

Examples

Fourth Grade Classroom. This newly hired teacher is extremely diligent about trying to make certain that her classroom is orderly and controlled. However, in her zeal to maintain a safe and orderly learning environment, she presents her students with so many rules and procedures that they appear overwhelmed by the list—and choose to ignore many of them because of their lack of understanding and buy-in. After discussing this problem with her mentor, the teacher decides to conduct a town meeting with her students. She revisits with them the importance of rules and procedures, as well as the significance of their assuming responsibility for how the classroom operates. At the conclusion of their discussion, the group identifies five key rules that everyone agrees are essential to maintain order, safety, and collaboration. She regularly revisits these five rules with students. As a result, her classroom becomes much more collaborative and productive, with all students "owning" the more limited list of rules. She also finds that procedures must be developed for a few of the less obvious rules.

University Preservice Teacher Training Program. This program is designed to prepare student teachers to work in urban schools with highly transient student populations. To prepare participants for their student teaching experience, professors all agree to reinforce two key tenets of effective classroom management: (1) the need to have students understand and contribute to the implementation of the rules and procedures for which they are responsible, and (2) the need to limit rules and procedures to a manageable number. Previously, many student teachers had become frustrated trying to get their students to follow a long list of rules for which the students refused to assume ownership. With this new approach, program participants find that students seem more aware of their individual role in sustaining a safe, orderly, and inviting classroom. Students also seem to benefit from their participation in the decision-making process. Their greater level of responsibility ensures that they are active—rather than passive—members of the classroom as a vibrant learning community.

Activity Box

Which rules and procedures that you currently have might be replaced? Which rules and procedures should you definitely keep? Why?

Interacting with Students About Classroom Rules and Procedures

When designing rules and procedures, it is important to interact with students about them. This is best done at the very beginning of the school year. Interaction about rules and procedures might be as simple as explaining each rule and procedure to students. This would involve discussing their logic and their importance.

Another approach is to present students with rules and procedures but then invite them to modify those rules and procedures. Students might be organized in small groups and asked to suggest changes. Each group's suggestions would be listed on the board, and all would be discussed by the entire class. Those suggested changes that gain consensus would be applied to the original set of rules and procedures.

At an even higher level of student involvement, the students can generate rules and procedures. In this scenario the teacher shifts responsibility for crafting rules and procedures to the entire class. The interaction usually begins with a whole-class discussion regarding the need for rules and procedures. Again, students are organized into small groups, each of which is charged with identifying an initial list. During a whole-class discussion, the students and teacher aggregate the list into one unified set. These are voted on by the class to obtain a consensus list. In subsequent discussions, procedures for those rules that are not obvious are designed by the class. This approach obviously takes more time but has the potential of maximizing student ownership of the class rules and procedures.

Examples

Seventh Grade Technology Education. A recurring problem in this classroom is students' perception that the workstations are difficult to access, resulting in their belief that resources are not equitably distributed. Because students are required to complete a minimum of six independent projects during the semester, the teacher decides to enlist student help in resolving the situation. At the beginning of the week, he announces that students will form small groups to develop a collaborative time line with completion benchmarks for each project. He shows them models and examples from previous academic years and allows them time to discuss the most viable ways for everyone to complete required tasks. They also explore the issue of limited workspace and the need to respect one another's time lines and individual needs. Once the small-group discussions are completed, each group presents its proposal. Finally, the class uses their small-group work to create a consensus-driven work plan that becomes the basis for making the workspace more efficient and productive. After the plan is implemented, the teacher sees a remarkable positive change in classroom climate and rates of project completion as well as decreased levels of tension and conflict.

High School Civics. This teacher uses the issue of classroom rules and procedures as a catalyst for reinforcing students' understanding of the role of law in social settings. She begins each year by having students develop a class constitution, articulating a limited number of clear, consensus-driven rules for whole-group, small-group, and independent work. Students are then asked to revisit their constitution on a monthly basis, examining how they are individually contributing to the operation of this microsociety and helping to amend the constitution as situations warrant changes. At appropriate times during the semester, the teacher also asks students to compare the operation of their class to the functions and processes of state and federal governments. By using this sustained analogy, the instructor reinforces key ideas and understandings related to social networking, rule of law, individual and group responsibility for social welfare, and consequences for citizens' failure to follow social norms, standards, and laws. Classroom management and collective responsibility become an integral part of the curriculum and day-to-day operations rather than being artificially separated from them.

Activity Box

How have you involved students in the design of rules and procedures? How might you involve them further?

Periodically Reviewing Rules and Procedures and Making Changes as Necessary

Periodic review of rules and procedures can prove extraordinarily useful in promoting students' ownership of their behavior. For example, impromptu class discussions—especially when on-the-spot situations warrant them—can be used to engage students in revisiting rules and procedures. Review is necessary when students seem to be systematically violating or ignoring rules and procedures. Rather than trying to remedy the situation by enforcing some type of negative consequence, the teacher calls the lapse in behavior to the attention of the students and asks for their suggestions as to how to get behavior back on track. This might lead to a reevaluation of the rule or a clarification of the behaviors that constitute following the rule. In some cases, a procedure might have to be designed so that all students know exactly what is expected of them.

In other situations, rules and procedures might be suspended or completely dropped, based on input from students. For example, students might view the rule of raising their hands before speaking out as overly restrictive. Based on this input from students, the teacher might suspend the rule to see how well this new protocol works in fostering more engaging classroom discussions. If the suspension of the rule does not produce the desired result, the rule can be reinstated.

Examples

Second Grade Art. This elementary teacher is dedicated to ensuring that her students have regular experiences involving the visual arts, including drawing, painting, sculpture, and other visual displays. She also helps them see cross-disciplinary connections by having students create nonlinguistic representations of key concepts and ideas. However, distributing materials can be challenging with young students, particularly when it comes to sharing supplies and space for larger art projects. So she makes certain that the class regularly revisits key rules and procedures before distributing art supplies. She also discusses with students how rules and procedures can be altered to make the class run more effectively. "How can we share our classroom supplies and space more effectively so that we all work well together? What rules should we change or delete to help everyone work more effectively?" As a result of these discussions, students grow in their ability to assume responsibility for rules and procedures. Throughout the year, students' experiences with art also complement their understanding of other content areas as well their capacity for self-regulation and self-monitoring within a community of learners.

Middle School Chorus. This chorus teacher understands that collaboration and mutual support are critical to the success of both in-class and schoolwide choral performances. In addition to stressing key elements of vocal technique and musical blending, she begins every unit with a brief class discussion of what works—and what doesn't work—in preparing for choral presentations. This process becomes a regular part of students' critique of their individual and collective performances. It also helps students perceive chorus as a training ground for collaborating in all types of group processes. When problems emerge with particular musical arrangements or preparations, the teacher takes time to conduct on-the-spot discussions of how rules and procedures might be modified. She also conducts individual and small-group coaching sessions to help students understand key rules and procedures and improve their contributions to the group's success.

Activity Box

Describe a time when you changed a rule or procedure that you had previously established. How did students respond to this change?

Using Classroom Meetings to Design and Maintain Rules and Procedures

To formalize the review of rules and procedures we advise scheduling regular classroom meetings for 10 minutes at the beginning of a class (e.g., every Friday). This "town meeting" approach reinforces the notion that the management of the classroom is the responsibility of students and within their control. In these meetings, the teacher and students bring up relevant issues. If students do not feel comfortable volunteering issues in front of the entire class, the teacher might use a suggestion box or might institute a policy whereby students can approach her individually and then she will anonymously bring up the student's issue at the class meeting.

Examples

Chemistry. This chemistry class is taught by a highly experienced teacher who begins his Friday classes with a collaborative debriefing on what is working and what needs to be improved in such areas as materials distribution, student interactions, and safety in the chemistry lab. These town meetings also help the teacher reinforce the habits of mind and professional protocols used by chemists in their professional settings. In effect, the town meetings become a structured and predictable venue to reinforce rules and procedures within the context of purposeful and authentic work. As students progress through the year under the teacher's guidance and coaching, these meetings help them observe changes in their own levels of independence. Chemistry becomes a class in which their capacity for self-management and responsibility is celebrated.

Interdisciplinary English–Social Studies High School Unit. Under the leadership of a new principal, teachers in the English and social studies departments at this high school have been encouraged to explore potential cross-disciplinary connections with their students. This principal wants students to understand how key themes and ideas interrelate and why these ideas are important. Teachers form cross-disciplinary pairs and design a series of project-based assessment tasks that require students to integrate key skills and habits of mind for language arts and social studies. At the beginning of each unit and at weekly town meetings, students revisit with both instructors key time line–driven benchmarks, protocols for independent work and media center research, and underlying rules and procedures for cooperative learning cadres. As students progress through the academic year, they become increasingly responsible for managing deadlines. The weekly town meetings also provide a context for celebrating successes in this area and for addressing and resolving emergent logistical issues.

Activity Box

How have you used classroom meetings in the past? If you haven't, how might you use them in the future?

Checking for Understanding

Use the following rating scale to assess your current understanding and comfort level regarding the strategies and processes presented in this module:

4 = I understand and already fully implement this strategy in my classroom.
3 = I understand this strategy, but I need to practice using it in my classroom.
2 = I can explain this strategy, but I am not fully confident that I can use it.
1 = I do not understand this strategy, and I do not currently use it in my classroom.

_____ 1. Establishing a small set of rules and procedures
Based on my rating, I may need to revisit the following:

___ 2. Interacting with students about classroom rules and procedures
Based on my rating, I may need to revisit the following:

___ 3. Periodically reviewing rules and procedures and making changes as necessary
Based on my rating, I may need to revisit the following:

___ 4. Using classroom meetings
Based on my rating, I may need to revisit the following:

Design Question 7

What Will I Do to Recognize and Acknowledge Adherence and Lack of Adherence to Classroom Rules and Procedures?

Module 18

Acknowledging Students' Adherence to Classroom Rules and Procedures

Module 19

Acknowledging Students' Lack of Adherence to Rules and Procedures

Design Question 7

What Will I Do to Recognize and Acknowledge Adherence and Lack
of Adherence to Classroom Rules and Procedures?

Module 18

Acknowledging Students' Adherence to Classroom Rules and Procedures

The Art and Science of Teaching emphasizes that when there are no consequences for following—or failing to follow—classroom rules and procedures, they do little to enhance student learning. Therefore, teachers should frequently reinforce students' adherence to rules and procedures rather than taking that adherence for granted. Similarly, teachers should acknowledge lack of adherence to rules and procedures. This classroom dynamic is addressed in Design Question 7: *What will I do to recognize and acknowledge adherence and lack of adherence to classroom rules and procedures?*

Notice that this design question basically has two parts: (1) acknowledging adherence to classroom rules and procedures, and (2) acknowledging lack of adherence to classroom rules and procedures. In the first case, teachers overtly recognize when students have followed a rule or procedure; in the second case, teachers overtly recognize when students have not. This module deals with the first part of the equation—acknowledging when students have followed a rule or procedure. Another way of saying this is that we address "positive consequences" in this module and "negative consequences" in the next (Module 19).

Reflecting on Your Current Beliefs and Practices

Before examining the strategies in this module, take some time to reflect on your current beliefs and practices by answering the following questions:

1. In your opinion, what are the most effective ways to recognize and acknowledge students' adherence to classroom rules and procedures?

_____

_____

_____

_____

2. What kinds of verbal and nonverbal acknowledgment do you use when students are adhering to classroom rules and procedures?

_____

_____

_____

_____

3. How do you acknowledge and reinforce positive individual and group behavior?

_____

_____

_____

_____

4. How do you involve parents or guardians in promoting students' adherence to classroom rules and procedures?

_____

_____

_____

_____

5. How would you summarize your overall approach to promoting student adherence to rules and procedures?

_____

_____

_____

_____

Recommendations for Classroom Practice

This module addresses the following strategies for Design Question 7:

- Using verbal and nonverbal acknowledgment
- Using tangible recognition when appropriate
- Involving the home in recognition of positive student behavior

Using Verbal and Nonverbal Acknowledgment

One obvious way to provide positive reinforcement when students follow rules and procedures is to use verbal and nonverbal forms of recognition. Stating to the class as a whole or to individual students that they did a great job in completing a task can go a long way to reinforcing a positive climate. Regular use of simple thank-you's and other social courtesies can become a catalyst for helping students replicate those behaviors in their own lives. Simple forms of verbal recognition of adherence to rules and procedures include the following:

- Thanking students for following a rule or procedure
- After students have followed a rule or procedure, explaining to them how that action contributes to the proper functioning of the class
- Describing to students exactly what they did that constituted adhering to a rule or procedure
- Contrasting current student behavior that adhered to a rule or procedure with previous behavior that did not

Teachers should also be aware of the powerful impact of nonverbal acknowledgments. Simple forms of nonverbal recognition include the following:

- Thumbs-up sign
- OK sign
- Smile
- Wink
- Nod of the head
- Pantomime of tip-of-the-hat
- Pat on the back

The combined and ongoing use of verbal and nonverbal reinforcements can greatly expand students' on-task behavior and their willingness to use such behaviors without tangible or external rewards.

Examples

First Grade Reading. In this 1st grade classroom, the teacher makes a concerted effort to use verbal and nonverbal reinforcement when students adhere to rules and procedures. "Class, you all did a great job in moving into your reading groups today," she states to students. She also selects individual students to receive verbal reinforcement for their contributions: "Sally and Frank, thank you so much for helping to distribute our materials today." Throughout whole-group, small-group, and independent reading activities, she makes certain to reinforce positive student behaviors via nonverbal cues, including smiles, nods, winks, and thumbs-up signs. About every 15 minutes, she describes for individual students ways in which they have positively contributed to class activities: "Allison, you are asking wonderful questions that help us all to understand what we are reading. Terrance, thank you for showing all of us how to work well with others when we are in small groups."

High School Drama. This class is heavily production oriented. Each unit of instruction culminates in some form of dramatic presentation to audiences made up of students from other classes. To ensure that all students support a collaborative and professional work environment, this teacher makes a conscious effort to verbally and nonverbally reinforce students' adherence to important rules and procedures. For example, at critical transition points in a lesson, the teacher describes whole-group and individual behaviors that contributed to successful outcomes. Additionally, he continually scans his classroom to discover commendable behaviors related to rules and procedures. Using both verbal and nonverbal signals, he tries to give every student at least one specific positive piece of feedback during every lesson. During every unit, he also uses student critique sessions to reinforce and build on students' growing ability to work successfully and collaboratively.

Activity Box

Are you better at using verbal or nonverbal acknowledgment? What are some things you can do to improve your weaker area?

Using Tangible Recognition When Appropriate

Use of concrete forms of recognition can become a form of "token economy" within the classroom. A token economy is a system in which students receive points for adherence to rules and procedures and lose points for lack of adherence. When students have acquired a sufficient number of points, they can be rewarded with some tangible recognition such as a certificate or a positive call home to parents.

Students themselves can play an active role in acquiring tangible recognition for their adherence to rules and procedures. A daily recognition form, for example, might award them a starting score of 20 points for a set of expectations (e.g., punctuality, preparation, on-task behavior, respect, and work completion), with points taken away for not following a particular expectation. At the conclusion of each class period, students can tally their total points, with the teacher recording daily totals in a separate ledger.

Teachers can also provide overt indicators of students' current behavior. For example, a teacher might establish a color code for behavior. A green card indicates exceptional adherence to rules and procedures. A yellow card indicates acceptable behavior with room for improvement. A red card indicates unacceptable behavior. All students start the class period with three cards at the top-left corner of their desks. At the beginning of the period, the top card is always green. During the class the teacher moves throughout the room changing the color of the card exposed on each student's desk to indicate the level of behavior exhibited. If the teacher exposes the yellow card or the red card for a student, the green card can always be reinstated when the student's behavior warrants the change.

Examples

Middle School World Geography. These middle school students have become more responsible for adhering to classroom rules and procedures as a result of a tangible rewards system recently implemented by their teacher. He provides concrete recognition in the form of "geography tokens." Each token is in the shape of a specific country or geographic region studied during that week. Students receive tokens for such behaviors as punctuality, preparation for class, and completion of homework and seatwork. If they receive a certain number of tokens, they are able to complete a puzzle map given to them at the beginning of the week. Completing it results in their receiving a certain number of points for that week. When they achieve a designated total of points over the course of several weeks, students receive specific tangible rewards such as coupons to buy juice in the cafeteria. Aligning the token system with concrete geographic locations provides a quick reminder of content addressed in class.

Third Grade Social Studies. To reinforce students' understanding of democracy as a political system, students receive tangible rewards for specific behaviors. Showing respect for others in the classroom, for example, can result in students' receiving a certain color-coded card that becomes a part of their academic notebook. Similarly, demonstrating appropriate behavior during voting activities leads to a certain number of points awarded. At key juncture points during the grading period, students review with their teacher their achievements as part of the classroom democracy. During conferences, students analyze what the range of color-coded cards and points they have received represents about them as a citizen and a contributor to the classroom environment. Periodically, students are asked to evaluate their adherence to the laws—that is, rules and procedures—of their classroom and how their emerging portrait as a citizen might translate into adult behaviors in a democratic system.

Activity Box

Some educators are in favor of the use of tangible recognition; some are against it. What is your position? Explain.

Involving the Home in Recognition of Positive Student Behavior

There are a wide range of strategies for eliciting support from parents and guardians for students' adherence to classroom rules and regulations. For example, notifying parents and guardians about students' positive behaviors is a strategy ranked highly by students as a reward for their positive behavior. This strategy can include a wide range of simple but productive interventions, including the following:

• *Phone calls home*—Establish the goal of making just one phone call home a day concerning one student's positive behavior, ensuring that over the course of the academic year every student's family receives at least one positive phone message.

• *E-mails*—This strategy can include messages composed for individual students or generic positive e-mails to parents and guardians of all students who behaved positively during a given week.

• *Notes home*—Write short notes home describing individual and group behaviors that were especially commendable. Be specific about how those behaviors reinforce a positive classroom environment and climate.

• *Certificates*—Certificates of positive behavior can communicate to parents and guardians that their children are behaving well in class. Specific certificates for specific types of positive behaviors can be preprinted and sent home to parents and guardians or given to students to bring home to parents and guardians.

Examples

Middle School English/Language Arts. To reinforce positive classroom behavior, this teacher actively involves students' homes in the recognition process. For every student, she attempts to make at least one positive phone call to parents and guardians over the course of the year. She also uses brief e-mail messages to parents and guardians to acknowledge whole-group achievements related to rules and procedures. When time permits, she creates short personal notes to acknowledge individual students' accomplishments in contributing to a positive classroom climate and atmosphere. At the conclusion of each grading period, she awards computer-generated certificates, organized according to categories of successful student behaviors: for example, being on time to class, being prepared for class, positive work habits, and meeting deadlines. Finally, she encourages students to reflect on their own contributions and progress via periodic journaling activities involving "notes to parents and guardians."

Sixth Grade Mathematics. As students grapple with complex mathematical concepts in preparation for taking algebra in 8th grade, their teacher encourages them to monitor their own attitudes about course content and how well they adhere to classroom rules and procedures. Whenever she identifies a student who is making outstanding contributions to the logistics, overall behavior, and operations of the classroom, she uses one of several means of acknowledgment. Students who seem to be making a concerted effort to improve their behavior, for example, are rewarded with a phone call home or an e-mail to parents or guardians recognizing their success. She uses notes home and certificates of behavior to reinforce students' willingness to be a productive member of the classroom learning community. With the cooperation of the school's technology coordinator, this teacher has also designed a class Web site. Parents and guardians can access the site to discover whole-group, small-group, and individual achievements related to mastery of learning goals as well as adherence to classroom rules and procedures.

Activity Box

Describe one specific way you have used home contingency to acknowledge students' adherence to rules and procedures. If you have not done so, describe how you might use home contingency in the future.

Checking for Understanding

Use the following rating scale to assess your current understanding and comfort level regarding the strategies and processes presented in this module:

4 = I understand and already fully implement this strategy in my classroom.

3 = I understand this strategy, but I need to practice using it in my classroom.

2 = I can explain this strategy, but I am not fully confident that I can use it.

1 = I do not understand this strategy, and I do not currently use it in my classroom.

___ 1.   Verbal and nonverbal acknowledgement
Based on my rating, I may need to revisit the following:

___ 2.   Tangible recognition
Based on my rating, I may need to revisit the following:

___ 3.   Involving the home in recognition of positive behavior
Based on my rating, I may need to revisit the following:

Module 19

Acknowledging Students' Lack of Adherence to Classroom Rules and Procedures

Like the previous module (Module 18), this module deals with Design Question 7: *What will I do to recognize and acknowledge adherence and lack of adherence to classroom rules and procedures?* Whereas Module 18 addresses recognizing and acknowledging adherence to classroom rules and procedures, this module addresses recognizing and acknowledging lack of adherence to those rules and procedures. Stated differently, this module deals with negative consequences, and the previous module deals with positive consequences.

Reflecting on Your Current Beliefs and Practices

Before examining the strategies in this module, take some time to examine your current beliefs and practices by answering the following questions:

1. To what extent do you demonstrate "withitness" by continuously scanning your classroom and intervening when students' inappropriate behavior threatens to become disruptive?

_____

_____

_____

_____

2. To what extent are there explicit and concrete consequences for inappropriate behavior in your classroom, especially when that behavior has progressed beyond a point where it can be addressed by withitness?

_____

_____

_____

_____

3. How do you involve parents/guardians and students in identifying and discussing behaviors that need to stop in class?

_____

_____

_____

_____

4. To what extent does your classroom reflect a coherent and sustained multitiered plan for classroom management issues extending from students' failure to follow rules and procedures?

_____

_____

_____

_____

5. How do you defuse volatile or high-intensity situations involving students' lack of adherence to rules and procedures?

_____

_____

_____

_____

Recommendations for Classroom Practice

This module addresses the following strategies for Design Question 7:

- Being "with it"
- Using direct-cost consequences
- Using group contingency
- Using home contingency

- Dealing with high-intensity situations
- Designing an overall plan for disciplinary problems

Being "With It"

Jacob Kounin's concept of "withitness" (see *The Art & Science of Teaching*, pp. 140–143) is one of the most powerful management tools teachers have at their disposal. Briefly, withitness involves being aware of what is happening in all parts of a classroom at all times by continuously scanning student behaviors, including when working with whole groups as well as small groups and individuals. It also involves intervening promptly and properly when inappropriate behavior threatens to become disruptive. Figure 19.1 summarizes key strategies associated with withitness.

FIGURE 19.1

Strategies to Communicate Withitness

1. *Talk privately to potentially disruptive students* before class starts and have brief conversations about expectations for the day.
2. *Use "stimulus cueing."* Provide a cue (e.g., a prearranged stimulus or sign) to selected students before inappropriate behavior occurs.
3. *Occupy the entire room physically or visually.* Move to all quadrants of the room systematically and frequently, making eye contact with all students.
4. *Notice potential problems*, such as small groups of students huddled together talking intensely, or one or more students not engaging in class activity for an extended period of time.
5. *Use a series of graduated actions.* Once a potential problem has been identified, seek out and extinguish the problem immediately.
6. *Look at suspected students.* Elicit their attention, confirming that you have noticed their behavior and that the behavior is not acceptable.
7. *Move in the direction of students.* If suspected behavior continues, move in the direction of offending students, still addressing the entire class but nonverbally communicating the message: "Please stop what you are doing and join in what we are doing in class. Your participation is welcome and needed."
8. *Stop the class and confront the behavior.* If students have not reengaged, directly and publicly confront their behavior in a calm and polite manner.

Examples

A New Teacher Takes Over a 5th Grade Classroom. One of the great challenges of teaching is to replace another teacher midway through an academic year. When a 5th grade teacher faced a health crisis requiring long-term hospitalization, this first-year teacher agreed to take over for her as a long-term substitute. Although her instincts were good, she quickly realized that students in the class appeared to be testing her and her ability to control the class. To ensure that she maintained order and reinforced rules and procedures, she used subtle but effective "withitness" cues to communicate that she was on top of everything happening in class. She would continually scan the classroom and respond quickly to potentially disruptive situations. She would have discreet side conversations with students who demonstrated inappropriate behavior. She made certain to circulate regularly through all quadrants of her room, signaling to students when they demonstrated positive or negative behaviors. Perhaps most important, she identified individuals and small groups of students who exhibited behavioral problems that could escalate to more serious problems and dealt with their behavior via conferencing and follow-up reinforcement. When whole-class intervention was required, she used appropriate but immediate interventions to reinforce the significance of classroom rules and procedures.

High School Special Education Self-Contained Classroom. This teacher made the reinforcement of "withitness" a regular part of her daily instruction. She began every class with a brief warm-up activity that reinforced students' understanding of rules and procedures and her expectations for how the classroom was to operate. Classroom discussions periodically focused on how everyone in the class could contribute to their learning community. She held conferences with students who exhibited acting-out behaviors, developing an action plan with them so that she could silently signal to them when they were escalating inappropriate behaviors. Throughout the lesson, she would circulate throughout the room, making certain that every student felt her physical presence and eye contact. Additionally, she used a series of graduated actions helping her to identify potential problems and work with students to seek out and extinguish the problem immediately. When necessary, she would stop the class and confront inappropriate behaviors.

Activity Box

How would you rate your withitness? Good? OK but can be improved? Poor? What are your strong areas? What are some new ideas you have?

Using Direct-Cost Consequences

Direct-cost consequences involve explicit and concrete consequences for inappropriate student behavior, especially when that behavior has progressed beyond a point where it cannot be addressed by using withitness strategies. We recommend two major interventions related to direct-cost consequences: (1) time-out and (2) overcorrection.

Time-out involves creating a place within or outside the classroom where students are required to go until they are ready to resume regular classroom activities. When students are removed to an external location, some form of concrete action plan should be developed before their return. That is, students should be required to describe exactly what they will do differently before they reenter the classroom. This helps students understand and control their offending behavior.

Overcorrection involves engaging students in activities that overcompensate for inappropriate behavior. Specifically, overcorrection is a viable intervention when a student has destroyed class property or has interrupted the entire class's opportunity to learn. For example, a student who has drawn on a classroom wall might be required to clean marks on all walls in that classroom. Similarly, a disruptive student might be required to summarize information from a teacher's lecture and distribute the summary to the entire classroom.

Examples

Pre-Algebra. This highly successful mathematics teacher uses a combination of disciplinary interventions to reinforce classroom rules and procedures. Usually, his use of withitness cues helps a majority of students maintain appropriate behavior and disposition toward learning. However, when potentially disruptive or inappropriate behaviors move beyond this stage, he uses two interrelated forms of disciplinary strategies. He maintains an in-class learning center with materials that students can use to reinforce their understanding of major algebraic concepts. This center can also become a time-out resource when students need to be removed from a small- or whole-group activity because of inappropriate behavior. He is also effective in using overcorrection. When students destroy or damage algebraic manipulatives, for example, they must rebuild or construct alternative versions that everyone in the class can use. In the process, they gain both a heightened sense of responsibility and a clearer sense of the value and purpose of these teaching tools.

High School Psychology. Students in this psychology class are asked to examine their own motives for inappropriate and disruptive behavior, reinforcing their ability to self-evaluate and self-regulate. When a student disrupts a presentation or lecture, for example, the student may be required to summarize information from the teacher's lecture and distribute the summary to the entire classroom. The teacher's emphasis on self-examination helps students expand their understanding both of themselves and of key psychological concepts and principles. He asks students to revisit such key questions as the following: *What are you attempting to gain by disrupting the class? How can disciplinary problems and acting-out behaviors reflect hidden psychological motives such as the need to be recognized, to control others, or to express displaced anger?*

Activity Box

How have you used time-out or overcorrection? What are some ways these strategies might be abused?

Using Group Contingency

The concept of group contingency rests on the premise that a successful community of learning holds the class as a whole responsible for the behavior of any and all members of the class. Two types of group contingency are most often found in educational research literature: interdependent group contingency and dependent group contingency.

With *interdependent group contingency*, the entire class receives positive consequences only if every student in the class meets a certain behavioral standard. Interdependent group contingency processes can be used to reinforce positive and extinguish negative group behaviors in regular classrooms.

With *dependent group contingency*, positive and negative consequences are dependent upon the behavior of one student or a small group of students who have been singled out for behavioral change. Dependent group contingency processes are generally reserved for clinical use with students who have severe behavioral problems.

Examples

Middle School Computer Applications. In a skills-driven and experiential learning environment such as her computer applications classroom, this teacher is very aware of the need to balance whole-group, small-group, and individualized instruction and tutorials. To ensure that this flexible grouping approach supports the learning of all students, she starts every unit with a discussion of how individual students can contribute to their own learning and that of their classmates. These interactions include explorations of learning goals, discussions of time limits and suggestions for what to do when individuals have completed activities ahead of others in the class. The entire class receives points and related positive consequences only when every student in the class meets agreed-upon performance targets and behavioral standards.

Fifth Grade Science. This teacher is balancing two complex challenges in teaching science to her 5th graders: (1) the need to help her students understand and productively deal with scientific instrumentation and biological specimens and (2) the presence in the class of a student with serious behavioral problems. She chooses to use a combination of interdependent and dependent group contingency strategies to ensure students' adherence to a limited number of rules and procedures. For example, her entire class receives positive consequences (such as opportunities to play computer simulation games) only if every student in the class meets a certain behavioral standard. She works closely—and continuously—with the behaviorally challenged student to implement an action plan to which he and his parents have agreed. During science lab days, for instance, this student understands that positive and negative consequences for the whole class are dependent upon how he conducts himself and interacts with the other students. Over the course of several months, this approach results in science classes characterized by collaboration, cooperation, and student self-regulation.

Activity Box

Dependent group contingency is a viable but controversial strategy. What are some potential negative consequences of using dependent group contingency? How can you guard against these negative consequences?

Using Home Contingency

This process begins with a meeting between parents or guardians, the teacher, and the student to identify and discuss student behaviors that need to stop in class. During such meetings, the student should have some input into both negative and positive consequences. Specifically, in consultation with parents or guardians and the teacher, the student identifies the positive and negative consequences associated with his behavioral changes in class. Such consequences should be implemented both in the classroom and at home so that the student perceives the teacher and the parents or guardians to be unified in their attempt to help him control his behavior.

Examples

Middle School World Geography. In this classroom, three students in particular seem to have a great deal of difficulty when instructional tasks require them to assume a level of independence and self-restraint. During cooperative learning activities, for example, these students often disrupt group activities or encourage other members of their group to engage in off-task behavior. After using a series of escalating interventions (from with-itness strategies to interdependent and dependent group contingency processes), this teacher concludes that home involvement is necessary. He sets up a meeting with each student's parents. At the meeting, the teacher, parents, and student identify behaviors that need to stop in class. The teacher believes that each student should have input into both negative and positive consequences for the identified behaviors, including opportunities for self-reflection as to the reasons for the disruptive behavior. At the conclusion of each meeting, the teacher, parents, and student develop an action plan for eliminating the behaviors, including performance indicators, consequences for continuing disruption, a clear time line, and ways in which the parents will monitor and support the action plan's implementation.

Third Grade Mathematics. A student in this classroom continues to act out and disrupt classroom activities whenever the teacher moves to the subject of mathematics. In spite of using a series of graduated interventions to help the student, the teacher sees the student's disruptions continue to escalate in their forcefulness and impact on other students. The teacher enlists the school counselor in setting up a parent-student-teacher conference. At the conference, the student and parents reveal the student's long history with math anxiety, including a series of failed tutorials and related interventions tried in previous years. This process results in the development of an intervention plan that combines diagnostic testing, after-school tutorials, and suggestions for ways in which the parents can help the student overcome her anxiety and reduce the level of disruption during mathematics lessons. The result of this intervention is that the student perceives mathematics in a less anxiety-driven way. The after-school tutorials are aligned with reinforcing her work on the objectives of lessons for that week. Weekly phone calls home also help to keep everyone apprised of the student's progress. Over the course of the next grading period, this teacher sees much-improved student performance and overall adherence to classroom rules and procedures.

Activity Box

In the previous module, we addressed involving the home in positive consequences for student behavior. In this module we address involving the home in negative consequences for student behavior. Which of these approaches do you use more? Why? What are some new ideas you have?

Dealing with High-Intensity Situations

Dealing with high-intensity situations requires the teacher to determine what level of intensity or crisis the situation represents. When a student is out of control and external resources (e.g., administrative) are not available, teachers can use the following series of strategies until help arrives:

1. First, recognize that the student is out of control.

2. Next, step back and calm yourself.

3. Listen actively to the student and plan action. Use active listening until the student calms down.

4. When the student is calm, repeat a simple verbal request (e.g., "Lois, I want you to go with me outside in the hallway to discuss this further. Can we please do that now?").

Examples

Elementary Chorus. Students in this chorus have been chosen for participation based upon auditions and their prior experience with choral music. During the first several weeks of working with these students, however, the chorus instructor notices incidents among various subgroups within the classroom. In discussing the various disruptive incidents with the students who commit them, she realizes that these incidents appear to be the result of tensions between different subgroups within the chorus. These tensions are carry-overs from community conflicts that seem to be affecting the ability of the students to get along and achieve collaborative musical goals. The teacher is especially concerned during several class sessions when verbal sniping and put-downs begin to escalate into physical confrontations. Before calling for administrative support, however, she uses a multistep intervention process. First, she acknowledges when an individual or a group of students is out of control. Next, she quickly steps back and calms herself so that her reactions do not contribute to escalating the situation. She then isolates the students and uses active listening to mirror their comments and feelings until they calm down. When the students are calm, she repeats a simple verbal request, encouraging them to go with her outside the classroom to discuss the situation and resolve the conflict peacefully.

High School Biology. As a result of lingering anger over an extended series of verbal put-down exchanges, two boys in this classroom continue to act out and disrupt instructional tasks. Although the interactions seem relatively low-key and amusing at first, the teacher is quick to understand that their anger has the potential to become a high-intensity disciplinary situation. She immediately develops an action plan to resolve their hostility. First, she revisits with the entire class the potential of verbal harassment to escalate into physical violence. Next, she commits to working with the two students to resolve their hostility. She recognizes whenever one or both of them may be bordering on becoming out of control. Stepping back and calming herself, she isolates the students during disruptive incidents and listens actively to both of them. She also reinforces that if they continue their behavior, she will need to remove them from the classroom and involve administrators in resolving the problem.

Activity Box

Describe a high-intensity situation you have handled in the past. Contrast your actions during that incident with those recommended in this section.

Designing an Overall Plan for Disciplinary Problems

Regardless of the level of intensity of disciplinary problems, an effective teacher should have a comprehensive plan for dealing with any disciplinary situation. Such a plan should outline steps for resolving conflicts with students and improving disciplinary behavior.

Figure 19.2 presents a model of an overall plan a teacher might develop. We recommend that every teacher develop such a plan. The plan depicted in Figure 19.2 is stated in terms of questions; however, it still provides the teacher with an overt framework or plan for addressing disciplinary issues.

FIGURE 19.2

Sample Overall Plan for Disciplinary Problems

I will start by examining my relationship with every student:

- With which ones do I have a poor relationship or no relationship?
- What can I do to improve these relationships?
- What will I do to remain "withit" during every class?
- What will I do to be consistent with positive and negative consequences?
- What is my strategy for dealing with high-intensity, dangerous situations?
- At what point will I bring administrators into a situation?

Examples

Sixth Grade World Geography. As students transition into middle school, they frequently experience anxiety and stress over the changes in their learning environment, schedule, and new peers. This seasoned middle school geography teacher is very aware of the influence of transitional anxiety upon new middle schoolers. She has developed an overall approach to discipline in her classroom. At the beginning of every academic year, her first priority is to share with her students her plan for promoting positive student behavior and classroom citizenship. She begins each year by discussing with her students a short list of essential rules and procedures and consequences for not adhering to them. This teacher also encourages her students' self-reflection and self-monitoring processes by asking them for suggestions about how the classroom can best become a true community of learning. At key points during the academic year (including weekly classroom town meetings), this teacher discusses ways of dealing with students' failure to adhere to rules and consequences, organized according to escalating levels of disruption and infraction. She uses a limited but effective number of clearly articulated protocols for specific behaviors that need to be curtailed, making certain that students understand and can describe their offending behavior when necessary. If offending behaviors continue, she actively involves students in identifying ways to curtail their disruptive behaviors. Although her commitment is to handling disruptive behavior internally with the students, her action plan also includes contingency processes for involving administrators and the home in modifying any disruptive behavior that moves toward high-intensity status.

Fourth Grade Reading/Language Arts. Aggregate and disaggregated testing results confirm that in this school, students' transition from 3rd to 4th grade often is accompanied by a decline in their academic performance and grades. It is during this transitional period that many students also exhibit heightened levels of acting-out behaviors. Teachers and administrators have concluded that a major cause of this decline is the increasingly academic nature of the 4th grade curriculum, including heightened emphasis upon students' analysis of whole-text literature and more complex forms of writing assignments. As part of their school improvement planning efforts, the faculty collaborates on an overall plan for addressing student underachievement and related disciplinary problems. Although this plan is initially designed to address the 4th grade achievement issue, the entire school benefits from all teachers agreeing to implement it. This whole-school plan includes strategies for ensuring that all students are clear about classroom rules and procedures and the consequences for not adhering to them. It also includes carefully articulated and research-based strategies for addressing student disruptions and misbehavior, including ways to encourage student self-reflection and self-monitoring. The plan contains strategies for dealing with students' failure to adhere to rules and consequences, organized according to growing levels of disruption and infraction. There are also processes for addressing escalating forms of behavior, including clearly delineated responsibilities for all staff members. The school also develops an early-intervention plan to identify students who may be experiencing either academic or social-emotional problems in their primary years. Through early instructional and counseling services, these students can receive support and assistance in avoiding or reducing the impact of the problems identified with their transition from 3rd to 4th grade.

Activity Box

Contrast your overall plan for disciplinary problems with that described in this section. What are some new ideas you have?

Checking for Understanding

Use the following rating scale to assess your current understanding and comfort level regarding the recommendations and strategies presented in this module:

4 = I understand and already fully implement this strategy in my classroom.
3 = I understand this strategy, but I need to practice using it in my classroom.
2 = I can explain this strategy, but I am not fully confident that I can use it.
1 = I do not understand this strategy, and I do not currently use it in my classroom.

___1.   Being "withit"
Based on my rating, I may need to revisit the following:

___2.   Using direct-cost consequences
Based on my rating, I may need to revisit the following:

___3.   Using group contingency
Based on my rating, I may need to revisit the following:

___ 4.   Using home contingency
         Based on my rating, I may need to revisit the following:

___ 5.   Dealing with high-intensity situations
         Based on my rating, I may need to revisit the following:

___ 6.   Designing an overall plan for disciplinary problems
         Based on my rating, I may need to revisit the following:

Design Question 8

What Will I Do to Establish and Maintain
Effective Relationships with Students?

Module 20

Communicating Appropriate Levels
of Concern and Cooperation

Module 21

Communicating Appropriate Levels
of Guidance and Control

Design Question 8

What Will I Do to Establish and Maintain Effective Relationships
with Students?

Module 20

Communicating Appropriate Levels
of Concern and Cooperation

Design Question 8 addresses teacher-student relationships: *What will I do to establish and maintain effective relationships with students?* The quality of relationships that teachers have with their students is a keystone of effective classroom
management—perhaps even a necessary condition for effective teaching. Problems
with classroom management frequently occur with a breakdown in teacher-student
relationships, when teachers establish a "we-they" stance with students. *The Art and
Science of Teaching* asserts that for teachers to promote and sustain healthy and
positive relationships with all their students, two types of behaviors are necessary:
(1) communicating appropriate levels of concern and cooperation within the classroom as a true community of learning and (2) communicating appropriate levels of
guidance and control to support the learning process. This module addresses the
first of these two categories of behaviors—communicating appropriate levels of concern and cooperation. The next module (Module 21) addresses the second aspect of
effective teacher-student relationships—communicating appropriate levels of guidance and control.

At the heart of communicating concern and cooperation is a teacher's commitment to helping students believe that they are valued as individuals. This is accomplished by ensuring that students perceive the teacher as being interested in them as
individuals and devoted to developing a culture of cooperation and mutual respect.

251

Reflecting on Your Current Beliefs and Practices

Before examining the strategies in this module, take some time to examine your current beliefs and practices by answering the following questions:

1. What do you do to keep informed about the students in your classes?

_____

_____

_____

_____

2. What do you do that demonstrates affection for each student?

_____

_____

_____

_____

3. How do you bring student interests into the content and personalize learning activities?

_____

_____

_____

_____

4. What types of physical behaviors do you use that communicate interest in students?

_____

_____

_____

_____

5. How do you use humor in class?

_____

_____

_____

_____

Recommendations for Classroom Practice

This module addresses the following strategies for Design Question 8:

- Knowing something about each student
- Engaging in behaviors that indicate affection for each student
- Bringing student interests into the content and personalizing learning activities
- Engaging in physical behaviors that communicate interest in students
- Using humor when appropriate

Knowing Something About Each Student

Students need to believe that their teachers value them as individuals and as human beings. One strategy for fostering this perception involves knowing things about students' lives, experiences, interests, and personal goals. There are many ways a teacher can obtain such information. For example, a teacher can use such strategies as interest surveys and opinion questionnaires. Individual teacher-student conferences are another source of information about students. A teacher can also use parts of parent-teacher conferences to ask about and listen for critical details regarding students and important information about their life experiences.

Becoming familiar with the local culture of students and how it may affect their learning can contribute significantly to how a teacher introduces, revisits, and reinforces students' understanding of key academic content. Weekly town meeting discussions in the classroom can incorporate questions like these: "Tell me about what's happening in your lives these days" or "What are some things students are talking about that teachers should be aware of?"

Armed with personal information about students, a teacher can do many things to communicate interest in students. *A Handbook for Classroom Management That Works* (Marzano et al., 2005, pp. 61–62) offers the following suggestions:

- Compliment students on important achievements in and outside of school. This may include commenting (and offering congratulations, when appropriate) on an achievement in another class, such as a well-written paper, an engaging class presentation, or a class-helper role that a student has assumed. It may also include offering positive feedback when students are involved in community projects such as a local recycling effort, a book drive at their church or synagogue, or volunteering at an animal shelter or a soup kitchen.

- Meet students at the door as they come into class and say hello to each student, *being sure to use the student's first name.* Simply saying "hello" or "good morning" to groups of students does not have the same impact as saying, "Good morning, Rosa," "Hi, Joseph," "Welcome, Susan," and so on.

- Find time to talk informally with students about their lives and their interests. These kinds of opportunities occur naturally over the course of a day or a week—for example, with students who arrive early to class or as students complete a classroom task at different times. This is a good time to give students unsolicited "strokes" regarding work, dress, hair, athletic accomplishments, or personal interests. You also might ask their opinions about the unit you are teaching, ask about their successes in other classes, or pass on compliments that you have heard about them from other teachers. If and when appropriate, give the student a hug.

- Make a positive phone call home with the student present.
- Take photos of students for room display.
- Attend an after-school function that involves the student.
- Single out a couple of students each day—for example, in the lunchroom—and talk with them. This can be as simple as beginning a conversation by saying, "How's your day going, John?" "What did you think about the class discussion today, Amber?" "Hi, Liana. Looks like it's going to be a sunny weekend. Do you have any plans?" "Hi, Jose. Are you excited about the play this weekend?" or "Thanks for offering that explanation today in class, Mariana. I think it helped make things clearer for everyone."
- Greet students *by name* outside of school if you happen to run into them at, say, the movie theater, a sporting event, or the grocery store. A long discussion is not necessary; just give a warm greeting that uses the student's name: "Hi, Alex. Nice to see you," "Hi, Meg. Enjoy the game!" or "Have a good weekend, Ben."

Examples

A New Elementary Teacher. This first-year teacher makes a concerted effort to get to know her 6th grade students. As part of that commitment, she administers a student-interest inventory at the beginning of the academic year. Throughout the year, she attempts to incorporate students' identified interests and personal goals into many of her units and lessons. She also asks students to revisit their responses and update their questionnaires. Her initial inventory asks students these questions: *What do you want to learn this year? What are your personal interests and hobbies? How would you describe your family? How would you describe your community? What are your personal goals for the coming academic year?*

Middle School English/Language Arts. This language arts teacher encourages her students to express their personal voice in their writing. As students learn about narrative and expository writing in her English class, they are periodically asked to respond to topics and issues related to their own culture and backgrounds. She also uses their interests and background experiences in shaping assignments and audiences. One of her writing prompts asks the following question: *How would you describe your favorite music to an older relative?* Another asks students to describe for a cousin in another state a local spot where they like to visit or congregate with their friends. She also reinforces the power of language in writing and the significance of vocabulary in communication by having her students explain to their parents slang expressions and idioms unique to their age level or peer group.

Activity Box

Identify one student in your class about whom you know very little. What are some ways you can gather information about that student?

Engaging in Behaviors That Indicate Affection for Each Student

Students need to know that a teacher likes them as individuals and as fellow human beings. Communicating appropriate but observable affection for each student can be as simple as greeting students at the door each day, acknowledging them and expressing interest in how they are feeling. A teacher can also take pictures of each student and post them on the bulletin board, attaching short statements from students that reflect their thoughts about the class and their personal goals for what they will be studying. When the schedule allows it, a teacher might attend after-school functions in which students participate. This can become an especially valuable intervention when dealing with alienated students who do not appear to be achieving their potential. Finally, as part of a daily and weekly planning process, teachers can develop a schedule to ensure that they regularly and personally interact with each student.

Examples

Geometry. This veteran teacher goes out of his way to make the abstractions of geometry both relevant and immediate to his students. He refers to them as "Geometry All-Stars" and posts their photographs on one of his bulletin boards. During each unit, students are asked to place sticky notes under their photos describing how they are experiencing what they are learning. He makes a point to read each note out loud when they are written. The students' photo wall and comments provide a great deal of humor for the teacher to play off of and help the teacher personalize the complexities of this mathematics subject area.

Elementary Science. A 5th grade teacher notices that one of her students seems to like science topics and activities but appears alienated and disinterested when studying other subject areas. The teacher makes a sustained effort to encourage the student to make connections between science and such content areas as social studies and mathematics.

She also finds science-related reading materials that connect to ideas and themes being addressed in reading and writing activities. As the science fair approaches, she encourages this student to participate and finds ways to support his integration of writing, reading, research, and social studies into his investigation of a local ecosystem. Over the course of the academic year, the student begins to appear more engaged and motivated.

Activity Box

When was the last time you engaged in a behavior that communicated affection for students? Specifically, what did you do?

Bringing Student Interests into the Content and Personalizing Learning Activities

A key component of differentiated instruction involves paying attention to student interests and learning profiles. Based on an understanding of these components, a teacher can make decisions about how both individual and group interests might be incorporated into task design and learning activities. For example, teachers can systematically draft classroom tasks that include student interests. Using processes such as a jigsaw cooperative learning group, WebQuests, and independent investigations, teachers can encourage students to identify specific topics of interest to them. When appropriate and feasible, teachers can encourage students to research and report to the rest of the class what they have learned about their topic and its connections to the core curriculum topic.

A teacher might also use simpler but effective strategies for incorporating student interests into daily activities, such as asking students to create visual representations, graphic organizers, and metaphors, similes, and analogies that play on their interests. Here are some examples: *Identify something in your life with this same pattern. Create a metaphor, a simile, or an analogy to represent this pattern. Design a visual organizer that represents the connections you have found between your interests and life experiences and those of the characters in this work of literature.*

Examples

Secondary Earth and Space Science. Teaching a content area with numerous abstract concepts and generalizations, this teacher continually tries to bring student interests into the content to personalize the learning activities. As students study geographic regions and land forms, for example, the teacher asks them to write postcards home, describing what they are observing and experiencing as if they were actually at the location. She also asks them to generate metaphors and analogies regarding the content. Students share their examples of figurative language as they review key unit concepts and store core curriculum content. The teacher also has students use reflective journal and think-log entries to personalize their experience of studying the content. Periodically the teacher asks students to include metacognitive reflections in their journals in response to such questions as the following: *How would you explain the key concepts and generalizations from this chapter to someone who had not studied them? Which aspects of this unit's content would you like us to review or study further? If you were teaching this unit, how would you make the content interesting to other students?*

Third Grade Interdisciplinary Art and Science. This teacher understands that primary students especially need to have fun with the content they are studying and process key information via nonlinguistic representations. Therefore, she integrates whenever possible students' science and art experiences. During art lessons, for example, she has students draw or paint visual representations of the science concepts studied that week. She also asks students to work in small groups to come up with examples from their own lives that seem to be similar to key science concepts they have just studied. As a small group, teams create visual expressions of the metaphors and analogies they have generated. When they finish, they are asked to explain their visual comparisons to help other students in the class understand and benefit from them.

Activity Box

Recall a time in your own K–12 school experience when you were allowed to investigate something of personal interest to you. What was your experience of that situation? What ideas does it give you for your own teaching?

Engaging in Physical Behaviors That Communicate Interest in Students

As part of their professional self-monitoring, teachers should consider how their nonverbal physical behaviors are—or might be—interpreted by their students. Additionally, they should consciously practice and engage in behaviors that communicate interest in their students. These include smiles, appropriate physical signs of encouragement, looking students in the eyes, standing close to communicate concern or interest without invading personal space, and looking interested in what students have to say.

Examples

Probability and Statistics. Students in this high school mathematics class frequently struggle with the complexity and abstract patterns they are asked to study. In addition to using strategies such as personalization, integration of student interests, and individualized learning goals, this teacher makes a very real and sustained effort to use a range of physical behaviors to communicate interest in students. When he detects that students are struggling or frustrated with abstract course ideas, he makes a concerted effort to use smiles, physical gestures of affirmation, eye contact with all students, and close proximity. The students seem to respond to these strategies, especially during challenging tasks and activities.

First Grade Reading. This teacher knows from experience that her students are continually interpreting her interactions with them to discern her mood and attitude toward them during reading lessons. She not only uses physical behaviors to communicate affect for students, but also explains to students how important these behaviors are in making others feel welcome and accepted. Students are asked to monitor their own responses during whole-group, small-group, and independent reading activities. They discuss and revisit the importance of smiling, making eye contact, looking interested, and being respectful during times of close proximity. In the process, students' reading performance seems to be enhanced, as well as their growing understanding of their responsibilities as a citizen in the classroom.

Activity Box

What is a specific physical behavior you use to communicate interest in students? With whom do you use that behavior? With whom do you not use that behavior?

Using Humor When Appropriate

Humor can take a range of forms and expressions. However it shows up in a particular teacher's classroom, it is a powerful tool in developing a positive and productive learning environment. When appropriate, for example, teachers can engage in playful banter with students, laugh with their students—including laughing at themselves—and use historical and popular sayings to make a point (e.g., "I'll be back" or "four score and seven years ago"). Similarly, cartoons and jokes can sometimes help to illustrate a point. Choices of language can also help students experience a teacher's humanity and care for them as individuals. For example, periodic use of puns and plays on words can provide a humorous approach to learning key content (e.g., "Always assess the acceptability of alliterations!").

Examples

World History. This wise teacher realizes that placing too much emphasis on declarative knowledge (i.e., facts, terms, and generalizations) in a one-year world history course can overwhelm students. He also knows that his implemented curriculum needs to focus on students' revisiting of big ideas and understandings that move within and across historical eras. One of the tools he uses to help students make these kinds of connections is humor. For example, he maintains a large electronic and print collection of cartoons that he shares with students at appropriate points in the course. He also asks student groups to examine his collection and select one or two cartoons that they think reflect key concepts and generalizations for a particular unit or set of units. Throughout the year, the teacher and students collect a class anthology of jokes, limericks, cartoons, and humorous anecdotes that can be shared with students taking the course in the future. He also has students collect interesting and humorous sayings and word play examples from other eras, which they periodically share with the whole class as they review key unit content and make connections across historical eras.

Physical Science. The challenges of teaching a middle school course made up of extensive technical vocabulary and concepts derived from such disciplines as chemistry and physics are enormous. In response, this science teacher decides to integrate humor as a key ingredient of her teaching. She starts every lesson with a joke of the day, which can include a play on words involving key concepts for that lesson. In partnership with her students, she collects cartoons, anecdotes, and humorous stories that exemplify big ideas and understandings related to physical science. When students are asked to present their findings after a lab experiment, they are encouraged to recount any amusing situations or incidents that occurred during the lab. The willingness of this teacher to bring humor into her classroom greatly enhances student motivation and engagement in response to a difficult and challenging body of curriculum content.

Activity Box

How comfortable are you using humor in your classroom? If you are not, what are some ways of using humor that you would feel comfortable with?

Checking for Understanding

Use the following rating scale to assess your current understanding and comfort level regarding the key strategies and processes presented in this module:

4 = I understand and already fully implement this strategy in my classroom.
3 = I understand this strategy, but I need to practice using it in my classroom.
2 = I can explain this strategy, but I am not fully confident that I can use it.
1 = I do not understand this strategy, and I do not currently use it in my classroom.

___ 1. Knowing something about each student
Based on my rating, I may need to revisit the following:

___ 2. Engaging in behaviors that indicate affection for each student
Based on my rating, I may need to revisit the following:

___ 3. Bringing students' interests into the content and personalizing learning activities
Based on my rating, I may need to revisit the following:

___ 4. Engaging in physical behaviors that communicate interest in students
Based on my rating, I may need to revisit the following:

___ 5. Using humor when appropriate
Based on my rating, I may need to revisit the following:

Design Question 8

What Will I Do to Establish and Maintain Effective Relationships with Students?

Module 21

Communicating Appropriate Levels of Guidance and Control

The previous module (Module 20) addressed strategies for communicating appropriate levels of concern and cooperation. As we have seen, this is one of the two critical aspects of establishing effective teacher-student relationships. This module deals with the other aspect—communicating appropriate levels of guidance and control.

The issue of locus of control is important in maintaining a positive and productive learning environment within a classroom. On one hand, students must perceive their teacher as providing sufficient guidance and control both academically and behaviorally. On the other hand, students must ultimately take responsibility for their own behavior. We believe students need to experience a gradual release of responsibility from the teacher toward them. This begins with students seeing that the teacher has clearly articulated and implemented rules and procedures and that the teacher maintains emotional objectivity. Students must also see that the teacher is committed to treating each of them fairly, equitably, and objectively. Over time, the teacher gradually makes students more responsible for monitoring and regulating their own behavior.

Reflecting on Your Current Beliefs and Practices

Before examining the strategies in this module, take some time to examine your current beliefs and practices by answering the following questions:

1. How consistent are you in enforcing positive and negative consequences regarding rules and procedures?

_____

_____

_____

_____

2. To what extent do you maintain a sense of emotional objectivity when working with difficult students?

_____

_____

_____

_____

3. To what extent do you maintain a cool exterior in difficult situations with students?

_____

_____

_____

_____

Recommendations for Classroom Practice

This module addresses the following strategies for Design Question 8:

- Consistently enforcing positive and negative consequences
- Projecting a sense of emotional objectivity
- Maintaining a cool exterior

Consistently Enforcing Positive and Negative Consequences

As suggested in previous modules, effective teachers establish clear learning goals, rules and procedures, and positive and negative consequences related to those rules and procedures. These strategies were addressed in Modules 16 and 17 in the discussion of Design Question 6. Effective teachers strive to ensure that their students perceive them as clear about the behavior they expect, and consistent and fair in the implementation of rules and procedures.

Although teachers might do a good job of initially articulating consequences regarding rules and procedures, if they do not consistently execute the established consequences, students soon conclude that consequences are not a serious part of classroom management. One way to ensure consistency in the execution of consequences is to engage in daily self-reflection by asking and answering questions like the following:

- Did I take every opportunity today to provide positive and negative consequences for student behavior?
- Did I strike a nice balance between positive and negative consequences as needed?

In addition to being consistent in the execution of positive and negative consequences, a teacher should also expect more and more of students in maintaining and controlling their own behaviors.

Examples

Fourth Grade Social Studies. Students this year are studying their state's history, including the role of law in their community, region, and state. Their teacher uses students' personal experiences and reactions as a springboard for discussing these topics. Whenever students fail to adhere to rules and consequences within the classroom, she uses the opportunity to talk about such concepts as equity, fairness, and ethical responsibility. She also uses end-of-lesson closure time to have students reflect on the class that day and the extent to which positive and negative consequences were both timely and appropriate. The teacher asks them questions such as the following: *Were you properly acknowledged when you followed our classroom rules and procedures? Did we apply appropriate consequences when rules were broken? How is the way we are conducting our class activities similar to a microsociety? How do we use our classroom rules and procedures in a way parallel to how communities and states use law and law enforcement?*

Middle School English/Language Arts. As one of their themes in literature this year, students in this class are exploring human actions, reactions, and consequences. They analyze characters' motivations and evaluate the extent to which the characters follow—or fail to follow—appropriate behavioral pathways. Whenever individual students or small groups appear inconsistent in following classroom rules and procedures, this teacher objectively but creatively integrates a discussion of consequences to human behavior and the choices we make as human beings. Gradually, students experience a powerful connection between their individual behavior and how it affects others, including the classroom as a learning community. This teacher also makes certain that the theme of actions and timely consequences becomes a periodic topic for students' personal writing, journal entries, and formal narrative and expository compositions.

Activity Box

At which are you better: consistently enforcing positive consequences or consistently enforcing negative consequences? What are some ideas you have for enhancing your weaker area?

Projecting a Sense of Emotional Objectivity

Projecting a sense of emotional objectivity is difficult for everyone in at least some situations. It is important to remember that emotions are natural and inevitable. Specifically, some students will elicit more of a negative response than others. Marzano and colleagues (2005) recommend the following process to help teachers examine why they might react negatively to certain students:

1. Mentally review the students in your class, noting your emotional reaction to each student.

2. For those students who arouse negative thoughts or emotions, spend some time trying to identify the specifics of your reactions. What specific negative thoughts do you have about those students? What specific negative emotions do you have about those students?

3. Try to identify events in your past that may be the source of your negative thoughts and emotions about those students. Does a specific student remind you of a previous student with whom you have had difficulty or a specific negative event that happened? (p. 88)

After identifying students who trigger negative emotions, teachers next try to reframe their beliefs about these students. Reframing is simply an attempt to view students' actions in a way that gives them the benefit of the doubt. Instead of viewing students' misbehavior as a personal attack, it is interpreted as a lack of self-assurance or control, both of which are not personal to the teacher.

Additionally, teachers must know their "hot buttons" and emotional triggers to maintain appropriate emotional distance from disciplinary incidents. Effective teachers continually look for ways to ensure they are thinking clearly about disciplinary issues and seek out ways to interact more productively with students.

Examples

Ninth Grade Spanish. This teacher loves the Spanish language and relishes opportunities to share the richness of cultural traditions, world regions, and history associated with regions of the world in which Spanish is spoken. However, she notices that when her students seem less than interested or fail to show the same level of enthusiasm she does—particularly when learning more complex linguistic concepts and principles—she tends to become angry, defensive, and defeated. She realizes that she needs to address this automatic response on her part. Therefore, she implements a plan to bring a sense of balance and objectivity to her reactions. When students fail to respond the way she would like, for example, she reframes her reactions, striving to explain her students' behaviors in a more empathetic and positive light, giving them the benefit of the doubt. She also becomes much more aware of her own hot buttons and emotional triggers, searching for ways to be clearer in her thinking, interpretations, and interactions with her 9th grade students.

Seventh Grade Mathematics. Early-adolescent students are wonderfully expressive and energetic, but they can also challenge their teachers and push their hot buttons fairly frequently. This 7th grade mathematics teacher finds himself experiencing a higher level of stress than usual. He examines what is happening in his classroom and in his reactions to students' behavior. He discovers that he frequently misinterprets students' motives and reactions. He realizes that his higher-than-usual levels of stress seem to result from a combination of family and classroom problems. Because of conflicts with his teenage son, he seems to be projecting his frustrations onto the adolescent males in his classroom. He makes a commitment to himself and his students to do a better job of monitoring his thoughts and emotions, examining his reactions to each student, and identifying the sources of his negative thoughts and emotions. Over the course of several weeks, his commitment to a higher level of awareness of both how and why he is reacting results in a heightened sense of objectivity and self-recognition. He becomes less stressed and much more capable of dealing with disruptions professionally and efficiently.

Activity Box

How would you rate your ability to portray a sense of emotional objectivity? Good? OK, but could be improved? Poor? What are some ideas you have for your classroom practice?

Maintaining a Cool Exterior

The final strategy to communicate appropriate levels of guidance and control involves teachers maintaining a cool exterior even when they are stressed internally. We advocate that teachers project a classroom demeanor that avoids extremes, especially when they are angry with a student. Of course, it is most difficult to maintain a cool exterior when dealing with a student who is agitated. Marzano and colleagues (2005) recommend the following teacher behaviors when dealing with a student who is agitated or on the verge of agitation:

- Speaking directly to the student in a calm and respectful tone
- Looking directly at the student without glaring or staring
- Maintaining an appropriate distance from the student
- Being conscious of the look on your face—keeping your facial expressions neutral (p. 89)

Marzano and colleagues (2005) also recommend *avoiding* the following teacher behaviors because they tend to provoke fear and anger in students:

- Pointing a finger at the student or shaking your fist at the student
- Raising your voice as you speak
- Squinting your eyes
- Moving toward or hovering over the student (p. 89)

Examples

A Second Grade Instructor. This first-year teacher has always dreamed of becoming an educator, but her first few weeks in the classroom have significantly challenged her expectations. She finds herself letting her emotional reactions get the better of her, often resulting in her students pressing back through tantrums and acting-out behaviors. Through the support of an assigned teacher mentor and professional coach, she develops an action plan for communicating a cool but caring demeanor with her students. While training herself to guard against volatile behaviors such as a raised tone of voice, glaring, or ridiculing disruptive students, she improves her ability to speak directly in a calm and respectful tone of voice. To project a sense of calm and objectivity, she looks directly at misbehaving students with appropriate facial gestures and physical distance. She also improves her sustained ability to use a calm and even tone of voice, commenting on observed behaviors rather than verbalizing her interpretations of students' motives.

Fifth Grade Science. The board of education for this teacher's school district has recently provided extensive new funding for the implementation of a science curriculum in intermediate classrooms. Part of this initiative involves students engaging in experimental-inquiry tasks via cooperative learning scenarios, simulations, and lab experiences. Because students are so new to these kinds of learning experiences, they lack the self-control and self-monitoring skills needed to work in small groups using a range of new scientific instruments and materials. Therefore, part of the professional development for implementing this new science curriculum involves training in strategies for teachers to establish and sustain emotional objectivity during science labs and other learning tasks. For example, science teachers are encouraged to discuss rules and procedures before every science class. Students discuss how they can contribute to the learning process and not distract from it. Teachers are also asked to point out specific student behaviors they consider to be offensive, disruptive, or inappropriate, framing feedback to students using "I messages" and reinforcing consensus-driven rules and processes. Teachers are also encouraged to identify their own instinctive or impulsive reactions associated with students' demonstration of offensive behaviors. They receive coaching in how to use a calm and even tone of voice when commenting on observed behaviors rather than presenting students with predetermined interpretations of their motives.

Activity Box

Describe a time when you didn't project a cool exterior. What were the consequences? What ideas do you have for your classroom practice?

Checking for Understanding

Use the following rating scale to assess your current level of understanding of key strategies and processes presented in this module:

4 = I understand and already fully implement this strategy in my classroom.

3 = I understand this strategy, but I need to practice using it in my classroom.

2 = I can explain this strategy, but I am not fully confident that I can use it.

1 = I do not understand this strategy, and I do not currently use it in my classroom.

___1. Consistently enforcing positive and negative consequences
Based on my rating, I may need to revisit the following:

___ 2. Projecting a sense of emotional objectivity
Based on my rating, I may need to revisit the following:

___ 3. Maintaining a cool exterior
Based on my rating, I may need to revisit the following:

Design Question 9

What Will I Do to Communicate
High Expectations for All Students?

Module 22

Identifying High-Expectancy
and Low-Expectancy Students

Module 23

Changing Behavior Toward
Low-Expectancy Students

Design Question 9

What Will I Do to Communicate High Expectations for All Students?

Module 22

Identifying High-Expectancy and Low-Expectancy Students

Research confirms that a teacher's beliefs about a student's chances of success in school influence how that teacher acts toward that student, which, in turn, influences the student's achievement. If a teacher believes that a particular student cannot succeed, the teacher might unwittingly behave in ways that subvert that student's success—or at least do not facilitate that student's success.

Key ways that teachers—often unconsciously—communicate expectations to their students include their (1) affective tone (i.e., the extent to which the teacher establishes positive emotions in the classroom and reinforces cooperative behavior) and (2) quality of interactions with students (i.e., behaviors such as creating more output opportunities for high-expectancy students when answering questions or responding to learning tasks). As long as students receive differential treatment regarding affective tone and quality of interactions, a teacher is not providing fair and equitable learning opportunities for all students. Obviously, teachers must strive to exhibit equal behavior with high- and low-expectancy students.

Changes in teachers' behavior toward students begin with identifying and understanding their expectations regarding students. Once differential expectations are identified, behavior can be modified. This module (Module 22) addresses specific steps teachers can take to identify those students for whom they have low expectations, how they are treating them differentially, and why they are treating them differentially. In the next module (Module 23) we address how to adjust behavior toward low-expectancy students.

Reflecting on Your Current Beliefs and Practices

Before examining the strategies in this module, take some time to examine your current beliefs and practices by answering the following questions:

1. In your opinion, how are expectations and student achievement related? How do you communicate your expectation levels for your students?

_____

_____

_____

_____

2. In your opinion, why do some students perceive themselves as "low expectancy"?

_____

_____

_____

_____

3. How do students' self-perceptions affect their performance and achievement?

_____

_____

_____

_____

4. How can educators help students to develop a sense of efficacy and high expectations for themselves?

_____

_____

_____

_____

Recommendations for Classroom Practice

This module addresses the following strategies for Design Question 9:

- Identifying expectation levels for students
- Identifying differential treatment of low-expectancy students
- Identifying the basis for differential expectations

Identifying Expectation Levels for Students

It is critical for teachers to become aware of their differential expectations for students. Although it can be disconcerting at times, this step helps teachers determine if they have any systematic bias regarding specific students. The process is simple. A teacher simply goes through her class list and asks herself, "How well do I expect this student to perform?" At this stage, the teacher inquires no further. Her purpose is simply to identify a differential pattern of expectations for her students.

A simple tool to this end is for a teacher to imagine that she has administered a comprehensive test on some of the more difficult content addressed in her class. As she goes through her class roster, she puts an *H* (High) next to the name of any student whom she imagines will do well on the test, an *L* (Low) next to the name of any student whom she imagines will do poorly, and *DK* (Don't Know) if she can't decide.

Examples

A New Middle School English Teacher. This teacher is new to both her middle school and the profession of teaching. She has been assigned to an urban site with a student population from a diverse range of ethnic, racial, cultural, and socioeconomic traditions and backgrounds. During the first few days of class, she realizes that she has quickly formed negative opinions about some students. Working closely with the teacher mentor assigned to her, this teacher commits to mentally examining her perceptions about students. She identifies a handful of students who she has already decided will probably not do well in class.

An Experienced High School History Teacher. This teacher has taught at this particular high school for several decades. Once considered to be an outstanding educator, he is discovering that as times change, he feels a need to examine whether his teaching has changed to meet the needs of his students. A particularly revealing focus point for him is the disparity in grades he assigns among certain classes he teaches. He notices that in those classrooms where his students demonstrate behaviors he associates with "the good old days" (e.g., conformity, group responsiveness, attentiveness regardless of assignment or task requirements), he tends to teach with higher levels of rigor and expectation. When he invites a colleague to observe his lower-performing classes, however, the observation data reveal that he tends to present less rigorous assignments and ask fewer open-ended questions.

Activity Box

List the students in your class for whom you have high expectations and the students in your class for whom you have low expectations.

Identifying Differential Treatment of Low-Expectancy Students

Teachers can communicate expectations for students in two general ways. One part of communicating expectations involves the affective tone that is established with students. Affective tone involves the emotional and relational interpretations students make in response to a teacher's tone of voice, proximity to them, and gestures made to emphasize an idea or a point. A teacher communicates a positive affective tone by eye contact, smiles, proximity, and playful dialogue with students. Expectations are also communicated by the range of questions posed to students. In general, more complex and robust questions are asked of higher-expectancy students. In addition, expectations are communicated by feedback provided to students after they have answered a question along with the follow-up probing and coaching.

Low-expectancy behaviors by the teacher can have a dramatic effect on students. Many withdraw, disengage, and fail to achieve because they lack a sense of efficacy. "If this teacher feels I can't do it, then I probably can't," a low-expectancy student may think. Amplify that reaction in that same student across multiple classes, and the problem becomes even more significant. Eventually the low-expectancy student may give up on school altogether.

Once teachers become aware that they, in fact, have different expectations for students, the next step is to identify how they treat them differently. One way to determine this is for teachers to keep track of their behavior with low-expectancy students for a few days or perhaps an entire week. A simple recording sheet like that in Figure 22.1 can be used. This informal observation form has a column for the names of low-expectancy students who are being observed. It has a column for observations regarding behaviors related to affective tone and a column that deals with behaviors related to the quality of interactions with students. Using this simple form, a teacher would make observations for a few days (or more) and then generate conclusions regarding how low-expectancy students are being treated differently.

FIGURE 22.1

Informal Observation Form for Teacher Expectations

Student Name	My Behavior in Terms of Affective Tone	My Behavior in Terms of Quality Interactions
Hank	I noticed that I didn't make eye contact with Hank.	I called on Hank once in class but didn't stay with him long.
Nancy	I talked to her briefly before class began, but I don't usually do this.	She never raised her hand, and I never called on her.

Examples

Fourth Grade Science. This teacher tends to favor experiential learning opportunities for his students, engaging all learners in science labs and field experiences involving observation, data collection, and analysis. However, when he collaborates with a colleague to design interdisciplinary projects involving language arts and science, his colleague informs him that she has observed certain differential treatment patterns when he interacts with certain students. Although initially taken aback with this assertion, he asks her to observe the next several science/language arts lessons they coteach and share her insights with him. The results are both eye opening and profound for him. His colleague shows him a sociogram she has completed for the two lessons. Clearly, the number of times she has observed him showing humor or moving toward certain students and asking higher-order questions of those same groups of students reveals an unconscious pattern of high and low expectancy. Together, they collaborate on ways in which he can make more eye contact, display physical proximity, and ask higher-order questions and follow-up responses of all students. After using this process for a month, both teachers agree that they see much more engaged and committed learning by a majority of the students they coteach.

Middle School Pre-Algebra. Teachers in this middle school are becoming increasingly anxious about their students' scores on standardized tests, particularly in mathematics. Therefore, they collaborate regularly on strategies and activities designed to enhance the achievement of their students. However, it is only after examining disaggregated test data patterns that the members of the mathematics department begin to reveal patterns of high expectation versus low expectation within and across various classrooms. The department as a whole institutes a process to identify differential treatment of low-expectancy students. The teachers each identify a minimum of five low-performing students in their individual classrooms and record their observations of their treatment of these students. After each teacher has created generalizations about the treatment of low-expectancy students, the department as a whole and teachers as individuals make plans for how to change treatment of low-expectancy students.

Activity Box

List some ways you treat your high-expectancy students differently from your low-expectancy students.

Identifying the Basis for Differential Expectations

Perhaps the hardest part of examining one's expectations is examining the underlying reasons. Certainly it is reasonable that a teacher might have lower expectations for students who do not perform well in the beginning stages of a class. However, as students demonstrate increased competence, this opinion should abate. This behavior by a teacher would *not* be an example of systematic differential treatment. What a teacher is looking for here is systematic patterns of expectations based on features like a student's ethnicity, appearance, verbal patterns, socioeconomic status, and the like.

The first step is to look for differential patterns of treatment of students, as discussed in the previous section. The next step is more difficult, more private, and potentially more intimidating. Here teachers note if they have any generalized low expectations for students because of the students' ethnicity, socioeconomic status, and the like. It is important to remember that if teachers do discover such patterns, it does not mean they are racists or bigots. According to *The Art and Science of Teaching*, all adults probably have preconceived notions regarding groups of people, simply because they were influenced by the biases and generalizations of the people with whom they interacted as children. As explained in *The Art and Science of Teaching*, these patterns of thought are very difficult to change because they are reactions that have been reinforced over many years. One might say that a bigot or a racist is one who knowingly or unknowingly behaves in accordance with such patterns. However, an individual who actively seeks to behave in a manner that is not controlled by biased patterns is anything but a bigot or a racist. To this end then, teachers can freely admit to themselves the existence of negative thought patterns and perhaps even try to ascertain the origin of these behaviors. For example, a teacher might discover that she has predetermined negative expectations for all students of a specific race and a specific socioeconomic status. Simply recognizing this tendency can provide some power over such patterns of thought.

Examples

Primary Music Class. A primary music teacher has noticed that she treats certain students differently in terms of her affective behavior and when she is interacting with them about the content in class. While looking for patterns with these students, she quickly notices that her low-expectancy students are all from lower-income families—they do not dress as well as other students in this predominately upper-middle-class school. Upon further scrutiny, she realizes that she has an assumption that becoming a good musician requires support from home and that children who come from low-income families will not receive the necessary support. Uncomfortable with this realization, she resolves to change her behavior toward those students.

Secondary Mathematics Teacher. A secondary mathematics instructor teaching an open-enrollment AP course notices that he has low expectations for a certain group of students who enrolled. All of these students tend to dress like gang members. He soon realizes that when the school initiated open access to advanced courses, he had a thought that "these types of students will ruin his AP class." He is initially embarrassed about his preconceived biases, but he resolves to do something about them.

Activity Box

What are your patterns of thought regarding low-expectancy students? For what specific types of students do you have low expectations? Where do you think these patterns and biases come from?

Checking for Understanding

Use the following rating scale to assess your current understanding and comfort level regarding key strategies and processes presented in this module:

4 = I understand and already fully implement this strategy in my classroom.

3 = I understand this strategy, but I need to practice using it in my classroom.

2 = I can explain this strategy, but I am not fully confident that I can use it.

1 = I do not understand this strategy, and I do not currently use it in my classroom.

___ 1. Identifying your expectations for all students
Based on my rating, I may need to revisit the following:

___ 2. Identifying differential treatment of low-expectancy students
Based on my rating, I may need to revisit the following:

___ 3. Identifying the basis for differential expectations
Based on my rating, I may need to revisit the following:

Design Question 9

What Will I Do to Communicate High Expectations for All Students?

Module 23

Changing Behavior Toward Low-Expectancy Students

Once teachers have identified their patterns of differential behavior toward low-expectancy students and explored the reasons for these patterns, they should move quickly to change their behavior. In fact, teachers can and should work on changing their behavior as soon as they notice that it is different from student to student. A consoling thought a teacher might keep in mind is that students cannot know what a teacher is thinking. Therefore, if a teacher has systematic biases, students will never be privy to those thoughts. However, students will interpret everything the teacher does and does not do as an indication of the teacher's opinions about them. This is good news in a sense. Even if teachers have low expectations regarding particular students, they can immediately begin to behave in a way that communicates high expectations.

Reflecting on Your Current Beliefs and Practices

Before examining the strategies in this module, take some time to examine your beliefs and practices by answering the following questions:

1. How might you change your current behavior toward low-expectancy students in terms of verbal and nonverbal communication of acceptance and respect?

_____

_____

_____

_____

_____

2. How might you change your questioning patterns with low-expectancy students?

_____

_____

_____

_____

3. How might you change your behavior patterns with low-expectancy students after they have answered a question incorrectly?

_____

_____

_____

_____

Recommendations for Classroom Practice

This module addresses the following strategies for Design Question 9:

- Using verbal and nonverbal indicators to communicate to students that they are valued and respected
  - Using questions to reinforce high expectations for all students
  - Responding to incorrect or incomplete responses to questions and tasks

Communicating to Students That They Are Valued and Respected

If teachers identify low-expectancy students in their school or classroom, they should strive to consciously and systematically behave in ways that convey that all learners are valued and respected. As we have seen, verbal and nonverbal actions can communicate a positive affective tone or a negative affective tone. For example, frequent eye contact overtly signals to students that they are an important part of classroom activities and the learning process. Lack of eye contact might convey the opposite message. Similarly, smiling at appropriate times enhances student motivation and engagement and contributes significantly to establishing a positive affective tone. Again, lack of smiling might convey the opposite message.

Teachers can also use occasional hand and body gestures to confirm acceptance of either individual students or the class as a whole. For example, a teacher can communicate a sense of acceptance by maintaining appropriate proximity to students. This requires teachers to circulate through various quadrants of their classroom on a regular basis, ensuring that all students—especially those in the back—are physically close to their teacher at various times.

When appropriate, a teacher should engage in playful dialogue with target students to enhance their sense of acceptance. Humor in a variety of forms can also reinforce student learning and promote a genuine sense that everyone in the class is respected and expected to succeed.

Examples

Eighth Grade United States History. This teacher has observed that some students in his classroom seem consistently alienated or disengaged from the rich variety of hands-on activities he incorporates into his teaching. The underperforming students enjoy the opportunity for experiential learning he provides, but they collectively feel less valued and respected than their more participatory peers. "You seem to like some of the class more than you like us," one of them declares. The teacher vows to be more consistent in sending out both verbal and nonverbal indications that all students are valued. He manages to ensure equitable eye contact with all learners and uses smiles, tone of voice, and proximity to acknowledge his respect for everyone in the class. In addition, he expands the level of playful banter and joking with underachieving students. The result is a markedly improved classroom climate and tone. Many students comment on how much more comfortable they feel in his classroom.

Fourth Grade Mathematics. This elementary teacher does not feel as comfortable teaching mathematics to her students as she does teaching them reading and language arts. As the year progresses, she realizes that the discomfort translates into a greater sense of rigidity and control during mathematics lessons. She comes to see that only the most cooperative and docile students in her class receive positive affirmation that they are valued or respected. After discovering her patterns of rewarding some students but detaching herself from others, she develops and implements an action plan to address this issue. An especially important part of her action plan is to provide individual recognition and affirmation to specific learners, particularly those for whom she has low expectations. She commits to smiling more at some students, standing closer to others, and monitoring individual student reactions. Perhaps most significantly, she discovers which interventions are most effective with specific low-expectancy students.

Activity Box

What nonverbal or verbal behaviors do you use to communicate affection toward students? What are some new techniques you might try, particularly with low-expectancy students?

Using Questions to Reinforce High Expectations for All Students

The questioning strategies used by a teacher play a very significant role in how students perceive themselves and how well they understand curriculum content. Specifically, teachers must ensure that the same quality of interactions is available to all students. At a basic level, the frequency of questions must be roughly the same from student to student. Similarly, all students must have the opportunity to respond to comparable levels of higher-order questions. Stated differently, teachers should not systematically ask harder questions of high-expectancy students. Parallel and comparable levels of follow-up probing and requests for evidence to support claims should also be a regular part of equitable classroom practice. Finally, teachers should avoid rewarding some students for less rigorous responses than those of their peers.

Examples

Secondary U.S. History. Teachers are struggling with a recently mandated high school accountability exam dealing with students' knowledge of U.S. history. In particular, students seem to have the greatest difficulty answering higher-order questions, particularly the constructed-response items on this exam. When they share insights and observations about student performance, the teachers recognize that there seems to be an inequitable distribution of questioning types in different classes. The differences appear to be closely aligned with the school's ability-level grouping system. In what are perceived to be "lower-ability-level" classrooms, teachers observe a tendency to emphasize factual-recall questions that stress student retention of information. In "college-bound" and "gifted" classrooms, however, most questions tend to skew toward the higher levels of thinking. The entire department commits to expanding their use of higher-order questions in all classrooms. They also decide to discuss question types and response follow-ups directly with their students. As a result, aggregate test scores improve greatly during the academic year. Disaggregated data analysis reveals that in what had been perceived to be "lower-level" classrooms, the expanded use of higher-order questions and related coaching strategies markedly improves test scores.

Fourth Grade. In this school, many male students show a decrease in academic achievement as they transition from 3rd to 4th grade, paralleling a national phenomenon. Teachers are both concerned and committed to effecting a change to eliminate this achievement gap. Therefore, they collaborate on a 4th grade action research project in which they assess the effect of changing rates of student questioning and the types of questions all students are asked to answer. Each teacher also commits to expanding the base of students who regularly respond to questions. For example, they eliminate predictable behavior related to calling on students, instead choosing to frequently call on students who have not raised their hands. They also create a data management system in which they give a check mark every time they call on a particular student and notate the type of question they ask. All of the teachers commit to raising students' perceptions of teacher expectations of them by systematically asking challenging questions of everyone in the classroom. The final action research summary report reveals a dramatic increase in motivation, engagement, and achievement levels in all classrooms, with the most dramatic increases occurring among students originally perceived as underachieving or underperforming.

Activity Box

What are some things you can do to ensure that low-expectancy students are asked difficult questions?

Responding to Incorrect or Incomplete Responses to Questions and Tasks

Inevitably, all students will at some point give an incorrect or incomplete response to a question or an assigned task. Unfortunately, teachers may vary their levels of response to such errors, depending on the expectancy level of the student with whom they are interacting. Teachers should spend as much time with low-expectancy students as they do with high-expectancy students when responding to incorrect or incomplete answers to a question or task. We suggest that teachers use elaborative interrogation strategies (described in detail in Module 6) with all students. Recall from Module 6 that examples of these follow-up questions include the following: *How do you know this to be true? Why is that so? What evidence can you give us to support that conclusion?* It is also important for teachers to use what students have communicated about what they understand—and do not understand—to help them overcome gaps and misinformation. Finally, there are a variety of general strategies teachers can use when responding to incorrect or incomplete responses from students, particularly low-expectancy students. These strategies include the following:

- Demonstrate gratitude for students' responses.
- Don't allow negative comments from other students.
- Point out what is correct and incorrect about students' responses.
- Restate the question.
- Provide ways to *temporarily* let students off the hook (e.g., "I'll give you time to think about that, and then I'll come back to you").

Examples

World Geography. Teaching a course with a high level of information can be a challenge, especially when also attempting to ensure both equity and excellence in the classroom. Many students in this teacher's classroom demonstrate a range of low-expectancy behaviors, especially a tendency to respond incorrectly to questions requiring their use of declarative knowledge (i.e., information such as facts, generalizations, and principles). He decides to work with students to "unpack" their thinking and identify the logic of their responses in light of content knowledge he has taught them. Therefore, he implements a system of elaborative interrogations in which he poses questions such as these: "Why do you think this to be true?" or "Tell me why you think that is so." This process allows the teacher to articulate basic generalizations the student has about the content and provide on-the-spot coaching to students to help them correct misunderstandings and reframe their knowledge and understandings.

Seventh Grade Life Science. This teacher has become tired of the many examples of students' failing to respond correctly to both knowledge/recall questions and questions requiring higher-order reasoning. She commits herself to developing and implementing an action plan to improve her students' ability to respond to a variety of question structures and follow-up probes. Her plan includes a range of simple but easy-to-use strategies, including showing gratitude for students' responses, not allowing negative comments from other students, and reframing student answers (emphasizing both what is correct and what is incorrect). This teacher also expands her use of question restatements and peer coaching and collaboration. The results are impressive, with a greatly expanded pool of students who are actively involved in responding to teacher-posed questions as well as providing accurate and correct answers with clear support for their conclusions.

Activity Box

What errors have you made in the past when responding to incorrect or partial responses by low-expectancy students?

Checking for Understanding

Use the following rating scale to assess your current understanding and comfort level regarding the key strategies and processes presented in this module:

4 = I understand and already fully implement this strategy in my classroom.
3 = I understand this strategy, but I need to practice using it in my classroom.
2 = I can explain this strategy, but I am not fully confident that I can use it.
1 = I do not understand this strategy, and I do not currently use it in my classroom.

____ 1.   Using verbal and nonverbal indicators to communicate to students that they are valued and respected
Based on my rating, I may need to revisit the following:

____ 2.   Using questions to reinforce high expectations for all students
Based on my rating, I may need to revisit the following:

____ 3.   Responding to incorrect or incomplete responses to questions and tasks
Based on my rating, I may need to revisit the following:

Design Question 10

What Will I Do to Develop Effective Lessons
Organized into a Cohesive Unit?

Module 24

Identifying the Focus of a Unit

Module 25

Developing Effective Lessons

Design Question 10

What Will I Do to Develop Effective Lessons Organized into a
Cohesive Unit?

Module 24

Identifying the Focus of a Unit

The first nine design questions in *The Art and Science of Teaching* deal with specific classroom behaviors. The 10th question is an omnibus question in that it asks how a teacher can use the previous nine questions to design effective lessons and then organize those lessons into a cohesive unit. There are a number of elements involved in such deliberation. One of the first is to think in terms of the overall focus of a unit. The focus of a unit can take one of three directions: (1) a focus on knowledge, (2) a focus on issues, or (3) a focus on student exploration. Each focus has implications as to how a unit plays out in terms of daily activities.

Each focus has a certain logic to it, and each has its own personality. A focus on knowledge is consistent with the current emphasis on standards. Acquisition of new information and skill is the driving force. A focus on issues places new knowledge in a supportive role. New information and skill is useful insofar as it helps illuminate an issue that is being examined. A focus on student exploration puts student interests at the center of planning. No set of issues or body of knowledge is preeminent. Rather, new knowledge and issues are used as stimuli to help students generate ideas and study topics of interest to them.

Reflecting on Your Current Beliefs and Practices

Before examining the strategies in this module, take some time to examine your current beliefs and practices by answering the following questions:

1. When you plan a unit of instruction, to what extent do you make enhancing students' understanding of subject-matter knowledge the focus of the unit?

_____

_____

_____

_____

2. When you plan a unit of instruction, to what extent do you make enhancing students' understanding of issues regarding subject-matter knowledge the focus of the unit?

_____

_____

_____

_____

3. When you plan a unit of instruction, to what extent do you make students' exploration of subject-matter content the focus of the unit?

_____

_____

_____

_____

Recommendations for Classroom Practice

This module addresses the following strategies for Design Question 10:

- Considering a focus on knowledge
- Considering a focus on issues
- Considering a focus on student exploration

Considering a Focus on Knowledge

A focus on knowledge might be thought of as a traditional approach in that its purpose is the development of new information and skill. This approach is in keeping with the standards movement in K–12 education. Throughout the United States, states have identified standards in multiple subject areas that are to be the focus of instruction. Figure 24.1 lists some typical standards statements for various subject areas at various grade levels.

FIGURE 24.1
Typical Standards Statements

Subject Area	Typical Content Found in State Standards Documents
History Grade 3	The student knows how a farm family from the early 1800s experienced daily life (e.g., work, clothing, tools, food, and food production).
Geography Grade 10	The student knows how the physical environment is affected by changes in human technology or behavior (e.g., changes in runoff and sediment, degradation of soil and air quality, habitat destruction, alterations in the hydrologic cycle, and increases in world temperatures).
Mathematics Grade 7	The student knows how number systems with bases other than 10 are structured (e.g., base 60 for telling time and measuring angles, Roman numerals for dates and clock faces).
Technology Grade 6	The student uses multiple Internet databases to expand on issues of interest.

When the focus of a unit is on knowledge, the learning goals come right from the standards statements. For example, the following goal might be designed from the 3rd grade history content in Figure 24.1:

> Students will describe the following things about farm families in the early 1800s:
> - The types of work they did
> - The types of clothes they wore
> - The types of tools they used
> - The types of food they ate and how they obtained their food

Similarly, the following learning goal might be designed for the 10th grade geography content in Figure 24.1:

> Students will explain how air quality in the city has been affected by population growth over the last 10 years.

Note that these goals address declarative knowledge and use verbs that specify how students will demonstrate their understanding (see Module 2).

As these examples illustrate, when the focus of a unit is on knowledge, learning goals are created by identifying specific components of the content in state standards documents. Addressing Design Question 1, then, is a fairly straightforward process when the focus is on knowledge. Teachers analyze benchmark statements from standards documents and design the goal or goals for a unit.

Within a unit that focuses on knowledge, Design Questions 2, 3, and 4 also focus directly on the knowledge and tend to play out in sequential order. That is, critical-input lessons come first and provide students with basic information about the knowledge goal or goals. To illustrate, consider the science goal regarding understanding how air quality has been affected by population growth over the last 10 years. Using Design Question 2, the teacher would provide some critical-input experiences that provide students with basic information such as the following:

- The characteristics of high-, medium-, and low-quality air
- The different ways population growth can affect the environment
- The different ways the environment can affect air quality

Next, using Design Question 3, the teacher would construct lessons that help students deepen their knowledge. These lessons might involve comparison and contrast activities and activities that require students to analyze the logic of information. Finally, using Design Question 4, the teacher would engage students in an experimental-inquiry task, a problem-solving task, a decision-making task, or an investigative task that is aimed at elaborating on students' understanding of the knowledge goal. For example, the teacher might provide students with the following investigative task:

Describe what you think would happen if the population of the city doubled over the next two years. Make sure you back up your conclusions with specific details about the relationship between changes in the environment and the quality of air.

Although this task requires students to apply what they have learned, its intent is to deepen their understanding of air quality, the various ways population growth can affect the environment, and the various ways the environment can affect air quality.

Examples

Primary Language Arts. The learning goal for this primary language arts teacher is for students to learn a general strategy for determining the meaning of words encountered while reading. During the initial lessons, students are presented with a clear model of the strategy. These critical-input experiences are immediately followed by a series of practice sessions in which students fine-tune and shape the new strategy. Finally, the teacher has students do a problem-solving task in which some of the aspects of the strategy can't be easily used due to the nature of the text. After this task is completed, the students reflect on how they might have to revise the strategy with different types of texts.

High School Art. The learning goal for this unit is for students to understand the characteristics of impressionism. The first few lessons provide students with information about the defining characteristics of impressionism. These are followed by lessons in which students compare impressionist paintings with other types they have studied. At the end of the unit, students do a project in which they experiment with different impressionist techniques as they create their own paintings. This task is designed to further develop students' understanding of impressionism.

Activity Box

Consider a unit you have presented in the past and describe how it would be organized if it were focused on knowledge.

Considering a Focus on Issues

When the focus of a unit is on issues, knowledge is still important. Using the previous geography example, the teacher would still have goals regarding how air quality is affected by population growth. However, given the focus on issues, the teacher would have an additional goal such as the following:

> Students will analyze the values and beliefs that encourage or underlie population growth.

A focus on issues usually involves the examination of attitudes, beliefs, or values that are the causes of a specific event or a specific situation—in this case, population growth. The sample learning goal illustrates this in that students are asked to examine the beliefs and values that support population growth. A variation of this learning goal would be one that requires students to compare and contrast the values underlying two perspectives around a controversial issue. For example, assume that a social studies teacher is preparing a unit on the two-party political system (i.e., Democratic versus Republican) used in the United States. Although the teacher will certainly want students to master some knowledge goals regarding the characteristics of the two-party system, she will also want students to understand why some people join a political party and some remain independent. Consequently, the teacher would construct a goal such as the following:

> Students will explore the underlying reason why some people join political parties and others remain independent, and examine their own tendencies.

Notice that the learning goal requires students to examine their own tendencies. This is probably one of the most powerful aspects of a focus on issues—it can be used as a vehicle with which students examine their own beliefs and values. To facilitate this type of analysis the teacher might assign a Design Question 4 task like the following:

> Describe what you think would happen if our country had not developed political parties. Then take and defend a position regarding whether parties are useful or detrimental to a democratic form of government.

A unit of instruction that focuses on issues has a different syntax from a unit focused on knowledge. With a focus on knowledge, the unit begins with the presentation of subject-matter content. A task in which students generate and test a hypothesis (Design Question 4) is presented at the end of the unit as a culminating activity. Conversely, when the focus of a unit is on issues, the unit begins with a task, like the example, involving generation and testing of a hypothesis. The issue inherent in the task frames the entire unit. Learning new subject-matter content is secondary to exploring an issue, which by definition involves exploring personal values and beliefs.

Examples

Middle School Technology. This teacher begins her unit by posing the following questions and accompanying tasks:

> Has the Internet increased or decreased the productivity of the typical worker? If you had to decide how to design an office, what provisions would you make for Internet use? Justify your decision using the criteria that formed the basis for the decision.

This decision-making task forms the basis of the entire unit. As students begin working on the task, they realize they need more information about current uses of technology. The teacher obliges by providing some critical-input lessons (Design Question 2) followed by some knowledge-deepening activities (Design Question 3). Although this new information is appreciated, the focus of the students' efforts is addressing the issue presented on the very first day.

Elementary Physical Education. This elementary physical education teacher begins her unit by presenting her 6th grade students with the following question: "Are you in shape or out of shape?" Students find that to answer this question they must determine what it means to be in shape and what it means to be out of shape for students of their age. They receive information from the teacher via critical-input lessons (Design Question 2) and knowledge-deepening lessons (Design Question 3), and then use this information to answer the initial question for themselves. Their answers are presented in a paper submitted to the teacher.

Activity Box

Consider a unit of instruction you have used before. Describe how it would look if it were organized around a focus on issues.

Considering a Focus on Student Exploration

The final type of focus for a unit of instruction is student exploration. A unit that has student exploration as its focus begins much like a unit that has knowledge as its focus in that knowledge goals are presented at the beginning of the unit. That is, the initial target of instruction appears to be learning new information and skills. However, soon after the unit has begun, the emphasis shifts. Once students begin to make progress on the initial knowledge goals, they are asked to identify a question they would like to answer or an issue they would like to explore. As described in Module 12, teachers would begin this process by posing questions like the following: "What are your initial questions and predictions about this (content/information)?"

Next the teacher would help students translate the initial questions into a specific type of task involving hypothesis generation and testing (Design Question 4) by asking stimulus questions like the following:

- Relative to my questions and predictions, is there an important hypothesis I want to test?
- Relative to my questions and predictions, is there an important problem I want to study?
- Relative to my questions and predictions, is there an important decision I want to examine?
- Relative to my questions and predictions, is there an important . . .
  - Concept I want to examine?
  - Past event I want to study?
  - Hypothetical or future event I want to examine?

By definition, a focus on student exploration requires the addition of a learning goal involving students' ability to plan and carry out an investigation. That additional learning goal might be stated in the following way:

Students will be able to identify a topic of personal interest and then plan and carry out an investigation of that topic.

This learning goal addresses procedural knowledge in that it requires students to execute the procedure of planning and carrying out an investigation.

When the focus is on student exploration, one of the main tasks of the teacher is to help students identify and construct tasks. For example, after developing students' knowledge regarding the topic of air quality and population growth, the teacher would present students with the stimulus questions in the bulleted list, offering examples of how each might be applied to the information that was introduced at the beginning of the unit. Students would then work individually or in small groups to brainstorm ideas about questions and predictions they might explore. Individual students or groups of students would then construct specific tasks they will complete by the end of the unit. For example, one student might identify the following task:

> I'm going to examine what they mean by "overpopulation." What is the number of people in the world that means we are overpopulated?

Examples

Elementary Music. The teacher begins the unit on playing the guitar by teaching some basic chords and hand positions. Once all students have a fundamental grasp of these basics, she asks each student to identify something they would like to explore about the guitar. Some students say they want to learn more about a particular artist. Others say they want to learn particular songs. Still others say they want to explore different fingering positions for the chords they have learned. The teacher helps each student translate these initial reactions into specific types of tasks involving generation and testing of hypotheses.

High School Science. After presenting information about atomic theory, this high school science teacher opens the class up to individual or group exploration. Some students want to study the development of the atomic bomb. Others want to examine the disaster at Chernobyl. Still others want to study possible changes in the use of atomic energy in the future. Students are organized into groups based on their interests. Stimulus questions provided by the teacher help the groups design specific tasks involving hypothesis generation and testing that are their focus for the unit.

Activity Box

Considering a unit you have used in the past, describe how it might look if it were focused on student exploration.

Checking for Understanding

Use the following rating scale to assess your current understanding and comfort level regarding key strategies and processes presented in this module:

> 4 = I understand and already fully implement this strategy in my classroom.
> 3 = I understand this strategy, but I need to practice using it in my classroom.
> 2 = I can explain this strategy, but I am not fully confident that I can use it.
> 1 = I do not understand this strategy, and I do not currently use it in my classroom.

____1.   A unit focused on knowledge
Based on my rating, I may need to revisit the following:

____2.   A unit focused on issues
Based on my rating, I may need to revisit the following:

____3.   A unit focused on student exploration
Based on my rating, I may need to revisit the following:

Module 25

Developing Effective Lessons

Once a focus for a unit has been developed, a teacher can think in terms of the lessons within the unit. As we have seen, three types of lessons occur in a unit: (1) lessons that focus on new knowledge—that is, lessons that involve a critical-input experience (Design Question 2); (2) lessons that focus on practicing and deepening knowledge (Design Question 3); and (3) lessons that focus on tasks involving generating and testing hypotheses (Design Question 4). Each has a different structure and, therefore, involves its own type of planning.

In addition to the types of lessons within a unit, effective planning involves considering the routine activities that will be part of a unit, such as reviewing learning goals and tracking student progress, as well as reviewing rules and procedures when necessary. Planning also involves being ready for things that might come up in every lesson, such as monitoring the extent to which students are engaged and taking action when they are not; acknowledging when rules and procedures have been followed, as well as when they have not been followed; attending to teacher-student relationships; and ensuring that students are given the message that high levels of achievement are expected from all of them. Finally, planning involves creating a flexible draft of daily activities.

Reflecting on Your Current Beliefs and Practices

Before examining the strategies in this module, take some time to examine your current beliefs and practices by answering the following questions:

1. When you plan lessons, to what extent do you plan differently for lessons that are focused on the presentation of new knowledge versus lessons that are focused on practicing and deepening knowledge versus lessons that are focused on long-term tasks that require students to generate and test hypotheses?

_____

_____

_____

_____

2. When you plan lessons, to what extent do you think in terms of routine activities that should be addressed every day?

_____

_____

_____

_____

3. When you plan lessons, to what extent do you think in terms of activities or behaviors you should be ready to execute on the spot?

_____

_____

_____

_____

4. When you plan a unit, to what extent do you develop a flexible draft of daily activities?

_____

_____

_____

_____

Recommendations for Classroom Practice

This module addresses the following strategies for Design Question 10:

- Planning for lessons focused on the presentation of new knowledge
- Planning for lessons focused on practicing and deepening knowledge
- Planning for lessons focused on tasks that involve generating and testing hypotheses
- Planning for routine activities that will be addressed systematically, or each day

- Planning for activities or behaviors that must be initiated on the spot
- Developing a flexible draft of daily activities for a unit

Planning for Lessons Focused on the Presentation of New Knowledge

An examination of Design Questions 2, 3, and 4 indicates that a lesson can have one of three foci:

- The presentation of new knowledge
- Practicing and deepening knowledge
- Tasks that require students to generate and test hypotheses

As we saw in Module 24, each of these has a distinct purpose and a distinct structure. In this section we focus on lessons generated from Design Question 2—lessons focused on the presentation of new knowledge. The purpose of lessons focused on the presentation of new knowledge is to introduce new content to students. We refer to these as critical input lessons. Obviously, for each learning goal, one or more such lessons must be developed.

To illustrate, assume that a language arts teacher has a learning goal regarding students being able to use a specific strategy for proofreading for subject-verb agreement. That learning goal might be stated in the following way:

Students will be able to proofread their essays for subject-verb agreement.

The first lesson addressing this goal would provide students with a model for proofreading for subject verb-agreement. As we saw in the modules for Design Question 2, to plan for these lessons, the teacher would consider how she will preview the strategy to help students make linkages with what they already know, how she will present the strategy in small chunks, how she will help students interact about the small chunks that have been presented, how she will help students summarize what they have learned or take notes on what they have learned, and how she will help them reflect on what they have learned.

For a strategy regarding proofreading for subject-verb agreement, one lesson focused on presenting the new skill might suffice. For some learning goals, more than one lesson might be required. To illustrate, consider the following learning goal identified by a 9th grade social studies teacher planning for a unit on the U.S. Constitution:

Students will understand and be able to explain the implication of the amendments to the U.S. Constitution with specific emphasis on how the 19th Amendment affected women in the United States.

When planning for this unit, the teacher might realize that it is best to present the new content for this learning goal in two lessons. The first critical-input lesson will address the specifics of the 19th Amendment, and the second critical-input lesson will present information about specific effects of the amendment. These two lessons would not be presented simultaneously; rather the first lesson might be followed by one or more lessons devoted to deepening students' understanding of the content.

One important thing to remember when planning for lessons involving critical-input experiences is to vary the mediums that are used to present the new content. Mediums include the following:

- Lecture
- Materials students read
- Physical demonstration
- Video or DVD presentations
- Field trips

It is probably safe to say that many teachers rely on lecture to present new content. Although this is a good medium, it is important that teachers vary the mediums they use. It is also important to remember that whatever type of medium is used, it can always be enhanced by stories and narratives provided by the teacher. Consequently, teachers should plan in a way that ensures they will use various modes of presentation.

To help plan for lessons that involve critical-input experiences, it is useful for teachers to ask themselves the following questions:

- Am I being sensitive to the need for a variety of mediums for critical-input experiences?
- How will I augment the critical-input experience by using anecdotes and narratives?
- What specific techniques will I use to ensure that students preview the content?
- How will I organize the content into small chunks?
- How will I facilitate students' discussions and interactions about the small chunks?
- What will I do to help students elaborate on the information in the small chunks?
- What will I do to help students summarize and represent the new content?
- What will I do to help students reflect on their learning?
- How will grouping be used in these activities?

Examples

High School Health. This high school health teacher is planning for a critical-input lesson regarding the effects of poor eating habits during adolescence on lifelong health. She decides that she will lecture to students but will also show some clips from a recent documentary aired on PBS. She will also tell a story about her own poor eating habits as a teenager. With these elements identified, the teacher considers how she will preview the content, organize it into small chunks, help students process information contained in the small chunks, elaborate on that information, summarize and represent the information, and finally reflect on their learning.

Elementary Physical Education. This elementary physical education teacher is planning for a critical-input lesson on how to execute an overhand throw. She will demonstrate the skill herself and show a video clip of the process broken down into fine detail. She has divided the video into three small segments or chunks. Before her lecture and the video clip, she will have students preview the content by describing times when they have played baseball. After the video, she will ask each student to draw a series of pictures or stick figures representing a good overhand throw.

Activity Box

Describe the most recent critical-input lesson you conducted. What would you do differently if you were to repeat that lesson?

Planning for Lessons Focused on Practicing and Deepening Knowledge

Design Question 3 addresses lessons focused on practicing and deepening knowledge. It is important to remember that the content in these lessons has already been introduced in a lesson devoted to introducing new knowledge via a critical-input lesson (Design Question 2). Here that knowledge is revisited, with an emphasis on practicing and deepening the new knowledge.

For the most part, each lesson focused on practice and deepening knowledge will begin with a brief review of the new content that was introduced. Practice activities typically accompany procedural knowledge. To illustrate, consider the example of teaching a proofreading strategy. This is procedural knowledge and would require practice for students to be able to use the strategy with any facility.

When a skill or strategy is first introduced, practice must be quite frequent—perhaps every day in the beginning. Consequently, the day after the teacher presents the strategy for proofreading, she would initiate a practice schedule. For example, the teacher might provide students with a brief exercise that requires them to edit for subject-verb agreement. That exercise might be based on contrived examples created by the teacher, or it might be based on an actual composition from previous students. The following day, the teacher would provide a similar exercise.

Before each exercise the teacher would review with the class the proofreading strategy and discuss possible changes and alterations in the strategy. Over time, the exercises provided by the teacher would be spaced out. Instead of providing a practice exercise every day, the teacher would wait one or more days before another exercise. The overall goal of a practice schedule that begins with exercises spaced closely together and ends with exercises spaced relatively far apart is to develop students' skills at proofreading (in this case) to a level where they can perform it somewhat automatically with relative ease and fluency.

Whereas practice is appropriate when teaching skills and strategies (i.e., procedural knowledge) such as proofreading, other types of activities are called for when information (i.e., declarative knowledge) has been the focus of a critical-input lesson. Consider the example of the critical-input experience involving information about how the 19th Amendment affected women in the United States. As opposed to "practicing" this information, the teacher would provide knowledge-deepening activities (e.g., activities involving analyzing similarities and differences, activities involving analyzing overall logic of information). Typically, far fewer knowledge-deepening activities are required for information than practice activities are required for skills and processes. Whereas teachers might have students do five or more practice activities (some of which might be assigned as homework), they might have students do only one or two knowledge-deepening activities. For example, the day after the critical-input lesson regarding the 19th Amendment, the teacher might engage students in a comparison activity in which they analyze the similarities and differences between the effect of the 19th Amendment and the effect of recent legislation that increased the minimum wage.

To ensure that the activity deepens students' knowledge, the teacher would select something with which the students are familiar to compare with the new information about the 19th Amendment. In this case, the teacher has selected an increase in the minimum wage because many students have summer jobs that pay minimum wage. A few days later, the teacher might provide students with another knowledge-deepening activity, this time one that requires students to examine the logic of a written commentary on the 19th Amendment.

Questions that teachers might ask themselves when planning for lesson segments involving practice and knowledge deepening include the following:

- What will I do to briefly review the content?
- What practice activities will I use, and what is my role during these activities?
- Am I using a variety of practice activities?
- What knowledge-deepening activities will I use, and what is my role during these activities?
- Am I using a variety of knowledge-deepening activities?
- What will the role of homework be during these activities?
- How will grouping be used in these activities?

Examples

High School Theater. This high school theater teacher has provided a few critical-input lessons in proper staging techniques. Now the teacher focuses on deepening students' understanding of these techniques. She plans to do so by providing students with a case study of how a play was staged. The students will be asked to determine which parts of the staging were done correctly and which parts were done incorrectly.

Elementary School Mathematics. Students have had some initial experience with three-column addition. Now the teacher is planning how best to help them learn this skill to the point where they can do it fluently. She sets up a three-day practice schedule. After the three days, she will continue to provide practice exercises, but they will be spaced with more time in between.

Activity Box

Describe a recent lesson you planned that involved practicing or deepening knowledge. What would you do differently if you were to do that lesson again?

Planning for Lessons Focused on Tasks That Involve Generating and Testing Hypotheses

The final type of content lesson that should be planned for involves tasks that require students to generate and test hypotheses about new content (Design Question 4). As we saw in previous modules, such tasks include the following:

- Experimental inquiry
- Problem solving
- Decision making
- Investigation (historical, projective, definitional)

To illustrate, consider the strategy for proofreading for subject-verb agreement. A task involving hypothesis generation and testing might involve asking students to identify the various types of errors that occur in subject-verb agreement and to rate each type in terms of how much trouble they have with it. This is fundamentally a definitional-investigation task in that students are required to articulate the "defining characteristics" of difficult as opposed to easy errors that must be corrected when proofreading for subject-verb agreement. To ensure that this task involves true hypothesis generation and testing, students would be required to make an initial guess as to what they will find and then verify that guess by actually analyzing their behavior when proofreading various compositions.

For the instructional goal involving the 19th Amendment, the teacher might engage students in a historical-investigation task in which they investigate controversies that surrounded the ratification of the 19th Amendment. Again, students would be asked to make some initial guesses as to what they might find and then verify the accuracy of their guesses based on the findings from their historical investigation.

Questions that a teacher might ask when planning for lesson segments involving the generation and testing of hypotheses include the following:

- What types of tasks for generating and testing hypotheses will be used?
- What will I do to facilitate the tasks?
- What will my role be during these activities?
- What will the role of homework be during these activities?
- How will grouping be used during these activities?

Examples

Middle School Social Studies. Students in this class have been studying the foundation and history of the United Nations. The teacher wants students to have a sense of how the structure of the UN allows it to do certain things but doesn't allow it to do others. She plans to engage students in a problem-solving task in which they must redesign the UN with the condition that it should make decisions in such a way that they enhance rather than hurt the global environment.

High School Visual Arts. In this high school visual arts class, students have been examining a variety of brushstroke techniques. The teacher plans an activity that will require them to decide which technique would be the best to create a specific visual effect. Each student will fill out a decision-making matrix and then defend the decision. Afterward, students will create a painting using the techniques they select.

Activity Box

To what extent do you use tasks requiring hypothesis generation and testing in your planning? What are some ideas you now have regarding changing your planning practices?

Planning for Routine Activities That Will Be Addressed Systematically, or Each Day

Planning for the three different types of content lessons (i.e., critical-input lessons, practicing and deepening lessons, and hypothesis generating and testing lessons) is certainly the focal point of unit planning. However, there are also routine activities that should be considered when planning. These include activities from Design Questions 1 and 6.

Design Question 1 asks the following: *What will I do to establish and communicate learning goals, track student progress, and celebrate success?* Although learning goals are established at the beginning of a unit, students might have to be reminded of these goals systematically or maybe even daily. Tracking student progress is something that is done pretty much every time students are assessed. If students are using the individual progress charts discussed in Module 3, then they will want to fill out those progress charts after each new formative assessment. Finally, celebrating success is something that should be done regularly. In a formatively based assessment system, teachers should be tracking gains in student knowledge. Knowledge gain can be celebrated at any point in the formative assessment process. Additionally, the teacher can develop a class progress chart by tracking the average score for students on a specific learning goal for the unit.

Questions teachers might ask themselves regarding routine activities for Design Question 1 include the following:

- *Communicating learning goals:* How will students be reminded about specific learning goals, or will new goals be set?
- *Tracking student progress on learning goals:* How will students be provided feedback (e.g., quiz, test, or informal assessment) on their progress on the learning goals for the unit? Will students be asked to record or reflect on their own progress toward learning goals?
- *Celebrating success on learning goals:* How will students be provided with some form of recognition for their progress on learning goals?

Design Question 6 asks the following: *What will I do to establish or maintain classroom rules and procedures?* Rules and procedures will be established at the beginning of the year. Students should be reminded of those rules and procedures systematically. For example, as a routine aspect of the beginning of each lesson, a teacher will have procedures for taking roll, collecting lunch money, and the like. At the end of class, a teacher might have routine procedures for passing in assignments, returning materials, and the like. In addition to systematically reviewing these procedures, it might be necessary for the teacher to change rules and procedures throughout the year. Questions that teachers might ask themselves to plan for the systematic review of rules and procedures or changes in rules and procedures include the following:

- What procedures and routines will be emphasized during this unit?
- Will students be reminded of specific rules and procedures, or will new ones be established?

Examples

Elementary Technology. An elementary school technology teacher is planning her upcoming classes for the week. She reminds herself of behaviors and activities she expects to do on a routine basis. As she goes over these behaviors and activities, she realizes that she has not reviewed classroom rules in quite a while, particularly those dealing with whole-class activities. She decides to go over these rules this week to remind students about agreed-upon expectations.

High School Economics. When reviewing routine activities, this high school economics teacher realizes he has become slack in tracking student progress regarding the two learning goals for the unit. He has not asked students to fill out their personal tracking charts in two weeks. He resolves to reinstate this practice starting tomorrow.

Activity Box

Which routine behaviors and activities do you review systematically? Which do you need to reinstate?

Planning for Activities That Must Be Initiated on the Spot

There are many behaviors that must be enacted as certain things occur in class. Such activities are addressed in Design Questions 5, 7, 8, and 9.

Design Question 5 asks the following: *What will I do to engage students?* At any moment a teacher must be prepared to employ some activity to get students engaged when their attention has been diverted or when their energy is low. Teachers might have to remind themselves about activities that might be used to reengage students. Questions teachers might ask include the following:

- What techniques for engaging students should I be ready to use during this unit?
- Am I being sensitive to the need for variety in these techniques?

Design Question 7 asks the following: *What will I do to recognize and acknowledge adherence and lack of adherence to classroom rules and procedures?* Whereas rules and procedures are established at the beginning of the school year and may be reviewed routinely during a unit of instruction, recognizing the extent to which students adhere to and do not adhere to rules and procedures must be addressed on a moment-by-moment basis. As the teacher observes the class or individual students following a specific rule or procedure, she will want to recognize this positive behavior in different ways (e.g., a positive comment or a physical gesture like "thumbs-up"). Similarly, if a teacher observes that a rule or procedure is not being followed, this too should be acknowledged on the spot in some way (e.g., a comment that makes students aware they are not following a rule or procedure; a reminder to students that there are consequences for ignoring rules and procedures).

Questions teachers might use to remind themselves of behaviors that address this issue include the following:

- What positive consequences should I be ready to implement during this unit?
- What negative consequences should I be ready to implement during this unit?
- Am I being sensitive to the need for variety in these activities?

Design Question 8 asks the following: *What will I do to establish and maintain effective relationships with students?* As discussed in Modules 20 and 21, addressing this question involves communicating both a sense of concern and cooperation and a sense of guidance and control. Behaviors that communicate concern and cooperation include using physical actions that express affection for students, making comments that indicate interest in students, and being playful with students. Behaviors that communicate a sense of guidance and control include establishing clear academic goals and establishing clear rules and procedures with accompanying positive and negative consequences. One aspect of effective relationships that teachers should monitor is the extent to which they are keeping a balance between behaviors that communicate guidance and control and those that communicate concern and cooperation. Planning questions that will help teachers address this design question include the following:

- Are my actions balanced between communicating a sense of guidance and control and a sense of concern and cooperation?
- What actions should I be ready to take to communicate a sense of guidance and control?
- What actions should I be ready to take to communicate a sense of concern and cooperation?
- Am I being sensitive to the need for variety in these actions?

Design Question 9 asks the following: *What will I do to communicate high expectations for all students?* The most important teacher behavior relative to this design question is being aware of those students for whom the teacher has low expectations and making a concerted effort to treat them in the same manner as students for whom the teacher has high expectations. Consequently, one question the teacher should ask when planning for a unit is this:

- Which students should I be paying particular attention to in terms of treating them in a manner that communicates high expectations?

Additionally, teachers should be aware of the type and variety of behaviors they use to communicate high expectations. These behaviors fall into two broad categories: those that communicate an appropriate affective tone, and those that enhance the quality of interactions with students. Questions teachers should ask regarding this issue include the following:

- What techniques should I be ready to use to establish an appropriate affective tone with low-expectancy students?
- What techniques should I be ready to use to enhance the quality of interactions with students?
- Am I being sensitive to the need for variety in these techniques?

Examples

Elementary Science. While reviewing various behaviors and activities that should be enacted on the spot, this elementary teacher realizes that she hasn't made much of an effort to keep her science class lively and high energy. She looks over the list of options and notices that she hasn't played any games with students in quite some time. She immediately starts planning for some games to use the following week. She also begins thinking of ways she can engage in some playful banter with students—particularly those who are having some trouble with the new content.

Secondary Physical Education. While mentally planning for the upcoming week, this physical education teacher becomes aware of the fact that she hasn't checked to make sure she is sending the message to all students that she has high expectations for them. She fears she has fallen into the trap of calling on the same students all of the time. She resolves to examine her patterns of calling on students and make necessary corrections.

Activity Box

Which activities that should be enacted on the spot do you address well? Which do you address poorly? What are some new ideas you have for your classroom practice?

In summary, planning from the perspective of *The Art and Science of Teaching* involves addressing a series of questions. These questions are listed in Figure 25.1.

FIGURE 25.1

Planning Questions

Planning for Content Lessons

A. Planning for lessons focused on new knowledge (critical-input lessons)

- Am I being sensitive to the need for a variety of mediums for critical-input experiences?
- How will I augment the critical-input experience by using anecdotes and narratives?
- What specific techniques will I use to ensure that students preview the content?
- How will I organize the content into small chunks?
- How will I facilitate students' discussions and interactions about the small chunks?
- What will I do to help students elaborate on the information in small chunks?
- What will I do to help students summarize and represent the new content?
- What will I do to help students reflect on their learning?
- How will grouping be used in these activities?

B. Planning for lessons focused on practicing and deepening knowledge

- What will I do to briefly review the content?
- What practice activities will I use, and what is my role during these activities?
- Am I using a variety of practice activities?
- What knowledge-deepening activities will I use, and what is my role during these activities?
- Am I using a variety of knowledge-deepening activities?
- What will the role of homework be during these activities?
- How will grouping be used in these activities?

C. Planning for lessons focused on tasks that involve generation and testing of hypotheses

- What types of tasks for generating and testing hypotheses will be used?
- What will I do to facilitate the tasks?
- What will my role be during these activities?
- What will the role of homework be during these activities?
- How will grouping be used during these activities?

Planning for Routine Activities That Will Be Addressed Systematically, or Each Day

---

A. Communicating learning goals, tracking student progress, and celebrating success

- How will students be reminded about specific learning goals, or will new goals be set?
- How will students be provided feedback (e.g., quiz, test, or informal assessment) on their progress on the learning goals for the unit? Will students be asked to record or reflect on their own progress toward learning goals?
- How will students be provided with some form of recognition for their progress on learning goals?

FIGURE 25.1

Planning Questions (*Cont.*)

B. Establishing or maintaining rules and procedures

- What procedures and routines will be emphasized during this unit?
- Will students be reminded of specific rules and procedures, or will new ones be established?

Planning for Activities That Must Be Initiated on the Spot

A. Engaging students

- What techniques for engaging students should I be ready to use during this unit?
- Am I being sensitive to the need for variety in these techniques?

B. Recognizing and acknowledging adherence and lack of adherence to classroom rules and procedures

- What positive consequences should I be ready to implement during this unit?
- What negative consequences should I be ready to implement during this unit?
- Am I being sensitive to the need for variety in these activities?

C. Establishing and maintaining effective relationships with students

- Are my actions balanced between communicating a sense of guidance and control and a sense of concern and cooperation?
- What actions should I be ready to take to communicate a sense of guidance and control?
- What actions should I be ready to take to communicate a sense of concern and cooperation?
- Am I being sensitive to the need for variety in these actions?

D. Communicating high expectations for all students

- Which students should I be paying particular attention to in terms of treating them in a manner that communicates high expectations?
- What techniques should I be ready to use to establish an appropriate affective tone with low-expectancy students?
- What techniques should I be ready to use to enhance the quality of interactions with students?
- Am I being sensitive to the need for variety in these techniques?

Developing a Flexible Draft of Daily Activities for a Unit

A unit of instruction is always a work in progress. Consequently, teachers should always be ready to adjust a unit to take advantage of learning opportunities that might come up. Additionally, teachers must be ready to change the direction of a unit if it is not working well. Although this implies the need for flexibility, it does not mean that a unit should not be well planned. To walk this middle ground between flexibility and thoughtful design, we recommend that teachers develop a flexible draft of the daily activities for a unit. This is depicted in Figure 25.2. In the figure, the teacher has recorded only those behaviors that address Design Questions 1, 2, 3, and 4. That is, the teacher has planned for the introduction of learning goals and their related formative assessments (Design Question 1), the critical-input lessons for the learning goals (Design Question 2), the practice and knowledge-deepening activities for the learning goals (Design Question 3), and the hypothesis generation and testing task (Design Question 4). The teacher has also considered activities that are routine (aspects of Design Questions 1 and 6) as well as activities that must be enacted on the spot (Design Questions 5, 7, 8, and 9), but has not recorded her plans in the matrix.

In this three-week unit she has one learning goal that is procedural (a specific decoding skill) and one learning goal that is declarative (information about the genre of tall tales). She uses formative assessments to enhance student learning. She has six short and informal assessments planned for the procedural goal; these are all coordinated with practice sessions for the decoding strategy. She has planned for four formative assessments for the declarative goal regarding the genre of tall tales.

This unit is probably best classified as focused on knowledge because the first week is devoted to the presentation of new content. During the second week students will start working on decision-making tasks, and they will present their findings the last two days of the third week. This task will be used as a final assessment for the learning goal regarding the tall tale.

Examples

Elementary Mathematics. This 2nd grade mathematics teacher plans for a unit on multicolumn subtraction. She has two learning goals—one dealing with the skill of multicolumn subtraction and the other dealing with a conceptual understanding of the processes of addition and subtraction. She plans for a series of critical-input lessons and practice sessions for the skill-oriented goal. Formative assessments will accompany each practice session, during which students can see the increase in their skill. For the goal regarding a conceptual understanding of subtraction, the teacher will rely on a few structured activities in which the process of multicolumn subtraction is compared with the process of multicolumn addition. Halfway through the unit the students will begin working on an investigation task in which they must explain how the processes of multicolumn addition and subtraction are similar. During the unit the teacher adjusts her unit design as needed.

High School Economics. This high school economics teacher plans for a unit on the concepts of supply and demand. She has three learning goals: one dealing with understanding the concept of supply, another dealing with understanding the concept of demand, and a third dealing with understanding the issue of recent changes in the United States regarding supply and demand for gasoline. She begins the unit with a

FIGURE 25.2

Flexible Format for Unit Design

Week	Monday	Tuesday	Wednesday	Thursday	Friday
1	• Read tall tale to students • Discuss other tall tales with students • Present two learning goals	• Critical-input lesson on decoding strategy • First assessment on decoding strategy	• Practice session on decoding strategy • Critical-input lesson on general tall tales	• Practice session and second assessment on decoding strategy • Comparison activity with tall tales	• Practice session and third assessment on decoding strategy • Another critical-input lesson on tall tales and first assessment
2	• Practice session on decoding strategy and fourth assessment • Metaphor activity with tall tales	• Second assessment on tall tales • Introduce decision-making tasks	• Practice session on decoding strategy • Students work on decision-making tasks	• Critical-input lesson on decoding strategy • Students work on decision-making tasks	• Practice session on decoding strategy and fifth assessment • Critical-input lesson on tall tales and third assessment
3	• Critical-input lesson on decoding strategy	• Sixth assessment on decoding strategy • Fourth assessment on tall tales	• Students work on decision-making tasks	• Students present results of decision-making tasks	• Students present results of decision-making tasks

decision-making task that will run throughout the entire two weeks. Critical-input lessons are planned for the concepts of supply and demand, along with a number of comparison activities to deepen students' knowledge of these two concepts. Although she has planned for a series of formative assessments, the decision-making task will also be used as a major form of assessment. Students will receive formative feedback on their projects. Each time their projects are scored by the teacher, students see their progress on the scales that have been designed for the learning goals.

Activity Box

Describe how you might plan for your next unit of instruction.

Checking for Understanding

Use the following rating scale to assess your current understanding and comfort level regarding key strategies and processes presented in this module:

4 = I understand and already fully implement this strategy in my classroom.

3 = I understand this strategy, but I need to practice using it in my classroom.

2 = I can explain this strategy, but I am not fully confident that I can use it.

1 = I do not understand this strategy, and I do not currently use it in my classroom.

____ 1.   Planning for lessons focused on new knowledge
Based on my rating, I may need to revisit the following:

____ 2.   Planning for lessons focused on practicing and deepening knowledge
Based on my rating, I may need to revisit the following:

___3.   Planning for lessons focused on long-term tasks that require students to generate and test hypotheses
   Based on my rating, I may need to revisit the following:

___4.   Planning for routine activities that will be addressed systematically, or each day
   Based on my rating, I may need to revisit the following:

___5.   Planning for activities that I must be ready to execute on the spot
   Based on my rating, I may need to revisit the following:

___6.   Developing a flexible draft of daily activities
   Based on my rating, I may need to revisit the following:

References

Hyerle. D. (1996). *Visual tools for constructing knowledge.* Alexandria, VA: ASCD.

Marzano, R. J. (2006). *Classroom assessment and grading that work.* Alexandria, VA: ASCD.

Marzano, R. J. (2007). *The art and science of teaching.* Alexandria, VA: ASCD.

Marzano, R.J. (2009). *Designing and teaching learning goals and objectives.* Bloomington, IN: Marzano Research Laboratory.

Marzano, R. J., Gaddy, B. B., Foseid, M. C., Foseid, M. P., & Marzano, J. S. (2005). *A handbook for classroom management that works.* Alexandria, VA: ASCD.

Marzano, R. J., & Kendall, J. S. (2007). *The new taxonomy of educational objectives.* Thousand Oaks, CA: Corwin Press.

Marzano, R. J., & Kendall, J. S. (2008). *Designing and assessing educational objectives: Applying the new taxonomy.* Thousand Oaks, CA: Corwin Press.

Marzano, R. J., Paynter, D. E., & Doty, J. K. (2003). *The Pathfinder Project: The power of one: Teacher's manual.* Cunifer, CO: Pathfinder.

Marzano, R. J., Pickering, D. J., & Marzano, J. S. (2003). *Classroom management that works: Research-based strategies for every teacher.* Alexandria, VA: ASCD.

Marzano, R. J., Pickering, D. J., & Pollock, J. E. (2001). *Classroom instruction that works: Research-based strategies for increasing student achievement.* Alexandria, VA: ASCD.

About the Authors

Dr. Robert Marzano is the CEO of Marzano Research Laboratory in Centennial, CO and Senior Scholar at Mid-continent Research for Education and Learning in Denver, CO. He is the author of 30 books, 150 articles and chapters in books, and 100 sets of curriculum materials for teachers and students in grades K–12. His works include: *The Art and Science of Teaching, Classroom Assessment and Grading That Work, What Works in Schools: Translating Research into Action, School Leadership That Works, Building Background Knowledge for Academic Achievement, Classroom Management That Works, Classroom Instruction That Works, Transforming Classroom Grading,* and *A Different Kind of Classroom: Teaching with Dimensions of Learning.*

During his 40 years in public education, Marzano has worked in every state multiple times as well as a host of countries in Europe and Asia.

John L. Brown is currently an educational consultant for ASCD in the division of program development. He is also a member of the national training cadres for Understanding by Design and What Works in Schools. He has extensive experience in public education, including previous roles as the director of staff development and director of program development for Prince George's County Public Schools, MD.

Brown has also worked in the fields of curriculum supervision, gifted and talented, and English/language arts. In addition, he has taught at both the secondary and college/university levels. He has been a consultant to school districts throughout the United States, Canada, and Barbados, conducting workshops and long-term coaching follow-up on Understanding by Design, What Works in Schools, Dimensions of Learning, learning styles, and standards- and research-based best practices in curriculum and instruction.

His publications include the recent ASCD book *Making the Most of Understanding by Design* as well as the best-selling *Observing Dimensions of Learning in Classrooms and Schools.* Brown is also the coauthor of the ASCD premium member book *The Hero's Journey: How Educators Can Transform Schools and Improve Learning.* He has developed a variety of electronic products for ASCD, including authoring five Professional Development Online courses and contributing to several videotape series.

Related ASCD Resources: The Art and Science of Teaching

At the time of publication, the following ASCD resources were available; for the most up-to-date information about ASCD resources, go to www.ascd.org. ASCD stock numbers are noted in parentheses.

Print Products

The Art and Science of Teaching: A Comprehensive Framework for Effective Instruction by Robert J. Marzano (#107001)

Classroom Instruction That Works: Research-Based Strategies for Increasing Student Achievement by Robert J. Marzano, Debra J. Pickering, and Jane E. Pollock (#101010)

Classroom Management That Works: Research-Based Strategies for Every Teacher by Robert J. Marzano, Jana S. Marzano, and Debra J. Pickering (#103027)

A Handbook for Classroom Instruction That Works by Robert J. Marzano, Jennifer S. Norford, Diane E. Paynter, Debra J. Pickering, and Barbara B. Gaddy (#101041)

A Handbook for Classroom Management That Works by Robert J. Marzano, Barbara B. Gaddy, Maria C. Foseid, Mark P. Foseid, and Jana S. Marzano (#105012)

Videos and DVDs

The Art and Science of Teaching Program 1: Effective Instructional Strategies (one 45-minute DVD) (#608075)

The Art and Science of Teaching Program 2: Effective Classroom Management Strategies (one 45-minute DVD) (#608076)

THE WHOLE CHILD The Whole Child Initiative helps schools and communities create learning environments that allow students to be healthy, safe, engaged, supported, and challenged. To learn more about other books and resources that relate to the whole child, visit www.wholechildeducation.org.

For additional resources, visit us on the World Wide Web (http://www.ascd.org), send an e-mail message to member@ascd.org, call the ASCD Service Center (1-800-933-ASCD or 703-578-9600, then press 2), send a fax to 703-575-5400, or write to Information Services, ASCD, 1703 N. Beauregard St., Alexandria, VA 22311-1714 USA.